No Place for Ethics

The Fairleigh Dickinson University Press

Series in Law, Culture, and the Humanities

Series Editor: Caroline Joan "Kay" S. Picart, M.Phil. (Cantab), Ph.D., J.D., Esquire

Attorney at Law; Adjunct Professor, FAMU College of Law; former English & HUM professor, FSU

The Fairleigh Dickinson University Press Series in Law, Culture, and the Humanities publishes scholarly works in which the field of Law intersects with, among others, Film, Criminology, Sociology, Communication, Critical/Cultural Studies, Literature, History, Philosophy, and the Humanities.

On the Web at http://www.fdu.edu/fdupress

Publications

T. Patrick Hill, *No Place for Ethics: Judicial Review, Legal Positivism, and the Supreme Court of the United States* (2021)

Caroline Joan "Kay" S. Picart, *Monsters, Law, Crime: Explorations in Gothic Criminology* (2020)

Elaine Wood, *Gender Justice and the Law: Theoretical Practices of Intersectional Identity* (2020)

Orit Kamir, *Betraying Dignity: The Toxic Seduction of Social Media, Shaming, and Radicalization* (2019)

Marouf A. Hasian, Jr., *Lawfare and the Ovaherero and Nama Pursuit of Restorative Justice, 1918–2018* (2019)

George Pate, *Enter the Undead Author: Intellectual Property, the Ideology of Authorship, and Performance Practices since the 1960s* (2019)

Victor Li, *Nixon in New York: How Wall Street Helped Richard Nixon Win the White House* (2017)

Marouf A. Hasian, Jr., *Kafkaesque Laws, Nisour Square, and the Trials of the Former Blackwater Guards* (2017)

Michaela Stockey-Bridge, *The Lure of Hope: On the Transnational Surrogacy Trail from Australia to India* (2017)

Ted Laros, *Literature and the Law in South Africa, 1910–2010: The Long Walk to Artistic Freedom* (2017)

Peter Robson and Johnny Rodger, *The Spaces of Justice: The Architecture of the Scottish Court* (2017)

Doran Larson, *Witness in the Era of Mass Incarceration: Discovering the Ethical Prison* (2017)

Raymond J. McKoski, *Judges in Street Clothes: Acting Ethically Off-the-Bench* (2017)

H. Lowell Brown, *The American Constitutional Tradition: Colonial Charters, Covenants, and Revolutionary State Constitutions 1578–1786* (2017)

Arua Oko Omaka, *The Biafran Humanitarian Crisis, 1967–1970: International Human Rights and Joint Church Aid* (2016)

Marouf A. Hasian, Jr., *Representing Ebola: Culture, Law, and Public Discourse about the 2013–2015 West Africa Ebola Outbreak* (2016)

Jacqueline O'Connor, *Law and Sexuality in Tennessee Williams's America* (2016)

Caroline Joan "Kay" S. Picart, Michael Hviid Jacobsen, and Cecil E. Greek, *Framing Law and Crime: An Interdisciplinary Anthology* (2016)

Caroline Joan "Kay" S. Picart, *Law in and as Culture: Intellectual Property, Minority Rights, and the Rights of Indigenous Peoples* (2016)

No Place for Ethics

Judicial Review, Legal Positivism, and the Supreme Court of the United States

T. Patrick Hill

FAIRLEIGH DICKINSON UNIVERSITY PRESS
Vancouver • Madison • Teaneck • Wroxton

Published by Fairleigh Dickinson University Press
Copublished by The Rowman & Littlefield Publishing Group, Inc.
4501 Forbes Boulevard, Suite 200, Lanham, Maryland 20706
www.rowman.com
6 Tinworth Street, London SE11 5AL, United Kingdom
Copyright © 2021 by The Rowman & Littlefield Publishing Group, Inc.

All rights reserved. No part of this book may be reproduced in any form or by any electronic or mechanical means, including information storage and retrieval systems, without written permission from the publisher, except by a reviewer who may quote passages in a review.

Fairleigh Dickinson University Press gratefully acknowledges the support received for scholarly publishing from the Friends of FDU Press.

British Library Cataloguing in Publication Information Available

Library of Congress Cataloging-in-Publication Data

Names: Hill, T. Patrick (Writer on legal ethics), author.
Title: No place for ethics : judicial review, legal positivism, and the
   Supreme Court of the United States / T. Patrick Hill.
Description: Lanham, Maryland : Fairleigh Dickinson University Press, 2021.
   | Series: The Fairleigh Dickinson University press series in law,
   culture, and the humanities | Includes bibliographical references and
   index. | Summary: "In No Place for Ethics, Hill argues the Supreme Court
   has an overriding obligation to ground its judicial review
   responsibilities not only in the Constitution but also in ethics,
   understood as the Constitution's ultimate justification. The text
   discusses a response to the question basic to all human beings: how
   should I behave?"—Provided by publisher.
Identifiers: LCCN 2021021821 (print) | LCCN 2021021822 (ebook) | ISBN
   9781683933236 (cloth) | ISBN 9781683933243 (epub) | ISBN 9781683933250 (pbk)
Subjects: LCSH: Legal ethics—United States—Cases. | Judicial
   review—United States. | United States. Supreme Court. | Constitutional
   law—United States. | Legal positivism.
Classification: LCC KF305.A52 H55 2021 (print) | LCC KF305.A52 (ebook) |
   DDC 174/.30973—dc23
LC record available at https://lccn.loc.gov/2021021821
LC ebook record available at https://lccn.loc.gov/2021021822

For AnnMarie

Contents

Acknowledgments   xiii

Abbreviations   xv

Introduction: Ethics and Law, A Complicated but Necessary Relationship   1

Chapter 1: *Lochner v. New York*, 198 US 45 (1905): Public Health and the Constitutionally Protected Right of Contract between an Employer and Employees   43

Chapter 2: *DeShaney v. Winnebago County Department of Social Services*, 489 U.S. 189 (1989): Liberty and the Due Process Clause of the Fourteenth Amendment   77

Chapter 3: *New York v. United States*, 505 U.S. 144 (1992): Wither the Social Contract?   103

Chapter 4: *FDA v. Brown & Williamson Tobacco Corporation*, 529 U.S 98 (2000): FDA Uses the *Food, Drug, and Cosmetics Act (FDCA) of 1938* to Claim Regulatory Authority Over Tobacco Products   133

Chapter 5: *United States v. Morrison*, 529 U.S. 598 (2000): Legal Formalism versus Human Rights, Federal Civil Remedies and the Victims of Gender-Motivated Violence   165

Bibliography   197

Index   209

About the Author   223

But laws founded singly on experience are like the mask in the fable, beautiful but hollow.

—Kant, *The Metaphysics of Ethics*[1]

---

1. Immanuel Kant, *The Metaphysics of Ethics*, trans. J. W. Semple, ed., and intro. Rev. Henry Calderwood (Edinburgh: T & T Clark, 1886), https://oll.libertyfund.org/titles/1445 (accessed October 10, 2020).

Acknowledgments

No book, including this one, is written in a vacuum. Without the unfailing support of Paul Armstrong, Franklin Gamwell, Larry Greenfield, Harry Keyishian, Robert Olick, Dona Schneider, Linda Stamato, and Raymond Szempruch who reviewed different early chapter drafts, the book as conceived might never have seen the light of day. I am also grateful to two of my students, Steven Mercadente and Justin Hyde for their invaluable review of the literature with regard to ethics commentary on court decisions. Their findings, confirming a dearth of analysis was justification for writing this book. In that vein, I cannot thank enough Caroline Picart, my editor at FDUP and Zachary Nycum my editor at Rowman & Littlefield. Throughout, they have been a source of indispensable advice and direction. As has my indefatigable and patient copyeditor, Sam Brawand.

Finally, it cannot be left unsaid how much I owe to my sister Ann, my daughter Katya and my son, St. John for their support and encouragement throughout this endeavor. One and all, in a thousand, unsuspected, eloquent ways give voice to what lies at the heart of this book—the pursuit of the good.

Abbreviations

ASH	Action on Smoking and Health
CDC	Centers for Disease Control and Prevention
CPSA	*Consumer Products Safety Act*
DSS	Department of Social Services
FCLAA	*Federal Cigarette Labeling and Advertising Act of 1966*
FDA	Food and Drug Administration
FDCA	*Federal Food, Drug, and Cosmetics Act of 1938*
FSLA	*Fair Labor Standards Act of 1938*
GFSZA	*Gun-Free School Zones Act of 1990*
HHS	Health and Human Services
IOM	Institute of Medicine
IPV	Intimate partner violence
LLRW	*New York State Low-Level Radioactive Waste Disposal Act of 1986*
NIMBY	Not-In-My-Backyard
NIRS	Nuclear Information and Resource Services
OSG	Office of the Surgeon General
PURPA	*Public Utility Regulatory Policies Act of 1978*
WHO	World Health Organization

Introduction: Ethics and Law, A Complicated but Necessary Relationship

The purpose of this introduction is to provide a framework within which the reader can assess the normative ethics that are applied in the analysis of the five Supreme Court of the United States decisions included in this book. The introduction is not intended to be a history of ethics. Nor is it intended to be a discussion of the various schools of ethics, such as utilitarianism, deontology, or teleology. Rather, it will provide the reader with an understanding of the ethics reasoning used to show that, though the decisions of the Court in these five cases, may be considered constitutionally sound, they cannot, despite that, be considered in all respects ethically sound.

In its decision *In the Matter of Baby "K" (Three Cases)* (1994),[1] the Appeals Court for the Fourth Circuit declared, "we recognize the dilemma facing physicians who are requested to provide treatment they consider morally and ethically inappropriate, but we cannot ignore the plain language of the statute because to do so would transcend our judicial function."[2] The Court went on to say in the same vein, "It is beyond the limits of the Court's judicial function to address the moral and ethical propriety of providing emergency stabilizing medical treatment to anencephalic infants."[3] As a result, respecting the plain language of the statute required the Court to insist that physicians do what they ought not do. Unfortunately, as the cases reviewed in this book demonstrate, this is not some aberration since it emanates from the positivist view of law that dominates contemporary American jurisprudence with consistently ethically unacceptable consequences.

Similarly, while testifying during the Senate Judiciary Committee hearings on her nomination to the U.S. Supreme Court, Judge Amy Coney Barrett referred, in her discussion of stare decisis, to certain decisions of the Court, such as *Brown v. Board of Education of Topeka (1954)*, as super precedents. The characterization was intended to suggest her belief that such decisions are as close to being beyond reversal as is thinkable because they are also beyond controversy. Considered logically, however, it drove a stake through the heart of the concept, precedent. If there is such a thing as a decision that is a super precedent, it follows that there is also a super, super precedent and so on into an irrational infinite regression. But if concepts like stare decisis and precedent are to be used, it must be in terms not of what is thinkable but unthinkable. If so, this excludes giving relevance to degrees of controversy that might accompany a particular decision. Even if there were controversy surrounding a decision, it would be unthinkable to consider a reversal. Were it otherwise, the invocation of stare decisis and precedent is a mere fig leaf for the relativism of legal positivism.[4]

Whether it is the case of Joshua DeShaney (*DeShaney v. Winnebago County Department of Social Services*) (1989) in chapter 2, Christy Brzonkala (*United States v. Morrison*) (2000) in chapter 5, or the bakers (*Lochner v. New York*) (1905) in chapter 1, the Court's constitutional reasoning resulted in grave injustices. And, if this cannot be explained away as the result of mistaken legal reasoning, how is it that the Constitution of the United States could be used to deny both plaintiff's what was owed them? Or, in *New York v. United States* (1992) in chapter 3, and *FDA v. Brown and Williamson Tobacco Corporation* (2000) in chapter 5, how could the U.S. Constitution be made to give precedence to an individual state's interests or those of a corporation over the common good of the United States?

Theoretically, one answer may be said to lie in the relationship between ethics and law. To explore this relationship it is useful to provide an outline of the development of natural law theory which consistently called for a necessary connection between ethics and law even as it insisted on seeing ethics and law as quite distinct. The concern was to avoid the danger of using law for purposes of ethics or of using ethics for purposes of law. Both place under obligation but whereas with ethics the obligation originates internally, in law it originates externally. Starting with Marcus Tullius Cicero (106–43 BCE), the outline will then take us to St. Thomas Aquinas (1225–1274) and from there to Hugo Grotius (1583–1645) who is considered to be the author of modern natural law theory. What that looks like in practice will then be outlined in a discussion of Thomas Jefferson, the U.S. Constitution, and its application by the U.S. Supreme Court in three decisions in the matter of slavery and racial segregation. The introduction will provide a review of some salient aspects of legal positivism as developed by H. L. A. Hart (1907–1992).

Introduction: Ethics and Law, A Complicated but Necessary Relationship 3

The introduction also includes in the discussion of ethics an outline of some aspects of R. M. Hare's (1919–2002) understanding of the language of morals that bear on the analysis of the Court's jurisprudence in the five decisions included in the book. Of particular relevance here will be Hare's concern that the logic of moral language be seen to render ethics as both objective and prescriptive. This discussion will be complemented by a review of Alan Gewirth's (1912–2004) argument for the same by establishing an irreducible principle derived from every rational person's inescapable rights to the necessary conditions of ethical behavior, liberty and a sense of purpose. Given that these rights are held in common within society, this gives rise to what he called a "community of rights" which, to be effective, requires a necessary connection between ethics and law.

Practically, another answer being advanced here, consists in two claims. The first is that these decisions result from the Supreme Court's history of distancing itself from an understanding of law known as natural law or law because it is just, in preference for a positivist understanding of law or law because it is so ordered. The second claim, closely linked to the first, is that this change in the Court's jurisprudence has resulted over time in abandoning the position that law is ultimately grounded in ethics.

In advancing the first claim, the goal, again, is not to provide a history of natural law theory but, more modestly, to examine the reasoning found at its core. In advancing the second claim, the purpose is to correct a pervasive understanding of ethics as without exception a matter of personal values, lacking any objectivity and therefore irrelevant in law. To begin, what then needs be said of law?

LAW

To ask the question, "what is law?" is in another manner to ask, "what is a human being?" One of the standard answers to the latter question, one that presumably gave rise to the natural law theory, is a rational animal. Human beings are a combination of mind and body, of reasoning and action, with action subject to reason as its measure or law because of the perceived preeminence of reason over action. Here, reason is understood to express itself in two modes. The first is pure reason, consisting in certain self-evident principles, such as the principle of non-contradiction, necessary and sufficient to engage in reasoning itself. The second is practical reason, again consisting in certain self-evident principles, such as do good and avoid evil, necessary but not sufficient for justifying human action.

Given that, the term *law*, as used in natural law, refers to the rational nature of a human being as the innate measure of actions proper to this nature. Since human beings are rational by definition, then acting as human beings means acting ultimately in a manner that is not contradictory to pure reason and as a consequence contradictory to their nature. It also means acting *in situ* (in the situation) in a manner that is not contradictory to practical reason, since practical reason as reason participates in pure reason. In this sense, it is correct to say that law as used in the *law of nature* does not mean quite the same as when it is used in the *law of the land*.

In his discussion of natural law, A. P. d'Entreves (1902–1985) observed that it inevitably prompts the question, "what is law?" as though its meaning is not as obvious as it might appear. Indeed, citing Immanuel Kant (1724–1804), he noted that to ask this question of "the jurist" is comparable in its difficulty to asking of "the logician," "what is truth?" Both are irreducible questions and as such their answers are to be found in pure reason which requires thinking from a universal perspective. In the case of the law question, it assumes the truth that before there were laws there is law which, as Kant noted, provides the justification for all possible *positive law* legislated by human beings.[5] Earlier than Kant, Aquinas, of whom more subsequently, worked from the same assumption in his treatment of natural law. More recently we find Sir Ernest Baker (1889–1975) making a similar argument: "It follows that law—in the sense of the law of the last resort—is somehow above lawmaking."[6] One way to appreciate this is to think of the concept, *law*, as a locus of inference controlled by the fundamental principle of pure reason, the principle of non-contradiction which allows for saying something like, "If law, then..." It might be thought of as law-thinking to distinguish it from law-making and helpful in distinguishing between law as understood in natural law theory and law as understood in legal positivism. According to d'Entreves, again citing Kant, this universal perspective illustrates the deficits of "legal empiricism" which, while it may tell you what concerns this or that law at a particular time or in a particular place, cannot say what law itself is.[7] This suggests that what practical reason necessarily is to pure reason, positive or human law necessarily is to natural law.

FORMULATION OF NATURAL LAW THEORY

The history of natural law theory reaches far back in time, but its enduring presence as a force in the discussion of the nature and purpose of law is even more significant. It is for this reason a source of dismay that its presence is so noticeably absent in the five decisions of the United States Supreme Court discussed in this book.

MARCUS TULLIUS CICERO (106–43 BCE)

One of the earliest expressions of this thinking about law is provided by Cicero. "There is a true law, a right reason, conformable to nature, universal, unchanging, eternal, whose commands urge us to duty, and whose prohibitions restrain us from evil."[8]

It is clear from this language that Cicero is entertaining a theory of law as such and not to be confused with what he referred to as the laws of "Rome" or "Athens," and which today would commonly be considered positive law. This is law as it ought to be, a necessary dialectic between human nature and human reason, issuing in behavior that is obligatory, because it is consonant with both as something to be done or not done. "Those who have been given reason by nature have also been given correct reason, and thus law, which is correct reasoning in ordering and forbidding. If law has been given, so has right."[9] But Cicero did not leave it there. Critically he added that since all have been so endowed, then it follows that "right has been given to all persons."[10]

This law is different from positive law in that its authoritative source is beyond the control of those authorized to make positive law. As Cicero put it, "Neither the senate nor the people can give us any dispensation for not obeying this universal law of justice."[11] And because of its authoritative source, this law is both universal and unchanging, further distinguishing it from positive law. That it is universal and unchanging follows from its origins, a nature at once common to and unchanging in human beings for whom consequently there is need of a corresponding law. It is also self-evident as there is no need to look beyond our "conscience" to interpret it.[12]

Affirming his belief in such a law, Cicero was taking issue with the Greek philosopher, Carneades (214–129/8 BCE), who had questioned the notion of natural justice. Carneades, a skeptic, had argued that "justice may be a civil right," but given the variety of expressions of justice between nations and cities, it could hardly be considered a natural and universal right, such that it, like "the elements of heat and cold, sweet and bitter" would be appreciated in the same way generally. With such consistent variety, if we assume a just and virtuous man should obey the laws, would that be obedience to "all the laws indifferently"? If virtue consists in obeying the law, how is virtue possible through indiscriminate obedience to laws that may be morally inconsistent? Indiscriminate obedience could only result from "fear of punishment," not the fulfillment of "justice," and that would be irreconcilable with "natural conscience." If "natural justice" is out of the question, Carneades concluded, then men cannot be naturally "just."[13] Carneades might have thought he was successfully demonstrating how untenable is the concept of natural justice. In fact, inadvertently, he was demonstrating the need for it.

To accept his position would undermine the principle of human equality central to natural law. As Cicero expressed it, "For there is nothing so similar, one-to-one, so equal, as all persons are among ourselves."[14] If justice is neither eternal, immutable nor universal, how could it be normative for fulfilling one's duties or restraining from doing evil?

Since Carneades' skepticism was directed against the certainty of Stoicism which Cicero shared, one needs look no further than to Stoicism to understand Cicero's response. When he declared that God is the author of the true law, he echoed the belief of Stoics that the universe "is formed and guided by a *logos* or reason."[15] Variously, the Stoics had spoken of this reason, using the terms "God," "nature," "fate," and "providence."[16] Thus, when Cicero wrote that whoever disobeys the true law "flies from himself and does violence to the very nature of man,"[17] he asserted unambiguously that law as an expression of human nature is itself normative of human behavior. In complying with this law, human beings are acting as human beings ought to act. This, in turn, confirms the Stoics' belief "that the individual mind is a 'seed' of the *logos* and the purpose of an individual life is a progressive grasp of, and adaptation to the overall purposes of the universe."[18] For Stoics "the ideal of conformity with logos implied an ethical cosmopolitanism: all human beings are by nature fellow-citizens of one world, divided only by artificial convention."[19] In other words, being ethical depends upon a clear appreciation of reality which requires the faithful pursuit of the truth of the human condition. The Stoics were well aware of how easily our sense perceptions can be misled and result in mistaken conclusions. Turning to Aristotle, they found a remedy for that in logic which enables us, applying his principles of propositional logic, to bring mental conceptions into alignment with the external world.[20]

It might be noted that Cicero was laying out his theory of natural law in parallel with a political discussion, one concerning the nature of a commonwealth. Scipio, at the urging of Cicero, had defined a commonwealth as a congregation of the people as a whole. There is after all no human being worthy of the name "who desires no community of justice, no partnership in human life with his fellow-citizens."[21] The association has less to do with some inherent inability of individuals to be self-sufficient and results ultimately from an inclination natural to human beings to be part of some social structure. According to Scipio, the human race is not made up of isolated individuals but is designed, even in the absence of any need for mutual assistance, for societal living.[22] Cicero was in agreement, concluding that societies of men, or states united by the law of natural "justice" could not be more concordant with reason.[23] Indeed, so concordant that the good person abided by it naturally, while the bad person, in resisting it, did violence to his "nature."[24] Accordingly, justice was societally indispensable since, among other things, it assured consideration for the interests of the whole human race generally, as well as the disposition to give everyone their due individually. This served to emphasize the transcendence of this law, further distinguishing it from positive law but without denying a clear relation between the two. Otherwise, how would one deal with the fact that "Wisdom urges us to increase our resources, to multiply our wealth, to extend our boundaries."[25] For this reason, the law of justice was not subject to other laws, lying as it did beyond the power of "senate" or "people" to change it.

The centrality of justice, universally applicable, assumed the equality of human beings as human beings. "Therefore, whatever definition we give of man, it must include the whole human race."[26] Manifest in this equality, Cicero insisted, was reason which was common to all human beings. As a result, there was not a human being anywhere who, "adopting his true nature for his true guide, may not improve in virtue."[27] This followed logically from Cicero's understanding of "nature" as a logos that "made us just that we might participate in our goods with each other, and supply each other's wants."[28] Nevertheless, he was quick to draw a critical distinction between nature, as understood here, "in its genuine purity and not in the corrupt state which is displayed by the depravity of evil custom."[29]

The distinction is critical if we are to acknowledge the implications of autonomy for human behavior. If human beings are free, then, when as human beings they act, if they act as human beings ought to act, their action cannot be predetermined. It must be a matter of their choice. Since law is a measure of action, the ethical implications of this for lawmakers, positive law and judicial review cannot be ignored. If positive law is such that it calls for or permits behavior that is incompatible with true law and results in a human being disowning himself then it has no warrant since we cannot be excused, whether by public opinion or government, from the prior obligations of true law. At the same time, if human beings enjoy autonomy, should they choose to, they can comply with positive law even at the expense of true law. They can do this even though they ought not to. And since as human beings we cannot not act, we live constantly in the face of these unavoidable alternatives. After all, it is only when you can do something that it is reasonable to ask whether you ought to do it. Indeed, the ability to do something is the condition, necessary, but not sufficient, for being in a position to pose the ought question. Unlike *can*, *ought* prompts the word *why*, setting in motion a process of reasoning in pursuit of justification which presupposes a normative principle of human behavior. While Cicero does not employ this linguistic distinction, we can infer it from the following:

For nature hath not merely given us reason, but right reason, and consequently that law, which is nothing else than right reason enjoining what is good and forbidding what is evil.[30]

But once more Cicero did not leave it there. If our "nature" was the measure of our behavior, so also was "justice." Having endowed all with "reason," nature had in the same way bestowed "the sense of justice on all."[31] And natural justice, as that which is owed, is the ethical foundation of all law in its unavoidably other-regarding purpose in society as a matter of ethics.

ST. THOMAS AQUINAS (1225–1274)

Essential to understanding Aquinas' formulation of natural law theory is that the natural law, according to Mark Murphy, consists in norms derived from practical reason as the measure of what particular human actions are to be considered "reasonable" or compatible with human nature. The natural law is concerned with those pursuits to which human beings are disposed under the direction of reason. That is, choosing to act rationally.[32] According to Aquinas, human reason moved between the general—where it functioned speculatively and in terms of the absolute, such as do good and avoid evil—to the specific—where it functioned practically in response to the contingencies to which human existence was subject. Whether one considered the general principles of "speculative" or "practical reason," Aquinas argued, their moral correctness was universally the same and known universally to be so. With regard to appropriate inferences to be drawn from "speculative reason," their moral correctness was again universally the same even though not necessarily known universally, as in the case of any of Euclid's theorems. With regard to inferences appropriately drawn from "practical reason," Aquinas noted some significant qualifications. For one, their moral correctness was not universally the same, and where it was, it was not necessarily equally known. Consequently, as a matter of "principle," it was morally correct to act on reason. If so, in the case where property had been given in care to someone, it was a reasonable conclusion that eventually the property would be returned to its owner. Unless, that is, restoration resulted predictably in some kind of harm. In that case, the principle of ownership would not apply and would give way, presumably to another principle more applicable under the circumstances. From this, Aquinas concluded that the general principles of the natural law, as true or morally correct, applied universally. And, similarly, so did the inferences drawn from them. However, and here Aquinas echoed Cicero, there were exceptions, as when someone's reasoning was compromised, as it might be, by greed or envy, for example.[33] The defect is not in the principles; it is in the person.

Given that Aquinas so unambiguously grounded his formulation of natural law theory in reason, the observation that it did not accommodate "relativist or conventionalist views" by which moral values were subject to particular social or cultural mores, was correct.[34]

Characteristic of natural law thinking is the "universal perspective" it demands. In agreement, Aquinas noted that viewed from this vantage point, a particular "order" asserted itself. For example, the first thing humans became conscious of when something came to mind was simply that they were. From this followed, as a matter of reason, the self-evident "principle" that the same thing cannot be and not be at the same time. This was the principle of non-contradiction without which reasoning itself would not be possible and from which all other laws of reasoning were derived. In parallel fashion, in regard to practical reason which directed immediately human behavior, a principle might be to always tell the truth. Based on reason as this principle is, it too is subject to the laws of reason. As Aquinas put it, since natural law was established by reason, the directives of the natural law functioned as an extension of practical reason, much as analytic statements were expressions of pure reason, since the two, pure reason and its practical counterpart were "self-evident" norms.[35]

If the primary directive of natural law ultimately consisted in doing good and avoiding evil, it followed that whatever the practical reason naturally understands to be to man's benefit or otherwise was included in the directives of the natural law as something to be followed or shunned. Further since the concept of "good," according to Aquinas, following Aristotle, was identified as an end in the same way that evil was identified as its very opposite, it followed that all those things to which humans were drawn by nature were, as a matter of reason, understood as good and consequently as something to be pursued. Anything that cannot be naturally understood as good was to be avoided.[36] In that case, the "order" of the directives of natural law was derived from the "order" of those predispositions inherent in humans. The first was self-preservation and included the means to secure it. Beyond self-preservation, there was the preservation of humans evident in the inclination to sexual intercourse and the subsequent formation of the young. Obviously, these predispositions were shared with the rest of the animate world. Peculiar to humans, however, was their predisposition to the "good," perceived by virtue of human reason, such as life "in society" with its social and political institutions.[37]

This brought Aquinas to his discussion of what he called "human law." He made it a point, in his discussion of natural law, to observe that "law" as a "measure" had two ways of being present in humans. The first was as present in the ruler, the one who measured. The second was as present in whatever was ruled, and in the degree that it was, by its nature, subject to the law.[38] He also maintained that "law is a measure" of action, positively urging it, negatively prohibiting it.[39] In the case of human action, the measure or law was "reason." Further, of all the actions humans were capable, only those were indeed "human" when they resulted from an interaction, controlled by the agent, between reason and "will." And if an act was willed, it was willed for some identified purpose perceived to be "good."[40] It would be hard to think of anyone acting if not for a purpose perceived to be good. This was not to say that the purpose was in fact good, only that it was thought to be good by the agent. Given the ambivalence this suggested, any action undertaken needed to be open to objective, rational assessment so that it was measured in itself and apart from the agent's subjective motivation for acting. At the same time, the action had also to have been willed by the agent if they were to be held accountable for their actions.

With these as essential conditions of law, Aquinas drew an analogy between how one arrived at knowledge of the sciences and how one made human law. In the case of the sciences, our knowledge was not innate but came with the use of the self-evident "principles" of pure reason. In the case of making "human laws," human reason proceeded from the directives of natural law, using them as self-evident principles, to the formulation of particular laws based on natural and therefore universal "justice." In both cases, it was a process of drawing inferences from relevant self-evident principles. In the case of law, the principles were innate to our nature.[41] The primary norm applicable to a practical matter like making law was, according to Aquinas, the consideration of the ultimate goal of human life which was "universal happiness" or the perfection of human nature. In this regard, Aquinas was echoing Aristotle who argued that law was just which secured the happiness of individuals, to be regarded as imperfect, but perfectible in and through their relationship with the state as the perfect community.[42] Evident here was that human law must be derived from the directives of natural law so as to secure conditions of justice embodied in the notion of a "common good" in which individuals as members of society participate.[43]

If one was to compare Aquinas' ethics as articulated in the formulation of his natural law theory with later developments in ethics theory, Murphy's observations are worth noting. Normative behavior is indeed grounded in norms for the common good, anticipating, if you will, utilitarianism. Not, however, without qualification, since Murphy claimed that Aquinas would not accept that acting rightly required of us to "maximize the good." Aquinas' concern, anticipating Kant, would have come from consideration of the actor's "intentions," since despite being good, they might compromise any outcomes and as a result fail to justify actions taken. Murphy added a third point of comparison here, this one with Aristotle who had argued that virtue consisted in acting between extremes. While Aquinas would have agreed on that score, he would have parted company with Aristotle who, according to Murphy, has generally been thought to believe that "there are no universally true general principles of right."[44] As Murphy put it, "the natural law view rejects wholesale particularism."[45] Since this would apply to lawmaking, as a human action, it would be hard to reconcile Aquinas' understanding of the necessary relation between ethics and law as found in contemporary legal positivism and its reliance on social acceptability as the standard for justifying law. Instead, in Aquinas, one has an early and very clear formulation of natural law rationally, and as a result, objectively grounded in ethics.

HUGO GROTIUS (1583–1645)

It is important to include Grotius in this discussion since he represented theoretically both a point of arrival and a point of departure in the formulation of natural law theory. While Cicero presented his formulation as participation in Stoic deism, and Aquinas framed his theologically as participation in Christian theism, Grotius unmoored his formulation from both of these *divine* origins, presenting it as a matter of unaided reason simply. In this secular guise, it was a ready candidate for reformulation as social contract theory in the rationalism of the following century when rights replaced reason as the immediate measure of human action. The result was the emergence of the individual as the subject of these rights. Inevitably, rights as claims to certain indispensable interests would replace practical reason, with its self-evident principles, chief of which was do good and avoid evil, as the justification of human action. The relativism inherent in the notion of contract theory replaced the absolutism inherent in natural law theory. Cynicism replaced idealism as a working assumption of the human condition. This change was evident in Thomas Hobbes' (1588–1679) formulation of the social contract in which humans were driven by self-interest. And because they were rational, they applied reason as a means to secure those interests. For this reason, a migration from life in the state of nature, in which everything was unpredictable to life in civil society, where law, based on reason as means, prevailed, was the pragmatic thing to do.[46]

Unlike Cicero and Aquinas, Grotius undertook his discussion of natural law indirectly, within a discussion of the right to wage war for purposes of securing peace. In the course of this discussion, he defined the concept of *right* variously. Basically it referred to whatever was "just" or, put negatively, as he preferred, something undertaken without "injustice" toward an "enemy," since injustice is unacceptable to the "Nature of a Society of reasonable Creatures."[47] This was a clear echo of Aquinas' discussion of "right" as the "object of justice." He had observed that the word *jus* or *right*, in its initial use, referred to the just thing itself as "a kind of equality" and was, as result, considered an objective denotation. Subsequently, it came to be used to refer to the means by which what was just was known to be just. Right, then, Aquinas concluded, was the "object of justice," which had to do with other-regarding behavior, one person to another or others, as in the case of paying what was owed for a "service" provided.[48] Since war for Grotius included conflict between individuals, that he should give as his initial example the appropriation of one person's property by another for personal gain was indicative of the possibility of a broader conceptualization of right that included personal interests. Robbery threatened the stability of society, but, what was more important, it violated the law of nature which established a "relation" between humans. Since the example presumed the existence of a right to property associated in some way with natural law, it also presumed a universal agreement that the protection of the interests of individual members of society was necessary for the protection of society itself. The point here was that humans were meant for society, the preservation of which depended on the well-being of its members. The assertion of a right, individually enjoyed as a guarantee of such well-being, should not go unnoticed if we are to appreciate how Grotius paved the way for the modern formulation of natural law theory. This was one that had less to do with the universal claims that certain indemonstrable principles of reason made of us in our behavior, than the claims that individuals made by means of their rights in the pursuit of personal interests, such as private property.

This outcome should not surprise since Grotius also gave right a moral quality to be tied to the person so as to entitle them to some privilege or to perform certain actions "justly."[49] A right was also a claim which individuals made for whatever they had of their own, such as autonomous "power" in the enjoyment of freedom.[50] There was also the notion of a right exclusive to the individual possessing some particular thing. At the same time, Grotius asserted also a right of the state, superior to individual rights, by which it made claims on individual members of society and their property in the interests of the common good.[51] Overall, this suggested a tolerance for a more subjective interpretation of right as a source of individual power to make claims on behalf of one's personal interests. A harbinger of social contract theory?

Ultimately, Grotius claimed, right was "law" understood in its most extensive sense and intended as a measure of "moral" behavior and therefore prescriptive of whatever behavior was deemed proper.[52] He declared further that the "obligation" to do what was proper, beyond what was just, meant that law embraced the substance of other virtues besides justice. In this form, right as law was the command of right reason by which human action, depending on its agreement or disagreement with rational nature was to be pursued or avoided. Since "God" is "the author of nature," this meant that ultimately it was God who required these actions to be pursued or avoided. Because of this, the "Law of Nature" was quite distinct from "Human Right."[53]

The essence of the distinction lay in that one was obliged without question to comply with the law of nature or betray one's human identity. With human law one agreed to comply with it, largely with a view to one's interests, whether they were as fundamental as self-preservation, or were more immediate interests, such as property or equal treatment before the law. Grotius referred to this as "civil right" which originated with the sovereign power of the state, perfect in its membership by "free persons" united in their pursuit of shared rights and benefits.[54] Ostensibly a political union, it was fundamentally a moral union because it was constituted in freedom of action, the unchanging measure of which in the case of humans was their rational nature. Indeed, it was so unchanging because literally it was unchangeable, even by "God," its author. Grotius did not deny that God was omnipotent. But he also insisted that there were certain things to which even that degree of power cannot reach. Were it to do so, it would result in unreason or contradiction. As he famously expressed it, that two plus two must equal four was beyond any power, even divine power, to be stated otherwise. Similarly, what was "intrinsically evil" may not be declared to be "not evil."[55]

Looking forward from Grotius, to subsequent developments in natural law theory, it is hard not to see the significant implications of unmooring it from its divine origins. It would stand intact, even if there were "no God." As Grotius himself put it, everything that has been said up to this point would be true, even if we were to concede the unthinkable, that "God" did not exist or that God had little or no interest in "human affairs."[56] The formulations of natural law theory produced in the seventeenth and eighteenth centuries were strictly rational and found no need for a theological framework. According to d'Entreves, Grotius' hypothetical was to become a thesis. "The self-evidence of natural law has made the existence of God perfectly superfluous."[57] It should not be forgotten that Grotius, unlike Aquinas, was not considering natural law from a purely speculative perspective. Having lived through most of the Thirty Years' War (1618–1648) that engulfed Central Europe, he found himself asking whether there was such a thing as war, waged by one country against another, that might be justified because it was waged as a means to peace.[58] After all, citing Seneca (c. 4 BCE–65 CE), Grotius declared that "men" should be supportive of each other, "since they are born for society" which depended for its survival on "mutual love and defense of the parts."[59]

For David J. Hill, the point Grotius was making was that "nations" represented concentrations of "individuals" who, despite their regional differences, shared a need for "justice which springs from the nature of man as a moral being."[60] Grotius, he argued, stipulated "humanity" as the foundation of a "true law of nations," resulting in a human solidarity that gave rise to what Hill called a "community of rights." Consequently, when war was declared between nations, it was only prosecuted within the restraints of "rights" to "assert rights."[61] Under conditions of war, while civil or human law might be suspended, natural law remained in operation. Serving as the law of war, its repudiation amounted to a repudiation of the rights and obligations with which human nature was innately endowed and burdened. It followed from this natural endowment that Grotius saw a clear distinction between an unchanging natural law, grounded in the rational nature of humans, and human law, derived from the consent of humans, and needed if individuals were to address the changing exigencies of life in society. This was in keeping with natural law theory which always acknowledged the need for positive law in the face of the immediate exigencies of life in society. But while natural law and positive law were distinct, they were not so distinct as to justify thinking of them as having no relation. On the contrary, there was a necessary relation between them that resulted in positive law being accountable to natural law. This explained why there was a necessary relation between positive law and ethics that resulted from the moral nature of natural law. From this discussion, it is clear that Grotius inherited a largely medieval formulation of natural law. His own formulation centered around rights derived from objective reason. But with the passage of time into the nineteenth century, those rights took up residence in persons, where becoming personalized, they were used to secure individual and competing interests, to the detriment of sharing these rights in common and using them to pursue the common good to which each justified a moral claim. In this significant change in direction for and eventual abandonment of natural law, aided an abetted by the emergence of the modern pluralistic and polyarchical society,[62] Thomas Jefferson played no small part.

THOMAS JEFFERSON (1743–1826)

Almost one hundred years later, Thomas Jefferson turned to the concept of consent to justify declaring the independence of the Thirteen Colonies from the rule of the British government. Invoking as something self-evident, namely, a divinely ordained equality among humans, he also posited certain unalienable rights—those to Life, Liberty, and the pursuit of Happiness—as inextricably linked to an essential equality universally shared among human beings. To secure, not originate, these rights, government was established and whatever powers it enjoyed derived from the consent of those to be governed. But should government fail in this purpose, the governed enjoyed the right to replace it with one that was considered most likely to fulfill its purpose. The influence of classical natural law theory was evident, particularly in the invocation of self-evident or irreducible reason and human equality. But the driving force had shifted significantly in the direction of rights as the measure of human action. Prudence, or the enlightened self-interests of the Thirteen Colonies, now dictated throwing off a despotic government and justifying a new one to provide for their future security.

This was a new constitution, essentially contractual in nature, more Hobbesian than Lockean[63] for its moral minimalism. One, that is, in which the moral imperative of classical natural law theory to do good and avoid evil as the measure of human action was replaced by rights, innate to individuals, as the measure of their actions. Thinking universally, in the natural law tradition, took second place to thinking locally in the form of convention. Further, it was a constitution in which monarchy was replaced by multiple sources of power exercised in and by rights. Accordingly, this constitution embodied a Federalist system of governance in which power was distributed on the basis of states' rights and federal rights so that its exercise ultimately was accountable to the electorate. As Justice Sandra Day O'Connor explained it in *New York v. United States*, "If the citizens of New York, for example, do not consider that making provision for the disposal of radioactive waste is in their best interest, they may elect state officials who share their view."[64]

A central argument of this book is that the constitutional framework outlined here has given rise to a jurisprudence distinct from one derived from natural law theory. In turn, this jurisprudence drives the process of judicial review which is the focus of the book in the five cases reviewed. Depending on their view of the role of the Constitution, justices may emphasize the defense of individual rights against unwarranted intervention from government. Their view of the Constitution may also dispose them to emphasize the need to defend community interests, even at the expense of individual interests. A third view disposes justices to adopt a deferential posture toward the legislature and government because of their accountability to the electorate. Any one or all three of these views might seem to reflect an underlying view of the political or mediating role of the Constitution within the context of a tri-part form of governance which seeks to secure what is often referred to as a more perfect union. In that role, the Constitution might be thought to embody a set of second order or universally dispositive principles against which all subsequent legislation is measured. As a consequence, justices might understandably see their judicial review as requiring in their decisions what is understood to be the original intention of those who wrote the Constitution.[65]

This raises a critical question. Does the Constitution embody principles at the level of a second order? If so, to what purpose? Is it not for purposes of securing consistency in understanding and applying the law, as postulated in the constitutional principle, *stare decisis* or precedent? Despite precedent, it is rare to see unanimous decisions handed down by lower courts, as well as the Supreme Court, suggesting that what is precedent for the majority is not precedent for the minority on the Court. Indeed, one could reasonably argue that a precedent is only as good as its next precedent. Precedent, it has to be acknowledged, based on the history of the Court, is not definitive. If that is the case, then positive law, including the Constitution, cannot be regarded as an irreducible or self-evident principle. What Jefferson declared about the human condition was not a matter of law, but a matter of reason which the Constitution did not originate but merely confirmed. As a result, it is constitutional because it is of reason, not the other way around. And since law is a measure of human action, it must measure according to ethics or practical reason embodying, as it does the self-evident principles intended for directing human behavior. Aristotle opened his discussion of ethics with the observation "that every activity, artistic or scientific, in fact every deliberate action or pursuit, has for its object the attainment of some good."[66] Since judicial review qualifies as a deliberate action, it can, presumably, fall within Aristotle's observation. Accordingly, we must ask of it what good is it seeking to attain? It cannot be the Constitution itself. Were that the case, it would result in unending contradiction, with, as, for example, in *DeShaney v. Winnebago County*, the majority of the Court saying due process is not constitutionally applicable, while the minority of the Court saying it is constitutionally applicable. But if one thinks it reasonable for the majority and the minority to draw these contradictory conclusions, it can only be so with the acknowledgment that the Constitution is not an end in itself but a means to an end—Aristotle's good. In that case, each justice must ask, in the process of judicial review, not what *can* my review do in the interests of the Constitution, as though irreducible, but what *ought* it do to achieve the good or end for which the Constitution serves as a means.

A brief review of three landmark decisions, two early and one much later, of the Supreme Court will illustrate a disposition to confuse matters of reason with matters of law, along with a related disposition to treat the Constitution as its own end rather than a means to an end. Adding to the problem is the pursuit of original intent as though definitive within the Constitution. The overall result is a pattern of logical inconsistency inherent in each decision.

The first case is *Dred Scott v. Sandford* (1856).[67] Here, the Court appeared intent on laying out the premise for the moral standing of the human person. It invoked the opening words of the Declaration of Independence that all men, as a matter of self-evident truth, were created equal and enjoyed by virtue of their divine creation certain inalienable or human rights, such as liberty. At the same time, the Court made three observations. One, these words included the entire human race. Two, were one to find these words in a constitution in 1856, that was how they would be accepted. But, three, given when they were originally uttered, "it is too clear for dispute that the enslaved African race were not intended to be included and formed no part of the people who framed and adopted this declaration."[68] Quite the contrary. The meaning of their language was clearly intended not to include members of the African race which, by common consent, had been excluded from civilized government and the family of nations, and doomed to slavery.[69] In the same originalist vein, the Court considered it quite clear, at least implicitly, that the framers had spoken and acted on the commonly accepted thinking of the day about the black race as property and marked by differences inherent to it. Moreover, the Court pointed to two clauses in the Constitution that explicitly spoke of the African race as "a separate class of persons,"[70] and not to be thought of as included among the people of the government. Combined, the Court concluded, these clauses meant only that the persons referred to and their descendants were never thought to be entitled to benefit from the provisions, whether those of liberty or of personal rights, of the Constitution.[71]

The reasoning of the Court was remarkable. Since the framers were men of integrity, and some happened to be slave owners, to have meant by their language to include the African race would have been dishonest on their part. "They spoke and acted according to the then established doctrines and principles, and in the ordinary language of the day, and no one misunderstood them."[72] In other words, so as not to prove them dishonest, it was justified to read the language that all men are created equal as actually saying that all men, except members of the African race, were created equal. This, however, appeared to contradict the Court's earlier observation that were one to see the words, all men are created equal, in a constitution in 1856, they would have been understood literally to include the entire human race. If so, that would have implied that established doctrine and ordinary language had changed, allowing the words, all men, to include members of the African race. Since it was established doctrine and ordinary language that justified excluding blacks in 1776, why, now that both have changed in 1856, cannot they be invoked to change the status of blacks so as to recognize their liberty and personal rights as protected under the Constitution?

There are two additional considerations. The Court used the words, *the entire human race*, not, note well, *the human race*. In context consequently, the use of the qualifying word, *entire*, would imply the inclusion of the African race, were it not for the fact that it had been doomed to slavery. Couple that with the Court's observation that "no one of that race had ever migrated to the United States voluntarily."[73] If it was recognized that they had not come voluntarily, then it followed logically that they came involuntarily. And that can only mean that, like the rest of the human race, members of the

African race were endowed with liberty. Furthermore, that they had all been brought to the United States as slaves, could have only meant that those who brought them did so intentionally to deprive them of the enjoyment of their innate liberty. And since this decision endorsed, by a significant majority, slavery in the name of the Constitution, it also represented a significant distancing from natural law, the source of the fundamental principles enshrined in the Declaration of Independence and given voice in the Constitution.

Plessy v. Ferguson (1896)[74] challenged the constitutionality of Louisiana's *Separate Car Act* (1890) which required blacks and whites, when traveling within the state by train, to ride in separate but identically equipped cars, on the grounds that it violated the Fourteenth Amendment.

According to the Court, the Fourteenth Amendment stood for the "absolute equality of the two races before the law."[75] Beyond that, however, it would be too much to expect of the Amendment that it erased "distinctions based upon color, or to enforce social as distinguished from political equality, or a commingling of the two races upon terms unsatisfactory to either."[76] As the Court expressed what it saw to be reality, "If one race be inferior to the other socially, the Constitution of the United States cannot put them on the same plane."[77] But if the Constitution cannot put the races on the same plane, then it cannot be understood to have been intended to do so. Does that mean that the Fourteenth Amendment addressed a substantial deficiency in the Constitution? Or did it address an oversight on the part of the framers by adding a provision that was compatible with the original formulation of the Constitution? Given the succession of amendments to the Constitution, the normative capacity of original intent was seriously questionable, confirming further that the Constitution was a means to an end, which end was normative of the Constitution itself.

Whether the statute violated the Fourteenth Amendment was for the Court a question of the reasonableness of the statute.[78] In this case, reasonableness was measured in the degree to which the statute reflected "the established usages, customs and traditions of the people … with a view to the promotion of their comfort and the preservation of the public peace and good order."[79] Assessed on this basis, the Court concluded that a law requiring blacks and whites to travel in separate but equal cars was neither unreasonable nor hostile to the Fourteenth Amendment.[80] Assessed, however on the basis of a necessary relation between law and ethics, it was far from reasonable. That the plaintiff, mistakenly, according to the Court, viewed the enforced separation of the races as a signal of the inferiority of blacks was, it concluded, simply a matter of a choice made by blacks. Nothing in the statute merited such a view.[81] The mistake was compounded, the Court added, because of the equally mistaken assumption it came from, namely, that "social prejudices may be overcome by legislation, and that equal rights cannot be secured to the negro except by legally enforced commingling of the two races."[82] If so, how illogical was it to argue from the assumption that legally enforced separation of the races might be thought to secure those same rights?

The real mistake is found in the Court's understanding of the relation between human equality and the role of law. In this regard, it is worth noting an observation made by the Court. Should Louisiana law require companies operating trains between states to extend to all passengers, regardless of race or color, traveling within the state, equal access throughout the train, then to deny to blacks, on account of color, access to a cabin set aside for whites would, where interstate commerce was concerned, be unconstitutional.[83] It appears to have escaped the attention of the Court that human equality was a matter of reason. As a result, it was not for law to function as though the originator of equality among humans, when, as subject to reason, its function was to confirm their equality, despite prevailing custom and societal mores. It was, in other words, a matter of conceding that the legitimacy of law depended on the extent it expressed the principle of universal justice, not the prevailing attitudes and preferences of society. Failing that, it is impossible not to see how mistaken the Court was when it declared, "If the civil and political rights of both races be equal, one cannot be inferior to the other civilly or politically."[84]

In *Brown v. Board of Education*,[85] the 1954 landmark case challenging school segregation, the Court felt the need to know what were the original intentions of the framers of the Fourteenth Amendment.[86] Were the U.S. Congress and the state legislatures that enacted the Amendment in 1868 intent on ending racial segregation with the promise that the states would guarantee "equal protection of the law," "due process," and "liberty"? But how, having promised any one or all three of these constitutional protections, could one think of them as not intended to end segregation? The premise of racial segregation, given its painful history, was inferiority. The premise of equal protection under law had to be the equality of those subject to the law, not because of the law as such but because of right reason which was to be reflected in the law and to which the law was accountable. The two premises were consequently irreconcilable. Racial segregation was a refusal to accept a shared humanity with others because of irrelevant differences, such as skin color, which were equated with inequality or inferiority. While the Court acknowledged this, it chose to ignore the logical implication that racial segregation, no matter where it was practiced—education, employment, housing—was unacceptable as a matter of reason and consequently must be unacceptable as a matter of law. Instead, the Court declared that it must focus on education and consider what effect segregation had on it. "Only in this way can it be determined if segregation in public schools deprives the plaintiffs of the equal protection of the laws."[87] Were it not the case that it did, where would that leave segregation? In that event, with the Constitution as the determinant, segregation would have been acceptable, even though, as the Court acknowledged, "the policy of separating the races is usually interpreted as denoting the inferiority of the negro group."[88] *Usually interpreted* unfortunately implied that it was not always interpreted as denoting the inferiority of black people. On those occasions the interpretation of inferiority would, it followed, have been acceptable, incurring, as a consequence, a contradiction. However, had the Court been disposed to turn to the natural law as right reason in conformity with nature, it would have avoided the contradiction that it courted in *Brown v. Board of Education*. The ambiguity of its jurisprudence has left a legacy of *de facto*, if not *de jure*, segregation. In other words, it was a serious mistake to treat matters of reason, such as segregation, as though they can be settled definitively as matters of law.

No doubt there is reason to applaud the decision, as decisions go, in *Brown v. Board of Education*. However, it was disappointing from the perspective of what could have been achieved had the argument been advanced in the terms of the natural law—right reason in conformity with nature. *Brown* recognized the difficulties the contradictory and therefore inconclusive interpretations the Fourteenth Amendment occasioned over time. "In approaching this problem, we cannot turn the clock back to 1868 when the Amendment was adopted, or even to 1896, when *Plessy v. Ferguson* was written."[89] But instead of turning to the natural law and its irreducible principles which revealed unambiguously that, whatever its expression, racial segregation by definition violated the principle of universal justice, the Court turned to the effects of segregation on education. This implied the mistaken proposition that education was an appropriate norm by which to determine whether segregation itself was acceptable, whatever the Constitution might say. If it was found in education, it was there as a symptom. Removing a symptom was not removing its underlying pathology. In this case, that called for a jurisprudence recast in the language of the natural law.

There is no doubt that the Constitution intentionally stands for certain fundamental values central to informing its underlying jurisprudence. But do the justices consider the Constitution to have originated these values or do they consider it serving only to confirm them? How they answer the question has implications for their approach to any legislation under judicial review. Where *original intent* as definitive controls the approach, it suggests, for all practical purposes, a view of the Constitution as source. The word, *intent*, is ambiguous, particularly here, where it can refer to the *meaning* of the words of the Constitution, or to the *purpose* of law. This latter sense has significant implications for the process of judicial review. An early example of this coincidentally was provided by Justice John Marshal Harlan I in his dissent in *Plessy v. Ferguson*. Apart from the importance of the Fourteenth Amendment

Introduction: Ethics and Law, A Complicated but Necessary Relationship   21

to his review of the case, what should not go unnoticed was Harlan I's assessment, for purposes of review, of the internal structure of the Louisiana statute. "However apparent the injustice of such legislation may be, we have only to consider whether it is consistent with the constitution of the United States."[90] But if the legislation was unjust, how was it at the same time consistent with the Constitution? Harlan I rejected the notion that courts should be concerned with the policy or the expediency of legislation. Statutes may be valid even though, relative to public policy, they were unreasonable. However, once the purpose of legislation was adequately determined, the sole responsibility for the courts was to carry out the will of the law-making power, constitutionally expressed. In other words, "if the power exists to enact a statute, that ends the matter so far as the courts are concerned."[91]

LEGAL POSITIVISM

Justice Harlan I's is an early expression of a central tenet of legal positivism that the existence of law and the merits of law are distinct because ultimately the validity of law resides in its originator. The same of course can be said in the case of natural law but with the acknowledgment that the word, originator, is being used differently. It refers to rational human nature in the case of natural law. In the case of positive law, it refers to this or that legislator with acknowledged authority to legislate. Therein lies an essential difference between natural law and legal positivism. "Whether a society has a legal system depends on the presence of certain structures of governance, not on the extent to which it satisfies ideals of justice, democracy, or the rule of law."[92] Instead, a society's laws reflect what are considered by its legislators as prevailing societal norms of behavior.[93] "The fact that a policy would be just, wise, efficient, or prudent is never sufficient reason for thinking it is actually the law, and the fact that it is unjust, unwise, inefficient, or imprudent is never sufficient reason for doubting it."[94]

Another difference, the one of primary interest in this book, is that whereas natural law theory sees a necessary connection between law and morals, legal positivism does not. According to Hart,[95] a leading proponent, legal positivism does not represent as a necessary truth that laws should reflect or meet certain moral injunctions, even though, as it happens, they have done this. Indeed, in its formulation "law" was always informed by current norms for acceptable behavior and the values promoted by certain organizations active in society, not to mention the influence of certain people whose value system saw farther than the prevailing moral standards.[96] But this suggested a contingent relationship between the two. Consequently, Hart believed it would be a mistake to think that in the relationship, any legal system, for its "validity" was required to be concordant with specific moral norms.[97] The contingency of the relationship derived, according to Hart, from five contingencies evident in the human condition. The first was "human vulnerability," which calls for a "morality and law" predicated on an institutional avoidance of violence, or tolerance. The second was a "law and morality" responsive to "approximate equality," with an acknowledgment that while humans differed in "physical strength" and intelligence, no one person should be able to control others indefinitely. A third was "rules of law and morals" predicated on "limited altruism," which recognized as false that humans are by nature self-centered, without any appreciation for the interests of others. However true that might be, it was even more true that altruism is far from being unlimited. The fourth was a morality and law built on "limited resources." Here the argument was that "human beings" require, as a contingency, such things as "food" and housing. Since neither was readily available to them in the way that it might be said air was, they had to be produced by someone. From this Hart derived the notion of "property" ownership and the need for its legal protection.[98]

Relative to any of these contingencies in the human condition, the "rules" involved were, according to Hart, "static." The duties they occasioned did not vary from one individual to another. But given the necessity of cooperation upon which the production of necessary "supplies" depended, "dynamic" rules were also required so that those involved were able to impose duties and construe commitments as equivalent to duties. "Where altruism is not unlimited, a standing procedure providing for such self-binding operation is required in order to create a minimum of confidence in the future behavior of others."[99]

The fifth contingency fundamental to the human condition and requiring a morality and law was "limited understanding and strength of will." Given their societal conditions, humans could appreciate the need for laws to secure the integrity of "persons, property and promises." Consequently, they were disposed for the most part to comply with them even when compliance came with cost. However, since there were unavoidable costs, most, if not all citizens, at some point balked at compliance. In which case, unless there were some punitive provisions in place, the likelihood of non-compliance was considerable. This was why there were penalties, not to motivate compliance, but to ensure that those who were willing to comply with the rules were not placed at a disadvantage by those who refused to comply. "Given this standing danger, what reason demands is *voluntary* cooperation in a *coercive* system."[100]

Hart saw these contingencies—he referred to them as "truisms"—as essential to appreciating "law and morals." In particular, they occasioned the critical question whether each formulation of law had to be accompanied by penalties as a matter of the logic of the term, "law," or simply as a matter of "fact." In the case of municipal law, sanctions were a "natural necessity," as sufficient at least, for the protection of individuals, possessions, and commitments. To be satisfactory, an account of law had to be conditioned by seeing human beings, and the world in which they lived, for what they were. Hart referred to this as a basic alternative appreciation of Natural Law.[101] Mistakenly, however, since natural law theory is predicated, not on human beings as they are but as they should be.

If these contingencies form the predicate for the real nature and purpose of law, they also illustrate for Hart the connection between laws and morality. A commonly shared sense of tolerance he argued, grounded both. It found expression in a variety of social structures and was enjoyed by a variety of individuals within those structures. Nevertheless, it might be the case, for example, that denying tolerance to some members of society, despite their being disposed to comply with coinciding limitations, would have constituted a breach of morality. At the same time, there was no requirement that either "law" or" morality" ensured that all persons within their embrace enjoyed equally the same level of tolerance. Hart offered slavery in the United States and apartheid in South Africa as examples of a structure of law and societal mores which failed to consider all human beings as equal and deserving of their physical security. Describing both as "painful facts of human history," he also concluded that they demonstrated something else. To endure, any society had to extend structures of reciprocal tolerance to a minimum number of its members, though it need not, regrettably, extend it to all members.[102]

But why should this be a matter of regret? For Hart it came down to societal viability and its need for sanctions. The right to impose law coercively was conditioned on enough citizens agreeing to comply with it. Secured on this basis, authority was exercised either punitively against those who choose to violate the law, or it was used against some citizens, whether a majority or not, as distinct from those whom Hart referred to as the "master group," to keep them in a state of unending subjugation, "victims" of both the law and the prevailing social morality.[103]

What then for tolerance? How is it possible to have, as a predicate of social morality, forbearance when this morality consisted in the contradiction of being at the same time tolerance and intolerance? How can law consist in the contradiction of being at the same time advantage and disadvantage? How is it possible for a morality to consist simultaneously in disrespect for the persons of slaves and respect for the persons of the dominant group in society? Earlier, Hart had cited with approval David Hume's (1711–1776) observation that as it was not possible for human nature to persist outside a social setting, so it was not possible for this social setting to succeed without consideration of the "laws of equity and justice."[104] This, we may recall, was at the center of Cicero's disagreement with Carneades. Aristotle's appreciation of human beings as social animals anticipated Hume's insistence on a substantive relation between human nature and social settings. Given the centrality of society to human nature, its structures, including law, must reflect this centrality. That requires something more than contingencies.

Comparing this formulation of the human good with Aristotle's "disinterested cultivation of the human intellect," or Aquinas' "knowledge of God," Hart saw Hume lower his sights because Hume saw in the purpose of "survival" a necessary component, if the language of natural law theory was to have meaning based on experience. Human beings need not think of "survival" as something to be desired for its own sake. It was nothing more than a matter of contingency. Human beings did in fact pursue it, but it could be otherwise. But even as a pragmatic good, "survival" coincided in significance, Hart insisted, with the significance accorded it in natural law theory. Indeed, in its contingent formulation, it had much more to contribute to our appreciation of "law and morals." Once born, if we were to continue living, how did we do that as members of society? What societal structures, whether of law or morals, assured the survival of human beings as we find them empirically? For Hart, this was to abandon the metaphysics of natural law, to be replaced with something more amenable to contemporary thought and compatible with common sense.[105] However, one could reasonably argue that Hart's call for empiricism had already been met by natural law in its embrace of the need for positive law, as evidenced above in Aquinas, for example. Unlike Hart, who used the minimalist good of survival, Aquinas used the maximalist good of self-preservation, extending it beyond the human individual to include the human species. Unlike legal positivism, which consisted in contingent law and a morality of contingencies, natural law made the argument that since human existence was contingent, it needed more than tolerance. It needed justice and needed it for reasons more fundamental than societal viability. It was needed as a declaration of the equality, universally recognized, of human beings. Otherwise, like Hart, we find ourselves in the unacceptable position of saying that, to be viable, society must extend tolerance to some minimum number of its members, but then having to add that regrettably it need not extend forbearance to all members.

The significance of Hart's use of the word, *unfortunately*, cannot be overestimated in this discussion. Although part of a sentence that appeared to be a statement of fact, its presence there rendered the sentence a value judgment. In effect, Hart was saying that it was not good that forbearance did not need to be extended to all, in much the same way as one might say that it is not good that contracts need not be honored. In either case, the use of the word *good* is prescriptive and not descriptive. That is, stated positively, the first sentence is saying that one *ought* to extend forbearance to all, just as the second sentence is saying that one *ought* to honor contracts. However, it is not clear in Hart's case where this prescriptive is coming from, except that it cannot be coming from the morality to which he referred since that morality consists in *not* showing forbearance to some members of society. Hart's point, with regard to tolerance, was that a minimum degree of it was required for any society to be viable. Viability called for members willing to comply with the status quo in sufficient numbers so that law, together with underlying social mores achieved compliance coercively from the rest of the members, even to their disproportionate cost and virtually no benefit. That was the legal order and social morality that gave rise, for example, to the anti-slavery and suffragette movements which declared in effect that just because one can secure the viability of society in this manner, it did not mean that one ought to. Nor should it be thought that the goal pursued in either case was simply an alternative version of viability, substituting one contingent formulation of it for another. As a result, it should give one pause to hear Hart state that, as a matter of fact, and therefore legitimately, law tended to follow social morality, if only to secure compliance. Those who called for the end of slavery, like those who demanded the vote for women, had had their fill of compliance with a social morality that would have continued to deny both demands. Their goal was justice as an absolute, irreducible principle of equality enjoyed universally by human beings living in society. That required a positive law to address human nature as one found it, but a positive law also grounded in ethics in recognition of the reality of human nature as it ought to be.

ETHICS

Ethics is possibly one of the most misunderstood methods used for assessing, in its very origins, human behavior. Some of this misunderstanding comes from confusing ethics with morality. Whereas morality is something we are born into, ethics is something we construct, using unaided human reason. Consequently, ethics consists in an on-going principled conversation between reason and human nature so as to distinguish between good and bad human behavior. Given the range of what, individually or collectively, human beings can do, coupled with the fact that so much of this activity affects others, it must be principled, or rational so as to be of universal application or ethically proportionate to its reach. From this perspective, the notion of ethics as subjective and relative is without merit if it results in the conclusion that the behavior of one individual is so subjective and relative in its motivation and consequences as never to be other-regarding, or not affecting others positively or negatively. Whatever about the life of the lone individual on a deserted island, that is hardly the experience of societal existence. But while the lone individual on a deserted island does not need law, he does need ethics so as not to turn his back on reason and his true nature. And since history confirms that it is possible for human beings, under the influence of law, to defy reason and debase their nature, law itself must be grounded in ethics.

R. M. HARE (1919–2002)

Hare's analysis of the language employed in ethics discourse[106] is of considerable relevance for the way it counters the appreciation of ethics as subjective and relative. "There are no absolutes in ethics" is not an infrequent observation made about ethics, the observer seemingly unaware that the logic of the language of the observation entails there is now at least one. To his everlasting merit, Hare has placed the laws of logic at the center of ethics, but without making ethics simply a matter of logic. Rather, his analysis of the language particular to ethics has made it possible to rescue ethics from what for it is the pointlessness of subjectivity and the uselessness of relativism. That is because, according to Hare, ethics exists to answer what for human beings is an unavoidable question, what "shall" be done in the way one might ask, what "ought" to be done?[107] Might they just as well ask, "what can be done?" Yes, if logically *can* functions in the same way as *ought* so that they are interchangeable terms. But they are not, since the use of *ought* signals a search for some norm or principle to direct our choice of what to do that is absent from *can*.

Human beings, as rational, live constantly in the face of the unavoidable alternatives, "can" and "ought." As observed earlier, it is only when one can do something that it is reasonable to ask whether one ought to do it. Indeed, the ability to do something is, for practical purposes, the condition for being in a position to pose the "ought" question. Since making law is a human activity, those so engaged cannot avoid considering the alternatives as the basis for their law making. Ought I to make this law, even though I can? does not seem to be a question that comes naturally to legal positivism.

Hare made the observation that to know how a person acts is the most telling indication of what are their ethical principles. Given particular circumstances that require taking action, and after considering various "courses of action," the particular action taken would tell us what "principles" informed their behavior since that is their purpose.[108] For this reason, Hare argued, the language used to present ethical issues calls for precision, since "confusion about our moral language leads, not merely to theoretical muddles, but to needless practical perplexities."[109]

Since the language of ethics revolves around words like "ought," "right," and "good," used prescriptively or as imperatives, it is designed to function as a form of reasoning, consisting in universal imperatives or "moral," as distinct from "non-moral" value-judgments to provide guidance to the moral agent. By comparing the two forms of prescriptive language where the same words are used, Hare's ultimate goal was to demonstrate that the laws of logic applied equally, ensuring, as a result, objectivity.[110] In other words, the logic of the moral command, "you ought to honor your contract," was identical to the logic of the non-moral command, "you ought to close the door." Having been commanded to close the door, if one accepts the command, it follows that one will close the door. Otherwise, one will have contradicted oneself. Having been commanded to honor one's contract, if one accepts the command, it follows that one will honor the contract. To do otherwise would also incur a contradiction. As far as the logic of the language in both the moral and non-moral commands is concerned, that one is a moral imperative and the other is a non-moral imperative is irrelevant. In the same vein, for A to tell B to honor contracts, while telling C *not* to honor contracts, would make sense neither logically nor normatively from an ethics perspective.

In his focus on the logic of the language used in ethics, Hare was also concerned to address a serious challenge to its prescriptivity. The issue here is the possibility of postulating a real distinction between language in the imperative mood and in the indicative mood so as to turn back the effort to think of imperatives as indicatives. That is, to say, "shut the door" is to say, "you are going to shut the door." As Hare observed, the difference between the two statements is clear. Explaining the difference, however, is not easy. Both have in common the idea of closing the "door in the immediate future." But grammatically it is clear they are not saying the same thing about closing the door. In the "indicative" form, the sense is X is occurring, whereas in the "imperative" form, the sense is let X occur.[111] The target here is what Hare referred to as the "naturalist" theory of language which wants to consider statements in the "imperative" mood as actually declarative or factual statements.[112] Were it to be successful, the implications for the possibility of ethics would be devastating since it is not possible to derive a prescription from a fact. Logically, one may not proceed from the indicative statement, "nuclear war is indefensible" to the prescriptive statement, "one ought not to conduct nuclear war." But if, as the naturalist theory of language contends, prescriptive statements are simply statements reflecting some attitude of whoever is speaking, this would mean that to say, "Nuclear war is wrong," means nothing more than "I disapprove of nuclear war." Used conversationally, Hare conceded, this is inconsequential. But used formally, the logical consequences are very considerable. Were someone to say to A, "conduct a nuclear war," as someone else said, also to A, "don't conduct a nuclear war," it would involve, incorrectly according to the naturalist argument, no contradiction, merely evidence of speakers with differing intentions. Nevertheless, as Hare would have observed, it does not alter the case that the words "conduct a nuclear war" have to do with conducting a nuclear war, and have little to do with what is going on inside the head of the "speaker."[113] Hare concluded that the disposition to treat an imperative statement as though an indicative statement was deeply rooted and based on "criteria of meaningfulness" deemed necessary to verify the truth of statements. "A sentence does not have meaning unless there is something that would be the case were the sentence true."[114] This is true of statements of fact, but is not the case with statements of command, which nevertheless are statements, though not factual statements. John Wilson provided a good example of this in his discussion of the legitimacy of the death penalty. While generally regarded as a just punishment for homicide, Wilson noted that there had been no attempt to demonstrate its effectiveness in preventing homicide. What was needed was empirical evidence of effectiveness based on "observation and experiment."[115] For effectiveness, maybe, but unless one equates effectiveness with justice, the only thing demonstrated would be that capital punishment is either effective or ineffective. Its justice would remain an open question, even if it were effective, less so, obviously, if it were ineffective. That capital punishment is ineffective is a statement of fact; that capital punishment is unjust is not a statement of fact. It is a value statement. They are quite different kinds of statements, the truth of which requires different ways of demonstrating their truth. Attempting to verify a value statement with the same method of verification used for verifying factual statements leads only to confusion.[116]

A second way imperatives are reduced to indicatives is to say they are designed to provoke certain emotions which then lead to a particular behavior. Again, Hare was prepared to say that conversationally, this was of little consequence. In formal uses of language, however, it was a matter of concern. A command is given to get someone to "do something." But in this case, the understanding of the command is that it actually causes what is commanded to occur. But as Hare noted, it is one thing to command someone to do something. Logically, however, causing this to happen is something else again. Confusing commanding with causing would render ethical behavior, which by definition is an act of the will in pursuit of some good, impossible. Indeed, the same distinction applies to statements of fact. Informing people of something factual is, as matter of logic, different from bringing them to a point where they accept it.[117]

To confuse the two would turn an act of informing into an act of indoctrinating. Hare concluded since ordinary commands and factual statements are subject to the rules of logic, it is reasonable to think that the same applies to moral imperatives or judgments, allowing for the fact that while moral imperatives function in some ways like ordinary imperatives, they also function differently.[118] The larger point here is that declarations of fact, ordinary commands, and moral judgments are rational statements directed to rational human beings with a view to their behaving rationally. To succeed, this requires that they are conveyed in and through language which is dependent for its intelligibility and objectivity on compliance with the laws of logic.

To demonstrate further the authority of logic, Hare examined what sorts of reasoning or inference-making can answer the ethics question, what is to be done? Until this is clear, little, he insisted, could be claimed for the obligatory nature of the inferences we make in ethics.[119] Inference rests on a principle of logic to the effect that a "valid deductive inference must consist in whatever is already present in the meaning of its 'premises.'"[120] From this, according to Hare, it follows that if the conclusion consists in an "imperative" then it should already be evident in the "premises."[121] To use Hare's example:

Take all the boxes to the station (imperative)

This is one of the boxes (indicative)

Therefore, take this to the station (imperative)[122]

This is because the logical outcome of a deductive inference is to make explicit what is implicit in the combination of the two premises. The conclusion, or what is deductively inferred, is contained already in the premises. In other words, deductively drawn inferences can be considered analytic in the same way that the statement, *bachelors are unmarried men*, is an analytic statement. Its truth is evident because of the meaning of the words used in the statement. As Hare explained it, if someone accepted the proposition that "all men are mortal and that Socrates was a man," but would not accept that "Socrates was mortal," it could only mean that he did not understand the meaning of the word "all."[123] Someone, having accepted that all men are mortal, and that Socrates was a man, cannot deny that Socrates was mortal without incurring a contradiction or being irrational. These two examples deal with non-moral issues but the same reasoning is applicable in moral settings as we can see in what follows.

When Socrates[124] was in prison and awaiting death at his own hand, he was visited by his good friend Crito who proposed a plan of escape. In his response to the proposal, Socrates used the same deductive reasoning to answer the ethics question, what should he do, escape or not? As Socrates saw things, the basic issue was not the fact of escaping but what merit escaping might possess. That is, "whether it is just or unjust for me to try to leave here, when I was not acquitted by the Athenians."[125] What merit, that is, if one thought one should never choose to behave unjustly, since that "is evil and shameful in every way for the person who does it."[126] What merit, if one thought there might be circumstances under which one could choose to act unjustly? Try as he would to identify them, Socrates could not. One must never behave unjustly, which in his situation would mean that by escaping he would be repaying an injustice with injustice.[127]

Socrates did not stop there. Should one be the cause of harm? Would leaving Athens, he asked, without the agreement of Athenians be harmful "to those whom we should least of all harm, or not?"[128] Since to harm someone is to do an "injustice," and since one should not be the occasion of injustice, then it follows that one should not cause harm.[129] Beyond this consideration, there is another. If someone has entered into an agreement that is just, should it be honored? This alluded to the agreement, both explicit and tacit, that he, as a citizen, had with the city of Athens. It should, was his conclusion. Otherwise, and here Socrates spoke for Athens, by escaping "aren't you planning to do nothing other than destroy us, the laws, and the civic community, as much as you can?"[130] Since one should never behave unjustly,[131] the conclusion for Socrates was inescapable: without the city agreeing to the escape, he would betray the agreement, thereby inflicting harm. From all of this, it is not too difficult to see Socrates' argument:

Always act justly (imperative)

Escaping violates one's agreements with Athens (indicative)

One should not escape (imperative)[132]

It is worth noting that while the integrity of the law was a central consideration for Socrates, he had no doubt that escaping, as a violation of the law, was unethical since it violated law as law because just, not law as law because simply so ordered. Otherwise, given the injustice of his sentence, he had every reason to accept Crito's invitation.

According to Hare, valid moral reasoning must result in an "imperative."[133] If one has asked the ethics question, "what should I do?" the ethics response is "you ought to do X." Evident in Socrates' argument, this is because the principles involved in reasoning and applied in ethics are intended to have prescriptive force. However, Hare observed that drawing inferences in an ethics context is more complicated. We are not dealing with the definition of words and their logical use; we are dealing with human actions and their normative direction. Consider, he suggested, that if someone declares, "never say what is false," and then asserts, "S is false," it follows logically to draw the valid conclusion that one should not say S.[134] Nevertheless, it is not clear, based on the meaning of the words themselves, in what sense *never say what is false* is self-evident as a principle directing one's conduct. Were it undeniable, it would be either because to do so would incur a contradiction, or it would be psychologically impossible. If the former, then the principle is *analytic* and incapable of directing behavior one way or the other. It would be equivalent, for example, to saying, "you ought to do your duty," that is, "you ought to do what you ought to do." If the latter, it would be contingent on the individual, possible for some, even though impossible for others. And since being impossible or possible is a matter of fact, there is no imperative derivable from it.[135]

What then is to be said for principles of conduct as rules of inference for what one ought or ought not to? If we are to use principles like "always act justly," or "never say what is false," we have, Hare argued, to show their difference from using the rules of logic to direct how we use words. The difference essentially lies in that principles of conduct are about matters of substance, captured in the factual premise, and not mere words.[136]

One difference, according to Hare, might be that principles of action as "rules of inference" are less rigorous in their application compared to those found in governing the logical use of words. If so, one might say, for example, "this is false, but say it," and since the principle is being applied less rigorously here, any contradiction is avoided. In which case, one can continue with "*S is false, therefore don't say S*," without logical difficulty. But, as Hare also observed, we can alternatively say, "S is false, but say it," without contradiction on the grounds that such rules of conduct are subject to exceptions, such as the protection of defenseless children from serious harm. Given the human condition, there may be particular cases which, as exceptions, would justify saying something false.[137] In Nazi Germany, some people concealed Jews in their homes from the Gestapo. If asked during a house raid, "are you harboring Jews?" would making an exception to the norm, always tell the truth, and deny it, be ethical? Clearly, it would.

Now, some will conclude from this line of argument that ethics is at once both relative and subjective. Neither is the case because, as Hare pointed out, the individual as moral agent, has to decide on what basis to make an exception in the particular circumstance presenting itself. It is, in effect, a decision of principle in the form of a modification of the principle. In other words, far from loosening the principle, one is making its application more precise by determining where and where not it actually applies. From this, Hare concluded that we should consider these rules of behavior as "provisional" rather than flexible. If we are to change them into precisely applied rules of conduct, correctly identifying where they do not apply in the process, we should count this as an indication of ethical development.[138]

This point is critical for both objectivity and universality in ethical behavior. Exceptions, though there may be to generally held principles, are also to be considered universal. Essential to reasoning in ethics is the final judgment that the moral agent makes. As Hare explained it, when an individual says either, "this is false, so don't say it," or "this is false, but I'll say it," making an exception to the general principle, something more than "inferring" occurs. On its own, whatever the "inference," it does not determine what is to be said or done in a particular circumstance. The inference goes as far as to determine that should one say what is false, one will be violating the rule. But having arrived at that point, it remains for the individual as moral agent to modify it or not. This means that rules of behavior necessarily call for specific "commands." As a consequence, for Hare, the issue was not a lack of rigor, but the formulation, and subsequent modification of our behavioral norms as rules with which to infer particular and precise commands directing our behavior.[139]

As brief as this discussion of Hare's linguistic and logic-based approach to understanding ethics is, it is sufficient to show the necessity of and merit for the argument that ethics, to be of real use in directing human behavior, particularly other-regarding behavior, has to be both objective and grounded in universally applicable norms.

ALAN GEWIRTH (1912–2004)

If we turn our attention now to the thinking of Gewirth,[140] we will see something very similar, though expressed differently. Like Hare, Gewirth sought to secure objectivity and prescriptivity for ethics. In this regard, he did not consider the individual's "judgment" as dispositive for deciding what is "morally good."[141] One of the main goals of his work, *The Community of Rights*, is to demonstrate the counterintuitive notion that individual "rights" and communitarianism are compatible because they function in complementary roles.[142] As Gewirth explained it, "rights" cannot be realized apart from "community." That is, he viewed the state as a means to secure the rights enjoyed equally by all. In this view, the state is not an end in itself, the viability of which is assured by a "solidarity" among members of society as they pursue shared interests.[143]

To justify his vision of the relations between the individual and the state, Gewirth developed an argument predicated on what he called "ethical individualism."[144] This consists in a "social relation" that renders the state a community of rights in which certain goods, equally enjoyed without exception by all its members, are to be claimed as "human rights" and a matter of "social concern." In this capacity, they serve, according to Gewirth, as the standard of what is the moral good, which he formulated in his principle of human rights. As he saw it, this principle was to stand in strong contrast to "ethical egoism" which consists in the pursuit of self-interests alone as a matter of rights. Rights, according to Gewirth, are "interests" that people enjoy and that merit protection. That these interests merit protection suggests that they are owed to the individual who controls them for their own sake.[145] He noted three characteristics of these rights. They are enjoyed universally across the human race. They are "mutual," in that they are enjoyed by each member of society in a "supportive" relation to all other members of society. And they are "reciprocal," in that there is an obligation for each member of society not to encroach on the rights of other members of society.[146] Unlike in the case of Hart, for Gewirth there is no minimal level of mutuality and reciprocity that will secure a society's feasibility. To be ensured, rights depend on society. At the same time, it is these same rights that give legitimacy to the functions of society. It is "a means to protect the equal rights of individuals rather than an end or good in itself."[147] Viewed as interests, they include "life, physical integrity, and economic security," among others.[148]

Gewirth used the word rights. But do humans have rights at all?[149] In his response, Gewirth noted two sources as justification for their existence. One is "social recognition" combined with "legal reinforcement." The other is a "moral justification." This, however, can be problematic, underscoring as it does the argument central to this book. Legally instituted and enforced "rights" may well lack ethical standing, as in the case of slavery. Similarly, ethically acceptable "rights" such as a woman's right to "own property," have lacked societal acceptance.[150] In both conflicts, the accepted procedure for resolution has been to hold the law or social mores accountable to moral norms, as we saw in natural law theory. While this may be true, Gewirth asked whether the procedure might be the other way round? In preference to using rights as the justification for human behavior, some turn, Gewirth suggested, to what Richard Rorty referred to as "culturally influenced intuitions."[151] The problem with this form of justification, as Gewirth noted, is the lack of consistency in "intuitions," clearly observable among societies. Another justification has been the claim that being human entails rights which would imply that the claim is analytic or self-evident logically. But that one can deny the claim without contradicting oneself is evidence that it is not. Further, there is the consideration that while one can say that an individual member of society enjoys "interests," it does not follow that other members have an obligation to support those interests. Having their own, they could fulfill them without having to recognize the interests of someone else, as we saw in Hart's view of a contingency-based society.[152] Another source of justification posed by Gewirth is the principle of "rational choice." Here, Gewirth hypothesized that if understanding what is a "rational" person refers to someone who, in pursuit of personal interests, selects the measure most certain to secure them, that person is likely to do that by invoking, as a matter of self-interest, certain "rights." Rational though that may be for any self-interested individual to do, it does not follow logically that others are under an obligation to comply with these claims.[153]

The elusive component in each of these sources of justification is prescriptivity. If then, we are to base justification in rights, the question will be whether they can be considered as prescriptive. For Gewirth, there are two indispensable conditions required of rights to fulfill this role. The first is that the "rights" claimed are themselves "normatively necessary." The second is that the principle itself on which these particular rights are predicated as justificatory has to be what Gewirth described as so dispositive as to override contradictory obligations derived from competing "interests" or "other norms."[154] Not surprisingly, Gewirth concluded that if individual interests and society are to be compatible, this condition is of paramount importance.[155]

This brings us to the consideration of the foundation of Gewirth's argument for rights as justificatory. Of necessity, he insisted, the foundation has to have the reach proportionate to the full extent of what might be considered moral behavior. And since it also has to be unavoidable for humans as "actual or prospective" actors, what alone qualifies as the foundation is human action itself. Humans as humans cannot *not* act. Accordingly, humans cannot avoid asking the question central to ethics, how they ought to act, with the reasonable expectation of receiving an answer since that is the function of the norms found in ethics.[156]

If action is constitutive of human being, one can infer that rights are derivable from interests persons have in being able to enjoy the conditions necessary for such action. The force of the argument stems from the nature of human agency itself. "For every agent logically must hold or accept that he has rights to the necessary conditions of action and successful action in general."[157] And if the question is how one ought, not can, act as a human being, the answer is with "freedom and well-being" as indispensable interests. As such these interests are the objects of the most powerful claims, that of a human right, that persons can make.[158] Consequently, freedom and well-being are the foundation of all ethical behavior. This is because what starts as an acknowledgment of a claim of self-interest or prudence logically becomes an acknowledgment of an identical claim of others, considered as actual or potential actors. If every agent acting as a human being has to acknowledge that to do so requires freedom and well-being, then it is also logically required of that agent to acknowledge the rights to freedom and well-being equally enjoyed by every other agent acting as a human being.[159] With the latter acknowledgment, according to Gewirth, the rights to freedom and well-being have become irreducible ethical norms, applying universally to the actions of every agent acting as a human being. To act solely on the basis of one's own interests, without due regard also for the interests of others, would be irrational, violating the principle of non-contradiction. If one claims as a right freedom and well-being for the sake of one's own human agency, to be rational, one ought not act so as to deny the same claim of all other agents made for the sake of their human agency. The inescapable logical conclusion is that all agents acting as human beings enjoy rights to freedom and well-being without exception.[160] This conclusion led Gewirth to formulate as foundational for ethics the norm that every agent act with respect for the "rights" of others, along with their own. He called it the *"Principle of Generic Consistency"* since it comprises two elements critical to normative ethics, logical coherence based ultimately on the principle of non-contradiction and substantive interests essential to, and "rights" claimed for, human agency.[161]

The implications of this are quite considerable for society and its laws. It is clear that Gewirth's vision of both as grounded in a prescriptive ethics, derived from his principle of generic consistency, is in marked contrast to Hart's contingency-based vision. Gewirth's vision is "communitarian," stressing a "solidarity" among persons that is feasible due to the mutuality characteristic of human rights.[162] The state, its institutions and its laws, function by way of securing and furthering the rights equally enjoyed by members of society. These rights, although housed in and exercised by individuals constitute a community of reciprocated rights.

At the center of his community of rights is what Gewirth called an "economic constitution."[163] He was using the term metaphorically so as to include a cluster of interests such as work, "property," and "political democracy." Accordingly, it can reasonably include *constitution* in its familiar literal sense, with "institutional" norms integral to a working "community."[164] Now since the constitution is there to secure the "economic rights" of members of society, it has to be regarded from two directions. The first is from that of the individual, where it amounts to a "biography" recording the enjoyment of "progressive" benefits in the exercise of their rights. The second is from that of society where the "constitution" is the embodiment of public policy, "legal" and "institutional," that furthers the "biography" as it ought to be furthered.[165] It is, in other words, a constitution with a necessary connection to prescriptive ethics in the long tradition of natural law theory.

John Dewey made the observation that "Democracy ... is a social, that is to say, an ethical conception, and upon its ethical significance is based its significance as governmental."[166] There is nothing in this discussion of Gewirth to suggest that he would not say, "amen."

***

It is clear, from even this cursory review of Hare and Gewirth, how mistaken the idea is that ethics is both subjective and relative, a matter of personal preferences irrelevant to law-making and jurisprudence. One of Hare's critical achievements was, according to Peter Singer,[167] the restoration of reason to ethical argument. A reasoning that merits necessary attention from the judiciary, who, in their jurisprudence, must address the question at the heart of ethics and unavoidable in any human behavior, what ought I do? For his part, Gewirth has rescued our use of rights as instruments exclusive to self-interest. Instead, he has cogently argued for understanding them as embodying a "mutualist and egalitarian universality"[168] by which society provides an ethics grounding for its laws and institutions.[169]

Since the judicial review undertaken by the U.S. Supreme Court, as human behavior, occurs within a Dewey democracy, it too is subject to ethics. There is then no escaping Kant. Jurists may declare what any law, specific to a time and place, calls for. But whether its prescriptions are just or unjust, and what norms recognize the difference, must remain unknown until they suspend temporarily their "empirical principles" and turn to "reason" itself as the final justification of "positive law," notwithstanding that it too can contribute to this effort. d'Entreves got the point. "Kant compared a "purely empirical theory of law" to "the wooden head in Phaedrus' fable, which may be beautiful, but alas! has no brain."[170] Fundamental to the problems in the decisions reviewed in this book is the unremitting reliance on a positivist theory of law, to the exclusion of natural law theory which stipulates the understanding of law as necessarily grounded in ethics.

NOTES

1. U.S. Court of Appeals, *In the Matter of Baby "K" (Three Cases)*, 16 F.3d 590 (4th Cir. 1994), https://h2o.law.harvard.edu/cases/4272 (accessed October 15, 2020).

2. *Matter of Baby "K"* at 596.

3. *Matter of Baby "K"* at 597.

4. David Leonhardt, *A Corporate Court,* New York Times, October 19, 2020

5. Alessandro Passerin d'Entrèves was an Italian philosopher and law historian. See Immanuel Kant, discussed in d'Entrèves, *Natural Law: An Introduction to Legal Philosophy* (London: Hutchinson University Library, 1964), 114.

6. Sir Ernest Baker, *Tradition of Civility* (Cambridge: Cambridge University Press, 1948).

7. Kant, cited in d'Entrèves, *Natural Law*, 115.

8. Marcus Tullius Cicero, *On the Republic*, in The Political Works of Marcus Tullius Cicero: Comprising his Treatise on the Commonwealth; and his Treatise on the Laws, in 2 vols., trans. Francis Barham, Esq. (London: Edmund Spettigue, 1841–1842), bk. 3, 270, https://oll.libertyfund.org/titles/546 (accessed October 15, 2020).

9. Marcus Tullius Cicero, *On the Laws*, trans. David Fott (Ithaca, NY: Cornell University Press, 2014), bk. 1, 33, https://www.ninrac.org/classical/cicero/documents/de-legibus (accessed September 5, 2020).

10. Cicero, *On the Laws*, bk. 1, 33.

11. Cicero, *On the Republic*, trans. Barham, bk. 3, 270.

12. Cicero, *On the Republic*, trans. Barham, bk. 3, 270.

13. Carneades, quoted in Cicero, *On the Republic*, trans. Barham, bk. 3, 262.

14. Cicero, *On the Laws*, bk. 1, 29.

15. *Penguin Dictionary of Philosophy*, ed. Thomas Mautner (London: Penguin Books, 1997), 542.

16. *Penguin Dictionary of Philosophy*, 542.

17. Cicero, *On the Republic*, trans. Barham, bk. 3, 270.

18. *Penguin Dictionary of Philosophy*, 542.

19. *Penguin Dictionary of Philosophy*, 542.

20. *Penguin Dictionary of Philosophy*, 542.

21. Cicero, *On the Republic*, trans. Clinton W. Keyes (Cambridge, MA: Harvard University Press, 1928), bk. 2, 26, 48. http://www.attalus.org/translate/republic3.html (accessed September 5, 2020).

22. Cicero, *On the Republic*, trans. Keyes, bk. 3, 31,43.

23. Cicero, *On the Republic*, trans. Keyes, bk. 3, 33, 45.

24. Cicero, *On the Republic*, trans. Keyes, bk. 3, 22, 33.

25. Cicero, *On the Republic*, trans. Keyes, bk. 3, 15.

26. Marcus Tullius Cicero, *De Legibus (On the Laws)*, in The Political Works of Marcus Tullius Cicero: Comprising his Treatise on the Commonwealth; and his Treatise on the Laws, trans. Francis Barham, Esq. (London: Edmund Spettigue, 1841–1842), vol. 2, bk. 1, 45, https://oll.libertyfund.org/titles/cicero-treatise-on-the-laws (accessed October 15, 2020).

27. Cicero, *De Legibus (On the Laws)*, trans. Barham, vol. 2, bk. 1, 46.

28. Cicero, *De Legibus (On the Laws)*, trans. Barham, vol. 2, bk. 1, 48.

29. Cicero, *De Legibus (On the Laws)*, trans. Barham, vol. 2, bk. 1, 48.

30. Cicero, *De Legibus (On the Laws)*, trans. Barham, vol. 2, bk. 1, 48.

31. Cicero, *De Legibus (On the Laws)*, trans. Barham, vol. 2, bk. 1, 48.

32. Mark Murphy, "The Natural Law Tradition in Ethics," Stanford Encyclopedia of Philosophy (Summer 2019), ed. Edward N. Zalta, https://plato.stanford.edu/archives/sum2019/entries/natural-law-ethics (accessed October 15, 2020).

33. St. Thomas Aquinas, "First Part of the Second Part," in *Summa Theologica*, 2nd and rev. ed., trans. Father of the English Dominican Province (New Advent, Online Edition, 1920), question 94, art. 4, https://www.newadvent.org/summa/2.htm (accessed October 15, 2020).

34. Murphy, "Natural Law Tradition in Ethics," 1.1.2.

35. Aquinas, "First Part of the Second Part," in *Summa Theologica*, question 94, art. 2. Note: "The principles of a demonstration must be true, indemonstrable, and such as to provide the reason for the truth of the conclusion, but they must also be necessary" (Aquinas, quoted in John Longeway, "Medieval Theories of Demonstration," *Stanford Encyclopedia of Philosophy* [Spring 2009], ed. Edward N. Zalta, https://plato.stanford.edu/entries/demonstration-medieval [accessed October 15, 2020]).

36. Aquinas, "First Part of the Second Part," in *Summa Theologica*, question 94, art. 2.

37. Aquinas, "First Part of the Second Part," in *Summa Theologica*, question 94, art. 2.

38. Aquinas, "First Part of the Second Part," in *Summa Theologica*, question 91, art. 1 and art. 2.

39. Aquinas, "First Part of the Second Part," in *Summa Theologica*, question 90, art. 1.

40. Aquinas, "First Part of the Second Part," in *Summa Theologica*, question 1, art. 1.

41. Aquinas, "First Part of the Second Part," in *Summa Theologica*, question 91, art. 3.

42. Aquinas, "First Part of the Second Part," in *Summa Theologica*, question 90, art. 2.

43. Aquinas, "First Part of the Second Part," in *Summa Theologica*, question 90, art 2.

44. Murphy, "Natural Law Tradition in Ethics," 1.1.3.

45. Murphy, "Natural Law Tradition in Ethics," 1.1.3.

46. Thomas Hobbes, *Leviathan* (1651*)* in *The English Philosophers from Bacon to Mill*, ed. Edwin A. Burtt (New York: The Modern Library, 1939), 163–67.

47. Hugo Grotius, The Rights of War and Peace, ed. Jean Barbeyrac and Richard Tuck, intro. Richard Tuck (Indianapolis: Liberty Fund, 2005), vol. 1, chap. 1, no. 3, https://oll.libertyfund.org/titles/1425 (accessed April 20, 2020).

48. Aquinas, "First Part of the Second Part," in *Summa Theologica*, question 57, art. 1.

49. Grotius, Rights of War and Peace, vol. 1, chap. 1, no. 4.

50. Grotius, Rights of War and Peace, vol. 1, chap. 1, no. 5.

51. Grotius, Rights of War and Peace, vol. 1, chap. 1, no. 6.

52. Grotius, Rights of War and Peace, vol. 1, chap. 1, no. 9.

53. Grotius, Rights of War and Peace, vol. 1, chap. 1, no. 10 at 1.

54. Grotius, Rights of War and Peace, vol. 1, chap. 1, no. 14.

55. Grotius, Rights of War and Peace, vol. 1, chap. 1, no. 10 at 5.

56. Grotius, Rights of War and Peace, vol. 1, "Prolegomena," no. 11.

57. d'Entrèves, *Natural Law*, 53.

58. Grotius, Rights of War and Peace, vol. 1, chap. 1, no.1.

59. Grotius, Rights of War and Peace, vol. 1, chap. 1, no. 3.

60. Hugo Grotius, The Rights of War and Peace, including the Law of Nature and of Nations, trans. from the original Latin of Grotius, with notes and illustrations from political and legal writers, by A.C. Campbell, A.M., intro. David J. Hill (New York: M. Walter Dunne, 1901), https://oll.libertyfund.org/titles/553 (accessed April 24, 2020).

61. Hugo Grotius, The Rights of War and Peace, including the Law of Nature and of Nations, trans. from the original Latin of Grotius, with notes and illustrations from political and legal writers, by A.C. Campbell, A.M., intro. David J. Hill (New York: M. Walter Dunne, 1901), https://oll.libertyfund.org/titles/553 (accessed April 24, 2020).

62. See Robert A. Dahl, *Democracy and its Critics* (New Haven, CT: Yale University Press, 1989), 280–98.

63. John Locke, *An Essay Concerning The True Original, Extent and End of Civil Government* (1690), in *The English Philosophers From Bacon To Mill*, ed. Edwin A. Burtt (New York: Modern Library, 1939), 404–9.

64. U.S. Supreme Court, *New York v. United States*, 505 U.S. 144 (1992), at 168, https://supreme.justia.com/cases/federal/us/505/144/ (accessed October 15, 2020).

65. Lawrence O. Gostin, ed., *Public Health Law and Ethics: A Reader*, 2nd and rev. ed. (Berkeley: University of California Press, 2010), 136–37.

66. Aristotle, *The Nicomachean Ethics*, trans. J. A. K. Thomson (Harmondsworth, UK: Penguin Books, 1965), 25.

67. U.S. Supreme Court, *Dred Scott v. Sandford*, 60 U.S. 393 (1856). https://caselaw.findlaw.com/us-supreme-court/60/393.html (accessed October 15, 2020).

68. *Dred Scott v. Sandford* at 410.

69. *Dred Scott v. Sandford* at 410.

70. *Dred Scott v. Sandford* at 411.

71. *Dred Scott v. Sandford* at 411.

72. *Dred Scott v. Sandford* at 410.

73. *Dred Scott v. Sandford* at 411.

74. U.S. Supreme Court, *Plessy v. Ferguson*, 163 U.S. 537 (1896), https://www.law.cornell.edu/supremecourt/text/163/537 (accessed October 15, 2020).

75. *Plessy v. Ferguson* at 13.

76. *Plessy v. Ferguson* at 13.

77. *Plessy v. Ferguson* at 25.

78. *Plessy v. Ferguson* at 24.

79. *Plessy v. Ferguson* at 24.

80. *Plessy v. Ferguson* at 24.

81. *Plessy v. Ferguson* at 25.

82. *Plessy v. Ferguson* at 25.

83. *Plessy v. Ferguson* at 17.

84. *Plessy v. Ferguson* at 25.

85. U.S. Supreme Court, *Brown v. Board of Education*, 347 U.S. 483 (1954), https://www.law.cornell.edu/supremecourt/text/347/483 (accessed October 15, 2020).

86. *Brown v. Board of Education* at 489.

87. *Brown v. Board of Education* at 493.

88. *Brown v. Board of Education* at 494.

89. *Brown v. Board of Education* at 492.

90. *Plessy v. Ferguson* at 34.

91. *Plessy v. Ferguson* at 42.

92. Leslie Green and Thomas Adams, "Legal Positivism," *Stanford Encyclopedia of Philosophy*, ed. Edward N. Zalta (Winter 2019), http://plato.stanford.edu/entries/legal-positivism/ (accessed April 29, 2020).

93. Green and Adams, "Legal Positivism."

94. Green and Adams, "Legal Positivism."

95. H. L. A. [Herbert Lionel Adolphus] Hart, *The Concept of Law* (1961) (Oxford: Oxford University Press, 2012).

96. Hart, *Concept of Law*, 185.

97. Hart, *Concept of Law*, 185.
98. Hart, *Concept of Law*, 194–97.
99. Hart, *Concept of Law*, 197.
100. Hart, *Concept of Law*, 198.
101. Hart, *Concept of Law*, 199.
102. Hart, *Concept of Law*, 200–1.
103. Hart, *Concept of Law*, 201.
104. Hart, *Concept of Law*, 191.
105. Hart, *Concept of Law*, 191–92.
106. R. M. [Richard Mervyn] Hare, *The Language of Morals* (1952) (Oxford: Clarendon Press, 1960).
107. Hare, *Language of Morals*, 1.
108. Hare, *Language of Morals*, 1.
109. Hare, *Language of Morals*, 1–2.
110. Hare, *Language of Morals*, 3.
111. Hare, *Language of Morals*, 5.
112. Hare, *Language of Morals*, 5 ff.
113. Hare, *Language of Morals*, 6.
114. Hare, *Language of Morals*, 8.
115. John Wilson, *Language and the Pursuit of Truth* (Cambridge: Cambridge University Press, 1969), 92.
116. Hare, *Language of Morals*, 8.
117. Hare, *Language of Morals*, 13.
118. Hare, *Language of Morals*, 16.
119. Hare, *Language of Morals*, 46.
120. Hare, *Language of Morals*, 32.
121. Hare, *Language of Morals*, 32.
122. Hare, *Language of Morals*, 28.
123. Hare, *Language of Morals*, 33.
124. Plato (ΠΛΑΤΩΝ), *Crito* (*ΚΡΙΤΩΝ*) (c. 399 BCE), trans. Cathal Woods and Ryan Pack (San Francisco: Creative Commons, 2007–2012), https://www.pitt.edu/~mthompso/readings/crito.pdf (accessed October 15, 2020).
125. Plato, *Crito*, 48b.
126. Plato, *Crito*, 49b.
127. Plato, *Crito*, 48b.
128. Plato, *Crito*, 50a.
129. Plato, *Crito*, 50a.
130. Plato, *Crito*, 50a.
131. Plato, *Crito*, 49a.
132. Plato, *Crito*, 49e.
133. Hare, *Language of Morals*, 46.
134. Hare, *Language of Morals*, 48.
135. Hare, *Language of Morals*, 41-42.
136. Hare, *Language of Morals*, 47.
137. Hare, *Language of Morals*, 50.

138. Hare, *Language of Morals*, 54.
139. Hare, *Language of Morals*, 55.
140. Alan Gewirth, *The Community of Rights* (Chicago: Chicago University Press, 1996).
141. Gewirth, *Community of Rights*, 97.
142. Gewirth, *Community of Rights*, 1.
143. Gewirth, *Community of Rights*, 97.
144. Gewirth, *Community of Rights*, 97.
145. Gewirth, *Community of Rights*, 9.
146. Gewirth, *Community of Rights*, 8.
147. Gewirth, *Community of Rights*, 97.
148. Gewirth, *Community of Rights*, 9.
149. Gewirth, *Community of Rights*, 10.
150. Gewirth, *Community of Rights*, 10.
151. See Richard Rorty, "Human Rights, Rationality, and Sentimentality," in *On Human Rights: The Oxford Amnesty Lectures, 1993*, ed. Stephen Shute and Susan Hurley (New York: Basic Books, 1993), 116, 117.
152. Gewirth, *Community of Rights*, 11.
153. Gewirth, *Community of Rights*, 11.
154. Gewirth, *Community of Rights*, 12.
155. Gewirth, *Community of Rights*, 13.
156. Gewirth, *Community of Rights*, 13.
157. Gewirth, *Community of Rights*, 18.
158. Richard Wasserstrom, "Rights, Human Rights, and Racial Discrimination," in *Human Rights,* ed. A. I. Melden (Belmont, CA: Wadsworth, 1970), 99.
159. Gewirth, *Community of Rights*, 18.
160. Gewirth, *Community of Rights*, 19.
161. Gewirth, *Community of Rights*, 19.
162. Gewirth, *Community of Rights*, 6.
163. Gewirth, *Community of Rights*, 100.
164. Gewirth, *Community of Rights*, 98.
165. Gewirth, *Community of Rights*, 100.
166. John Dewey, *The Ethics of Democracy*, University of Michigan Philosophical Papers, 2nd ser., 1 (Ann Arbor: Andrews & Co., 1888).
167. Peter Singer, "R. M. Hare's Achievements in Moral Philosophy," Talk for Memorial Service at St. Mary's Church, Oxford, May 25, 2002, *Utilitas* 14, no. 3 (2002): 1–10, https://www.utilitarian.net/singer/by/20020525.pdf (accessed October 15, 2020).
168. Gewirth, *Community of Rights*, 6.
169. Gewirth, *Community of Rights*, 6.
170. A. P. d'Entreves, *Natural Law: An Introduction to Legal Philosophy*, 115, citing Kant, *Einleitung in die Rechtslehre*, sec. B. See Immanuel Kant, *The Metaphysics of Ethics*, trans. J. W. Semple, ed. and intro. Rev. Henry Calderwood, 3rd ed. (Edinburgh: T and T Clark, 1886), https://oll.libertyfund.org/titles/14437 (accessed October 31, 2020).

Chapter 1

Lochner v. New York, 198 US 45 (1905): Public Health and the Constitutionally Protected Right of Contract between an Employer and Employees

Pope Leo XIII (1891) said, "If through necessity or fear of a worse evil, the workman accept harder conditions because an employer or contractor will afford him no better, he is made the victim of force and injustice."[1]

In 1905, the U.S. Supreme Court issued two decisions that, from the perspective of the public's health, could not have been more different. The first was *Jacobson v. Massachusetts* in February, the second was *Lochner v. New York* in April.[2] Both were in response to appeals to state legislation— in *Jacobson*, an appeal against state-required vaccination; in *Lochner*, an appeal against state-required limitations on the hours of work in bakeries. In *Jacobson*, the Court found for the State of Massachusetts, and in *Lochner*, the Court found against State of New York. And whereas Justice John Marshall Harlan II wrote the decision for the Court in *Jacobson*, he wrote the dissent in *Lochner*. Of the two decisions, *Jacobson* has been more lasting in its constitutional implications for public health, particularly in light of contemporary opposition to vaccination. But *Lochner* is of considerable importance for the way it raised the issue of the justification for regulating commerce in the interests of the public's health. In so doing, it gave its name to the so-called *Lochner*-era, 1890 through 1937, during which the Supreme Court adopted an expansive interpretation of the Due Process clause so as to protect economic rights. To this end, the Court was disposed to "strike down economic regulations of working conditions, wages or hours in favor of laissez-faire economic policy."[3] In *Lochner v. New York*, the Court concluded that New York legislation that prohibited employees from working in bakeries in excess of "sixty hours a week or ten hours a day" was in violation of the constitutionally protected "right of contract between the employer and employees."[4]

IDEOLOGY UNDERMINING CONSTITUTIONALITY

Unlike any of the other decisions discussed here, *Lochner* was informed by an ideology having as much to do with economics as with the Constitution of the United States. It was the outcome of the Court's belief "that Americans had fundamental unenumerated constitutional rights," which were "protected by the Fourteenth Amendment's Due Process Clause."[5] According to Cass R. Sunstein, one can see three elements in the *Lochner* Court's understanding of substantive due process. As we know, the Clause as formulated, is intended to prevent legislation that encroaches on life, liberty, or property interests of individuals. For the Court that meant protection for individual rights against government action. The right in question in *Lochner* was the liberty interest in the purchase and sale of labor. The second element amounted to an acknowledgment that since the liberties included under due process are not absolute, they can be subject to regulation to secure, for example, "health or morals." A third element was a recognition of the Court's responsibility to review legislation for its suitability as an appropriate balance between securing the legitimate goals of governance and avoiding unwarranted limitations on market choices. "Market ordering under the common law was understood to be a part of nature rather than a legal construct."[6]

The legislation in question was the labor laws enacted in 1897 in the State of New York. While six sections, specifically 110, as well sections 111 through 115, were cited in the decision, it is noticeable that the Court focused exclusively on the section dealing with hours of employment and ignored the other five sections which addressed the public health goals of the legislation. Section 110 prohibited employers from requiring or permitting employees, employed in a biscuit, bread or cake bakery, or confectionery establishment, to work more than sixty hours in the course of a week, or more than ten hours in the course of a day, unless the purpose was to make the last day of the work week shorter. Section 111 dealt with such issues as proper drainage, plumbing, and ventilation of bakeries, while section 112 laid down specific requirements for rooms used for the manufacture of flour, or flour meal products. They were to be at least eight feet high with impermeable flooring of cement or tiles laid in cement, or in addition, wood flooring treated with linseed oil. The section also specified cleaning requirements for utensils and their storage in a manner that did not interfere with the proper cleaning of the rooms which needed to be dry and airy for the storage of manufactured flour and meal food products. Section 113 called for employee washrooms, bathrooms, and sleep rooms that were separate from bake rooms. Section 114 provided for safety and health inspections, the procedures for which required issuing certificates of compliance. Finally, section 115, assuming that alterations were needed for compliance with the legislation, called for the inspector to issue a written notice to the owner of the bakery specifying the alterations to be made and requiring that it be done within sixty days of receipt of notice.[7]

It is telling from the perspective of this analysis of the *Lochner* decision, how inconsistent from the outset was the Court's approach to it. The Court acknowledged the inclusion of these five provisions, all essentially having to do with health, only to deny that the act itself was concerned with health law. From there, in a giant leap of logic, it concluded that the act had to be considered an unwarranted encroachment on the right of individual employees and employers to make labor contracts.[8] But due regard to the logic of this proposition would require us to say that if the act can be considered a health law then it was not the unconstitutional interference that the Court declared it to be. Given the content of sections 111 through 115, it seems clear that they were about conditions conducive to the health of employees. And if section 110 is placed within the context of those five following sections, its restriction on the number of hours an employee in a bakery may be required to work amounted also to a condition conducive to the health of the employee. According to evidence cited by Justice Harlan I in his dissent, "The labor of the bakers is among the hardest and most laborious imaginable because it has to be performed under conditions injurious to the health of those engaged in it."[9] Harlan I harbored no doubts that the statute was intended to safeguard the physical safety and health of those employed in bakeries.[10] The same can be said for the decision of the State of New York's Appellate Court.[11] Whatever this restriction might have to do with contractual agreements between employer and employee, it did nothing to interfere with the making of such contracts so long as their terms were not a threat to the health of the employee. As the Appellate Court ruled, "the statute does not prohibit any right but regulates it, and there is a wide difference between regulation and prohibition, between prescribing the terms by which the right may be enjoyed and the denial of the right altogether."[12]

THE FACTS OF THE CASE

At the time of this case, most bakeries in New York City were located in the basements of tenement houses where rents were low and the floors sufficiently strong to support the heavy ovens used for commercial baking. However, these basements had never been designed for baking on a commercial scale. Sanitation was wholly inadequate. For example, the sinks, baths, and toilets available in the tenement buildings themselves drained into sewer pipes in the basements and were prone to leaking and causing foul odors. Basement ceilings typically were five and a half feet above the floor, causing anyone working there to have to stoop constantly. Heat during the summer and cold during the winter were extreme. Due to little or no ventilation, the dust from flour and fumes from the ovens remained trapped in the basement, exposing workers to associated health hazards. There was general agreement that these bakeries were unhealthy places of work and the bread baked in them posed health risks to consumers. Since it was not unusual for those employed in these bakeries to work seventy-four, possibly more, hours a week, the New York State Assembly adopted legislation modelled on British law of 1863 that established basic sanitation standards and specifically restricted the hours of work in bakeries to no more than ten a day and sixty a week.[13]

In 1901, Joseph Lochner, owner of Lochner's Home Bakery in Utica, New York, was fined $50 for permitting an employee to work in excess of sixty hours a week, thereby violating section 110 of article 8 of the then recently enacted 1897 New York State labor laws. Claiming that the legislation was unconstitutional, Lochner appealed the fine unsuccessfully to the Appellate Division of the New York Supreme Court. He then appealed to the New York Court of Appeals where he was similarly unsuccessful. Finally, he appealed to the U.S. Supreme Court.[14]

Lochner based his appeal on the constitutional protections afforded by the Fourteenth Amendment which prohibits "any State from depriving any person of life, liberty or property without due process of law." The question then is whether section 110 of article 8 was a legitimate exercise of the police powers of the state in the interests of the public's health or an unwarranted intrusion on the right of autonomous contractual employment between the individual seeking work and the individual providing it. It is clear, depending on how the various courts involved in the case answered this question, judges either affirmed or denied the original conviction. For example, in dissenting to the affirmative decision of the New York Court of Appeals, Judge Denis O'Brien declared, "There is nothing on the face of the law nor in its manifest operation to show that it has any relation to the public health."[15] In contrast, in concurring in the same decision, Judge Irving Vann concluded that where legislation has deemed a particular employment harmful to health so that no person should be allowed or required to work more than a certain number of hours a day or a week it "is a health law and is a valid exercise of the police power."[16]

Accordingly, Justice Rufus Peckham, who wrote the opinion of the U.S. Supreme Court, picked up where Judge O'Brien left off. Since Lochner was charged with violating the 1897 labor laws of the State of New York by allowing and requiring an employee to work more than sixty hours in one week, the sole issue for the Court in this case was the freedom, under the Fourteenth Amendment, an employee enjoyed to sell his labor and the freedom the employer enjoyed to buy it. This was the right of contract which is known as the contract clause in article 1, section 10 of the U.S. Constitution. While it failed, according to David E. Bernstein, to secure "a general right of freedom to contract," there was evidence at this time that the "courts" were disposed to favor "a right to contract," secure from unwarranted legislated restrictions under the "Due Process clause of the Fourteenth Amendment." Nevertheless, in 1898, the U.S. Supreme Court, in *Holden v. Hardy* (1898),[17] saw fit to confirm a law restricting hours of work in mines as a legitimate exercise of the state's police powers even as it encroached on liberty of contract.[18] Similar judgments, supporting greater latitude for the police powers of the state to regulate working conditions continued to be handed down. Invariably, Justice Peckham could be found in opposition to these judgments.[19]

THE PECKHAM ARGUMENT

In writing the *Lochner* decision, Peckham was, from the outset, intent on emphasizing that contracts were by definition free. For this, he noted that the word, *require*, as used in section 110, was not intended to suggest the exercise of physical force on the part of the employer to secure the labor of the prospective employee. Further, he contended that there was no real distinction between the meaning of "required" and "permitted," which, he concluded can only mean that the language of the statute, "*no employee shall be required or permitted to work*" was equivalent to "*no employee shall contract or agree to work*" more than ten hours per day. And since section 110 did not allow for any exception, it had to be understood as an absolute prohibition upon the employers permitting under any circumstances more than ten hours' work to be done in their establishment.[20]

Here is a good example of legal positivism, as it might have been written by Herbert Lionel Adolphus Hart, who regarded the legal system as "a closed, logical system in which correct decisions can be deduced from predetermined legal rules without reference to social considerations."[21] Although unemployment rates were low at the beginning of the twentieth century in the United States, it would be wrong to think of low unemployment as equivalent to job security. On the contrary, this period was noticeable for "fierce competition for jobs due to immigration, job insecurity, no protection or compensation for those who were injured on the job, no retirement income."[22] Under such conditions, the last thing employers had to worry about was resorting to involuntary labor! Being unemployed was the nightmare and to avoid it, one can imagine how exploitable prospective workers were, and how likely it was they could be reduced to "wage slaves"[23] when seeking employment. It was also the case that workers worked long hours and received low wages. Employment was at the will of the employer, something employees were never allowed to forget, and working conditions were anything but good. Under those circumstances, the words, *required* or *permitted* must have meant something rather different to workers than the meaning which Peckham was advancing.

It is reasonable to think that Peckham knew of the prevailing working conditions and the serious disadvantage under which they placed workers seeking employment. If so, it is equally reasonable to think that from the beginning he was asking the wrong question, the answer to which would be the basis for his decision. As he put it, when the State exercises its police power in order to limit the right to labor or the right of contract between an employer and an employee who are *sui juris* (independent), which of the two deserve to prevail? Should it be "the right of the individual to labor for such time as he may choose, or the right of the State to prevent the individual from laboring or from entering into any contract to labor beyond a certain time prescribed by the State?"[24]

The question, as worded, is unanswerable because its formulation is so simplistic. Before the law, it may have been the case at the time that employer and employee were in principle *sui juris*. Whether that was the case in fact is questionable. For example, were an employee injured while working in 1900, the only remedy was to sue for damages. Largely unsuccessful, such lawsuits secured compensation in slightly less than 15% of the cases.[25] But that prospective employees were that independent economically as to be able to enter on equal terms into a contract to labor with an employer was hardly the case. In 1880, the Journeymen Bakers Union of New York was formed. At that time, the typical work week for bakers was 108 hours. Of those, sixteen hours a day was the norm between Monday and Friday. That jumped to twenty-three hours on Saturdays and culminated in five hours on Sundays. That meant that it was not unusual for bakers to sleep on the premises. Given this extended exposure to prevailing working conditions, the incidence of rheumatism, baker's asthma, and other illnesses was noticeable. In 1881, the union called a strike that led to some improvement. The workday, Monday to Friday, was reduced to twelve hours and Saturday's hours dropped to fourteen. Although approximately 3,200 bakers joined this union, fewer than thirty-six bakeries were unionized four years later.[26] Emerging so recently from such a history of exploitation, it is hard to imagine the level playing field between employer and employee that was central to Peckham's argument for the priority of right of contract over the police power of the state in the interest of employees specifically and the public's health more broadly.

What then was the strength of the right of contract? Constitutionally, it was not an absolute right since the Court had imposed limits. One instance mentioned earlier was *Holden v. Hardy*. In that decision, as Peckham acknowledged, the Court found for a Utah statute limiting the hours of work of underground miners and smelters to eight hours a day, unless there was imminent danger to life or property. In the Court's judgment, the statute represented a valid exercise of the state's police power. Peckham, however, characterized it very narrowly. "It was held that the kind of employment, mining, smelting, etc., and the character of the employees in such kinds of labor, were such as to make it reasonable and proper for the State to interfere to prevent the employees from being constrained by the rules laid down by the proprietors in regard to labor."[27] Clearly, Peckham cited *Holden* only to conclude that since the Utah statute applied exclusively to workers subject to conditions of labor peculiar to mining and smelting, there was no need "to discuss or decide whether the legislature can fix the hours of labor for other kinds of employment."[28] Earlier, however, he had declared that the legislature limiting labor hours was a valid exercise of police power because it was intended to protect workers against being constrained by the employer's rules with regard to work. On the one hand, if the justification for the exercise of police powers derived from the conditions of work peculiar to miners and smelters, then arguably the justification might not extend to conditions of labor for bakers. But if the justification derived from an intention to protect workers from restraints accompanying employers' rules with regard to conditions of labor, there was nothing in the logic of the language to prevent the justification from being extended to bakers. Since the two justifications advanced were not necessarily compatible, Peckham's reasoning here was open to question. It is clear that the limitations imposed on working hours in mines by Utah came from a recognition of the health hazards posed by underground mining and that the longer miners were exposed to those risks the greater the probability they would suffer harm. It is just as clear that the State of New York was persuaded by similar reasoning. There were health hazards peculiar to baking, and the longer a baker was exposed to them, the greater the risk of suffering harm. If it was a constitutionally protected exercise of police power in the case of miners, why not then in the case of bakers? That would presumably depend on the degree of hazard associated with working in a bakery.

WORKING CONDITIONS IN BAKERIES

In Peckham's estimation, "the trade of a baker, in and of itself, is not an unhealthy one."[29] That, however, is not the point. Were it otherwise, regardless of its resulting benefits, presumably people would avoid engaging in it. The issue was the conditions under which at the time commercial bakers practiced their trade. That was what was unhealthy. That was why several sections of the statute were devoted to improving the physical conditions of bakeries. Unlike Peckham, Harlan I, in his dissent provided evidence, available at the time, in support of the view that the work of bakers was "very hard work, not only because it requires a great deal of physical exertion in an overheated workshop and during unreasonably long hours, but more so because of the erratic demands of the public, compelling the baker to perform the greatest part of his work at night."[30] Other evidence referred to such health hazards as inflammation of the lungs and bronchial tubes caused by flour dust; rheumatism, cramps, and swollen legs due to long hours of work were also common. A basic source of hazard was attributed to bakers' "irregular and unnatural mode of living, whereby the power of resistance against disease is greatly reduced."[31] Further, Harlan I captured explicitly the public health dimension of the New York statute when he cited the "Eighteenth Annual Report of the New York Bureau of Statistics of Labor": "Shorter hours of work, by allowing higher standards of comfort and pure family life, promise to enhance the industrial efficiency of the wage-working class—improved health, longer life, more content and greater intelligence and inventiveness."[32] While Harlan I admitted that much of this was open to debate, none of it suggested that it was unreasonable for the State to intervene in the interests of the public's health. As a result, where the U.S. Congress and many other states had considered the number of hours of labor in specific occupations with a view to the health of those employed in such occupations, they had for the most part set eight hours as the limit for the work day.[33]

There are two important constitutional considerations informing what Harlan I was saying here. The first had to do with the separation of powers between the judicial and the legislative branches of government, which, in part, found expression in the deference the judicial branch showed to the legislature with regard to the enactment of law, " unless such enactments are plainly, palpably, beyond all question, inconsistent with the Constitution of the United States."[34] There should be no presumption that New York State had acted in bad faith, without due deliberation, or without considering the fullest evidence available and the common good.[35] The second consideration was that to view the New York statute as violating the Fourteenth Amendment amounted to expanding its scope in ways never originally intended. "A decision that the New York statute is void under the Fourteenth Amendment will, in my opinion, involve consequences of a far-reaching and mischievous character: for such a decision would seriously cripple the inherent power of the States to care for the lives, health and wellbeing of their citizens."[36]

In his separate dissent, Justice Oliver Wendell Holmes Jr. expressed a similar concern. He believed it perverted the meaning of liberty in the Fourteenth

Amendment if it is used to reject democratically enacted legislation, unless it was clear such legislation "would infringe fundamental principles as they have been understood by the traditions of our people and our law."[37] Decisions like *Northern Securities Co. v. United States* (1904)[38] and *Otis v. Parker* (1903),[39] both of which confirmed legislative restrictions on the freedom of contract, pointed, according to Holmes, to the fact that "a constitution is not intended to embody a particular economic theory, whether of paternalism and the organic relation of the citizen to the State or of laissez-faire."[40] On the contrary, it had to embrace people who think quite differently about any one issue. Since the differences of opinion concerning this or that statute, were accidental, they had no bearing on deciding whether a particular statute was incompatible with the Constitution.[41] "The Fourteenth Amendment does not enact Mr. Herbert Spencer's Social Statics."[42]

THE NEW YORK STATUTE AS VALID LABOR LAW

A significant part of Peckham's decision took up the question of whether the New York statute was a valid labor law. The premise of the question was that since no one was claiming that bakers, as a class, were not as intelligent or as able as men in other trades or manual occupations, there was no reasonable justification to interfere with their personal liberty or right of free contract by restricting their hours of labor. Like their peers in other manual labor occupations, bakers were capable of asserting their rights without assistance and protection from the State. "They are in no sense wards of the State."[43] Consequently, since this act served no purpose in the public interest, it could not be considered valid as labor law.[44]

In their essentials, labor laws have been seen as needed to protect employees' rights and set forth what employers were responsible for with regard to workers and their conditions of employment. Included in this were the conditions of employment, such as provisions for promotion and salary raises, as well as workers' health broadly defined. Of particular interest in the present discussion is the provision for unionization. In 1935, the *National Labor Relations Act* (the *Wagner Act*) was passed to protect employees from interference in their pursuit of an improved environment for themselves.[45] According to Otto Kahn-Freund, the relation between employee and employer "in its inception is an act of submission, in its operation it is a condition of subordination, however much the submission and subordination may be concealed by the indispensable figment of the legal mind known as the 'contract of employment.'"[46] Unlike Peckham, who appeared to see labor law as a countervailing force to protect the employee from his lack of intelligence, Kahn-Freund insisted that the main purpose of labor law is "to counteract the inequality of bargaining power which is inherent and must be inherent in the employment relationship." Employer and employee were related within a construct he called "collective laissez-faire," with the employer powerful and the employee powerless. [47] The premise of the question, as Peckham put it, was misleading. Rather than intelligence, it should have been inequality of bargaining power. But inequality of bargaining power, to be clear, was only symptomatic of an illusionary "view of society as an agglomeration of individuals who are coordinated as equals." The implications of such a view for relations between employer and employee were serious, since the one thing known of "industrial societies" was their "unequal distribution of power." As if, one might say by way of compensation, "the law does and to some extent must conceal the realities of subordination behind the conceptual screen of contracts considered as concluded between equals."[48] In light of Kahn-Freund's observations, one's view of the nature and purpose of labor law gives rise to a critical question. Since the paramount issue here was the conditions of labor operating within an employment relationship between un-equals, how well designed was labor law to secure justice for workers, despite the institutional inequality? In Peckham's decision, what evidence was there that he recognized how the law actually obscured the conditions of subservience behind the veil of contracts? Indeed, was there any evidence that in his dissent Harlan I recognized this? Harlan I was willing to allow that the origin of the New York statute was due to a belief that the needs of employees working in bakeries "often compelled them to submit to such exactions as unduly taxed their strength."[49] If so, it added additional support for the justification of the statute as a legitimate exercise of the State's police power on behalf of the public welfare. Despite his allowance, Harlan I qualified it. Whatever the merits in considering inequality in employee-employer relations as the origin of the New York statute, there could be no doubt that the statute had to be understood as a statement of belief that working more than sixty hours a week in bakeries was injurious to the health of those working there. In that case, it should not be a surprise that even Harlan I seemed to give the benefit of the doubt to the merit of the notion of a contract of employment.[50]

So far, in this analysis, Peckham's decision has been considered on its own terms and there found wanting. It is hard to see why the Utah statute restricting the hours miners can work is constitutional, but not the New York statute restricting working hours for bakers. Unless, that is, you are prepared to accept as authoritative Peckham's positive assessment of the safety of commercial baking. But if safety was relevant to bolster his negative constitutional assessment of the New York statute, why were not prevailing labor conditions that undermined equality of bargaining power as a necessary condition of a right of contract relevant for a positive constitutional assessment of the New York statute?

HARLAN I AND HOLMES DISSENTING

Peckham's inadequacies aside, even though both Harlan and Holmes have the better of the constitutional argument in *Lochner*, they too made assertions which, grounded as they were in legal positivism, impoverished the concept of law in general and the Constitution in particular. Harlan, for example, asserted that in the American system of government the courts had no stake in the wisdom or policy of legislation. Consequently, when it considered the power of the state to encroach on liberty of contract, it needed only ask whether the means chosen were appropriate for reaching the end— in *Lochner*, protecting the health of those working in bakeries—lawfully. However, unless we have criteria other than the law with which to answer the question, what Harlan was saying was that the goal was legal because it can be reached legally. In other words, if the means was to be appropriate, it was appropriate if, when used, it achieved its goal legally. But this is to say that the means, here police power, was legal because it was legal. This is a tautology. It begs, but it does not answer the question which Harlan correctly saw as central to this case. Alternatively, must there be more to be considered to determine the warrant of a particular law than the legal process of enacting it? Slavery in the United States was made legal by means of an enactment that was legally carried out. Subsequently, it became illegal by means of an enactment also carried out legally. Does it matter, relative to the principle that the end does not justify the means, that we used the same means to secure slavery as we did to abolish it?

To be clear, to justify something is to declare it "right." As Mortimer J. Adler explained it, "nothing in the world can justify a means except the end which it is intended to serve."[51] Hence the question: as a means, will X achieve Y? If not, why use it? It would not be the "right means." Adler proceeded with the obvious observation that a particular end, let us say slavery, may be "wrong." Nevertheless, intent on achieving it, society might have concluded that a duly enacted law would secure that goal. And our history shows this to be correct, at least as a matter of convenience. If so, ought society choose any means that might serve to secure its goal of slavery? Not unless it wants to reject the principle, "since a bad end is one that we are not morally justified in seeking, we are not morally justified in taking any steps whatsoever toward its accomplishment."[52] To think other than this with regard to the law would reduce it to a matter of moral indifference, an instrument of expediency. Yesterday it was for slavery, today it is against it. But at the very least, as an instrument of social mediation, law must ever be considerate of its consequences for members of society, members, that is, who are moral agents, possessed of rights whose exercise by one rights-holder may affect the ability of other rights-holders to exercise their rights.

For this reason, one has to question Justice Holmes' appreciation of the notion that citizens are free to do as they choose so long as it does not interfere with the liberty of others as a "shibboleth." As evidence of this he cited the interference suffered by the citizen from school laws, the Post Office, indeed from "every state or municipal institution which takes his money for purposes though desirable, whether he likes it or not."[53] Holmes was likely referring to the so-called Harm Principle, enunciated by John Stuart Mill in his "On Liberty," published in 1859. At its center was the need to "make the fitting adjustment between individual independence and social control."[54] For Mill, that required asserting a fundamental "principle" of absolute authority to guide the use of coercion by society in its relations with individual members of society. Whether this coercion took the form of "legal penalties" or "public opinion," its guiding "principle" is "That the only purpose for which power can be rightfully exercised over any member of a civilized community, against his will, is to prevent harm to others."[55] This power, to be used individually or collectively, extends, according to Mill, to a variety of steps taken to benefit others, including those taken in the interests of the "defenseless" against exploitation.[56] Far from being of no further use, the harm principle, as an ethics norm, can reasonably be seen to ground the constitutional notion of substantive due process, at the heart of which is government's burden of proof of compelling interest to interfere with an individual's constitutionally guaranteed rights, in this case the right of "contract."[57] And the compelling interest here, justifying government intervention, was the well-being of bakers, otherwise at risk in an unregulated commercial arena of exploitation.

Had Holmes looked deeper, he would have seen there was considerably more to Herbert Spencer's *Social Statics* than an argument for political liberalism, something that possibly even Spencer failed to recognize. At its center was the understanding that social evolution was a matter of "increasing individuation" resulting from the development of "human societies" into "industrial societies" built on a "division of labor" that requires "voluntary cooperation" from their members. The upshot is a state of affairs in which society functions for the benefit of its members rather than the other way around.[58] Ultimately, this is an argument for the moral primacy of the individual and gives rise to its legal expression in the form of due process.

Alan Gewirth, as we saw earlier, called this "ethical individualism" and derived it from the "principle of human rights to freedom and well being." It involves a "social relation" between the purposes of society, its "policies and institutions," and the equally-enjoyed "rights" of individuals in which these rights as human rights serve as the moral standard by which society and by extension its policies are measured. These rights then are also "social concerns" in the pursuit of which the state is a means only. It is clear from this that because human rights, although located in individuals and exercised by individuals, are reciprocal, they give rise to a "community of rights." As rights, they are claims to goods that are constitutive of human being and in the absence of which human being is intrinsically compromised. The resulting "social solidarity" this brings to society, with its members acknowledging and pursuing needs held in common, lead Gewirth to the conclusion that "rights require community" for their realization, while "community requires rights" to justify its purpose.[59]

Of course, the harm principle, whether in Mill's or Spencer's thinking, lends itself to an argument for as little government interference as possible and as much independence for the individual as possible. According to Albert Jay Nock,[60] Spencer believed that the organizing principle of society should be "voluntary cooperation," not "compulsory cooperation." In practical terms, government activity with regard to the individual member of society should be confined to enforcing contractual "obligations" or assuring ready access to "justice." For Spencer, the goal was to establish "individualism" rather than "Statism."[61] Both presuppose the participation of the individual as moral agent. That is, the individual enjoys freedom as the necessary condition for voluntary cooperation, and the individual possesses rights as the justification for claims made in their interests. Spencer's argument assumed that everyone had the resources enabling voluntary participation. The development of an "industrial society" signaled for him the arrival of a social "order" sufficiently balanced to meet the "needs of all" members of society. As a result, there was no need for legislation regulating, for example, "hours of work, sanitation, or education," which sowed the seeds for a future of enslavement.[62] For Spencer, "The function of true liberalism in the future will be that of putting a limit to the powers of parliaments."[63] However, in the face of the dystopia that characterized the lives of the "poor" as a result of the economic conditions unleashed by the Industrial Revolution, Spencer's utopia was hardly credible.[64] Government intervention to create conditions conducive to the well being of society itself was necessary to protect those members of society whose rights to freedom and well being were falling victim to economic interests over which they had no control.

RIGHT OF CONTRACT

Of this, the *Lochner* decision showed no awareness in its preoccupation with securing the right of contract as a constitutional matter. But worse than that was its neglect of the fact that the right of contract was a derivative of the human right to freedom and well being and, as such, found its ultimate justification, not in the Constitution but in this human right. And since the Constitution itself served to confirm such human rights, there was no conflict with the Constitution by interpreting it within this larger framework of human rights. That is to say that the right to contract was certainly not self-justifying. Nor was it justified ultimately by reference to the Constitution, particularly where, as in *Lochner*, the Constitution was open to an interpretation that put employees working in bakeries at the mercy of their employers, thereby rendering the Constitution an instrument of injustice. That a minority on the Court interpreted the Constitution differently only demonstrates the need for appeal to that larger conceptual framework within which the Constitution sat, rather than being satisfied with the illusory finality of its decision based on the contingency of the Court's 5 to 4 majority.

It will be argued that this suggestion of yet another appeal is an invitation to some kind of legal infinite regression. The suggestion is not contemplating an appeal to a court higher yet than the U.S. Supreme Court. Rather, the suggestion contemplates an imperative on the part of the Court's justices to conduct their analysis of the Constitution's provisions within its originating conceptual framework which provides those second order principles against which first order constitutional principles, such as due process, equal protection under the laws, and rights of contract and privacy, should be assessed for justification under whatever particular circumstances are present. Given a broader frame of reference with which both the spirit of the Constitution and its letter, are consistent, the reasonable expectation would be for greater consensus and sounder judgment.

The notion of a contract suggests some level of freedom to enter into an agreement between or among parties, regardless of any constitutional sanction to this effect. According to Henry James Sumner Maine, individuals have made a transition from membership in traditional groups in which relationships and obligations are matters based on the status afforded by birth to a status of autonomous agency in which they are free to enter into contracts as equals with whomever they choose. As he observed, it amounted to a development in law and in society "from status to contract."[65] It seems clear that Maine saw freedom of contract as derivative from the freedom inherent in being a human and, as such, enjoyed equally by all humans as humans. If equally free, then it must be the case that as parties to any contract they enter into, both are equal. This is required by virtue of the human right to freedom and would supersede other freedoms, such as an employer's freedom, derived from economic advantage, to hire from among a number of individuals competing to be hired. This freedom, encroaching as it does on the human right to freedom, would result in a contract in which one party is not equal because they need the employment more than the employer needs one particular employee. The disadvantage is obvious and renders the would-be employee vulnerable to the unwarranted power of an employer, and in no position as a single individual to secure the balance of power that should inform a legitimate contract. If the individual lacks the resources to secure this balance necessary for freedom of contract, then who should secure it on their behalf, if not government exercising its police powers, also known as governmental paternalism.

Paternalism is a response, predicated on the authority of the response, to potentially harmful human behavior. Human behavior can be considered either "self-regarding" so that its effects do not go beyond the agent, or "other-regarding," in which case they do and as a result affect others. The same behavior can be either "voluntary" or "non-voluntary." Using this framework, the ethics problem raised by paternalism is then fairly obvious since it consists in an encroachment by government on the liberty of its citizens either to prevent them from harming themselves or to protect them from sources of harm over which they have no control. It has been said already that ethics is concerned with human behavior as it affects others and asks the unavoidable normative question, what should we do when what we do will likely affect others? Accordingly, it would seem clear that where the behavior is "voluntary and self-regarding" there would be little justification for paternalistic interventions on the part of government Yet, in the case of "other-regarding voluntary or non-voluntary" behavior resulting in harm, there would seem to be a *prima facie* (presumed) justification for paternalistic intervention. In Lochner, the working conditions of bakers were such that the 1897 labor laws constituted a legitimate act of paternalism by government to protect the bakers from themselves and their powerlessness, and to prevent the risk of harm posed by employers over which employees had no control. What, however, under these circumstances, constituted, voluntary and non-voluntary behavior may be difficult to determine. Where, moving on a continuum from voluntary to non-voluntary might, for example, economic forces so influence behavior that it ceased to be voluntary and became non-voluntary?[66] The point is important because, as we can see from Peckham's language, no consideration was given to it. "There is no reasonable ground for interfering with the liberty of person or the right of free contract."[67] Surely, he presumed too much here. The enjoyment of liberty of person and right of free contract within the conceptual framework of the Constitution might indeed have been expressed in this manner as though existing independently of any external influences. This is hardly the case in real life, where liberty of person or right of free contract is subject to external influences to such an extent that either is at most enjoyed conditionally. And when that occurs, it will result from an awareness that whatever the outcome, it will include harm unavoidably.

Determining that the degree of harm is substantial is a necessary condition to justify any paternalistic intervention since that cannot be undertaken without encroaching, not on the principle of liberty of person or right of free contract but on the practical enjoyment of either.

As we saw earlier, there was sufficient evidence at the time that the conditions under which employees in bakeries worked were harmful. In an 1895 study, health conditions in bakeries in New York were deemed exceptionally bad, while employees worked what were described as inhumanly long hours, often in excess of one hundred hours a week. The same study reported that some 11% of the workers had been ill during the previous year, hardly a coincidence since two-thirds of the bakeries inspected had been determined to be totally unfit.[68] What was described here with regard to bakeries was simply a particular reflection of the widely dangerous and unhealthy conditions under which employees worked in America's age of industrialization between the Civil War and World War I, and which called out for a broad range of government intervention. A series of investigations by state labor bureaus into the dangers prevailing working conditions posed for the safety and health of employees resulted at the state level in systematic factory inspections and their resulting improvement in the safety and healthiness of working conditions. By 1900, things had reached the point where the Progressive movement turned its attention to the campaign for labor reform, reinforcing the call for improved safety and health, while supporting the need for workers' compensation, and industrial commissions to be responsible for regulation. It is not surprising that with this amount of activity, the issue of industrial health became the focus of attention from both the general public and the scientific community.[69]

COURT INDIFFERENCE

What was surprising about the Court's decision was how unaware it showed Peckham to have been of a widespread concern over working conditions, particularly those affecting safety and health, and of a broad legislative agenda for significant improvement. Worse, however, was his misrepresentation of the central problem when he declared, "We think there can be no fair doubt that the trade of a baker, in and of itself, is not an unhealthy one to that degree which would authorize the legislature to interfere with the right to labor and with the right of free contract."[70] But the baking trade itself was not the cause of concern. It was the conditions under which it was conducted that were calling for reform. The misrepresentation did not however end there. "There must be more than the mere fact of the possible existence of some small amount of unhealthiness to warrant legislative interference with liberty."[71]

And if not, "are we all, on that account, at the mercy of legislative majorities?"[72] Unavoidably, Peckham concluded, there would be no way of earning a living, whether it be as a banker, a broker, or a lawyer, that would not escape the unrestrained intrusion of government should the legislation before the Court be assumed to be valid.[73] On that assumption, Peckham continued, it was but a short step to contest that employees, such as lawyers or bank clerks, contracting to work more than eight hours a day for their employers would be invalid. Should that number be deemed unhealthy, should the legislature feel, "in its paternal wisdom," that it must have the right to limit such hours, only to be challenged, then all it has to do is to justify its intervention as a health law, thereby placing it beyond the scrutiny of the court.[74] Once here, we would be on a slippery slope where "the protection of the Federal Constitution from undue interference with liberty of person and freedom of contract is visionary (impractical) wherever the law is sought to be justified as a valid exercise of the police power."[75] Having restricted the work hours of employees, what, Peckham asks, was to prevent restricting the work hours of employers, doctors, lawyers, or scientists for that matter? The legislation, he concluded, was not a health law but an unwarranted interference with the rights of employees and employers to enter into labor contracts on terms they deem in their best interests. The only way to rescue this legislation from being a "meddlesome interference with the rights of the individual," would be to say that unless work hours were restricted, there would be real danger to the public health or to the health of those working in bakeries. If this was not the case, and clearly it was not for Peckham, then this legislation was invalid and the Constitution's protection of liberty interests and right to contract prevailed.[76]

It is clear from this line of argument why Peckham rejected the notion that this legislation was a health bill. Yet in the same breath he acknowledged approvingly of provisions of the legislation to secure healthy conditions for working in bakeries. "All it could properly do has been done by it with regard to the conduct of bakeries."[77] Some eight health provisions in all, as discussed earlier, they were nevertheless not enough for Peckham to regard the legislation as health legislation. Rather, they were merely incidental to its real purpose which was to interfere with constitutionally protected interests under the guise of securing conditions conducive to the public's health. As noted earlier, there was nothing in the legislation that interfered with the freedom to contract unless it could be said that there were no circumstances under which any contract was not subject to those restrictions deemed necessary in the public's interest or that of one or both of the parties to the contract.

It is remarkable how little attention was given to the particular circumstances of the contract under consideration and how they affected it so negatively as to warrant some restraint imposed by government. The

Constitution may guarantee the right of free contract, but the Constitution neither guarantees nor can it guarantee the circumstances required for the free exercise of the right as envisioned in the Constitution. That requires the broader understanding of law, not only as law so ordered, but also law as just, or law as answerable to ethics. Contracting, by definition, is other-regarding human behavior which in *Lochner* involved employers and employees, with employers offering employment and employees seeking it. Placed within the framework of law understood as so ordered, whatever it contained only told the parties to the particular contract how to be compliant with the law. There was nothing to tell them how they ought to act toward each other considered as moral rather than merely legal agents, relative to the terms of the contract. The reason for this lay with the assurance provided by the notion of legal rights, or "a claim recognized and delimited by law for the purpose of securing it."[78] But how credible was such assurance? Given Peckham's position, it was quite reasonable to think that a contract between bakery owners and bakers would be legal even though it meant that bakers were obliged under the terms of the contract to work in working conditions seriously adverse to their best physical and mental health interests. Were it not for the fact that ethics is a necessary condition of law, there would be considerable difficulty explaining that these interests were owed to the bakers, not because they possessed legal sanction but because they were the object of claims derived from rights and for that reason lawful, meriting protection from the law.[79] The distinction is critical if we are to appreciate the significance of considering contracting as a right. But before that, it is more critical to consider what is meant here by right.

There is a contract clause in article 1, section 10 of the Constitution, prohibiting state governments from interfering with contractual obligations.[80] Given that, it has been argued that this clause "had the making of a general right to freedom of contract."[81] Nevertheless, in an 1827 decision, the Supreme Court interpreted the clause to refer only to impairments after the fact. It was not to be understood as applicable as a general exercise of police power to future contracts.[82] However, between the time of this decision and the close of the nineteenth century, there was clear evidence of American courts using the Due Process clause of the Fourteenth Amendment to provide protection to a right to contract without fear of unwarranted interference from government. The first decision to find a state law unconstitutional for interfering with freedom of contract came in 1897.[83] In that decision, Peckham "firmly established liberty of contract as a right protected by the Fourteenth Amendment's Due Process clause."[84] That did not prevent the Court,[85] the following year, from limiting freedom of contract in the interests of health and safety of underground miners, to be followed by a succession of similar decisions concerning work-related legislation.[86] If only for this precedent, it is understandable why *Lochner* struck contemporaries as a constitutional course reversal.

From *Lochner* to today, the constitutional history of freedom of contract has waxed and waned depending on prevailing political trends, as well as court appointments influenced by these trends.[87] With the appointment of "four conservatives by President Warren Harding," it waxed. But in the aftermath of the Great Depression, it waned. As the cumulative outcome of President Franklin D. Roosevelt's appointments, the Court consistently regarded "economic" statutes interfering with "freedom of contract" as subject to the minimum of judicial review. But even that was thought, during the course of the "New Deal," to be too much. In this regard, Bernstein cited *Williamson v. Lee Optical of Oklahoma* (1955) as illustrative. In its decision, the Court declared that provisions in an Oklahoma statute making it unlawful for anyone except licensed optometrists or ophthalmologists to fit lenses to a face or replace lenses into frames, and unless with written prescriptive authority of an Oklahoma licensed ophthalmologist or optometrist did not violate the Due Process clause of the Fourteenth Amendment. Giving a perfect example of legal positivism, Justice William O. Douglas, delivering the opinion of the Court stated, "The day is gone when this Court uses the Due Process clause of the Fourteenth Amendment to strike down state laws, regulatory of business and industrial conditions because they may be unwise, improvident, or out of harmony with a particular school of thought."[88]

The constitutional history of the right to free contract is reflected precisely in the following explanation of the phrase, obligation of contracts, as stated in article 1, section 10:

> [The] obligation of a contract referred to here is a legal not a mere [*sic*] moral obligation; it is the law which binds the party to perform his undertaking. The obligation does not inhere or subsist in the contract itself, *proprio vigore*, [on its own merits] but in the law applicable to the contract.[89]

Unfortunately, it is this hollowing out of the moral properties of human behavior, such as contracting, that results from legal positivism. The obligations do inhere in the terms of the contract by virtue of the nature of a contract, law or no law. What would be the point of entering into a contract where it is standard practice to have no intention of honoring its terms? It would be irrational and spell the end of this other-regarding behavior. Attributing the binding force of a contract exclusively to applicable law is to render it hostage to the vagaries of the law, as the history of constitutional contract law recounted above so clearly demonstrates. So once more, we see the critical importance of understanding law as just, or as consonant with the rationality and nature of the behavior to which it is being applied. This is all the more important if the behavior we are talking about is deemed to be engaged in as a right. It is worth mentioning here how, according to Mary Ann Glendon, Europe, in the aftermath of Hitler's national socialism, undertook a thorough-going review of its legal foundations. "Legal positivism, the notion that one's rights are no more or less than what the law says they are now seemed untenable."[90] The systematic attack under Nazi Germany on a broad front of human and civil rights was carried out, following, for the most part, long-standing parliamentary procedures, presumably legitimate and therefore legitimizing, at least according to legal positivism, the legislative results.[91] But surely to accept this is to pervert the role of law in relation to rights.

RIGHTS

There are rights only in relation to things that are valued and they are accompanied by a disposition to honor whatever is valued as a right. It is the case however in the real world that the enjoyment of rights may be curtailed or even denied. Denial may be warranted. But a denial of the enjoyment of a right is not to be confused with the notion that the right ceases to exist because of the denial. Otherwise, the denial would not be what it is, an encroachment.[92] The concern here is that we are treating rights as *prima facie*, the unavoidable upshot of which is that when infringement is justifiable it is not all clear where infringement may not be justifiable. "Our moral framework is unnecessarily and undesirably impoverished by the theory that there are such rights."[93] And this is indeed the outcome when the right to free contract is regulated by law understood as so ordered only, the understanding central to the *Lochner* decision.

The explanation is not complicated upon consideration of the nature of rights, specifically human rights. Rights are ultimately "moral commodities" that function to honor certain interests on the basis of a "claim of right." Such a claim is to be clearly distinguished from claiming something on the basis of some advantage due, for example, to social status or personal wealth.[94] "To have a right to something is, typically, to be entitled to receive, or possess, or enjoy it now, and to do so without securing the consent of another."[95] Proportionate to the strength of such claims of right is that their objects are things of consequence. For that reason, to have a right to something is to be able to invoke the right itself as justifying acting in the enjoyment of the right. "To exercise one's right is to act in a way that gives appreciable assurance of immunity from criticism."[96] That is, exercising one's human rights is to act right-fully or in accord with reason and human nature. If we are to understand contracting correctly, especially in the context of Lochner, it has to be seen as involving the human right to freedom and well-being. That is to say, it has to be genuinely voluntary on the part of the employees and not the result of accepting employment but at the cost of an involuntary endurance of working conditions posing serious risk of harm. Just as Peckham was disposed to consider baking theoretically, removed from any of the physical conditions surrounding its practice, so too was he disposed to think of contracting. As a result, he objected to state interventions of the kind New York had called for on the grounds that they were likely to interfere with his positivist legal, as distinct from a moral, conception of contracting.

In any contract, at least two parties find common cause for their activities but usually for different reasons. Consequently, there can be little doubt that contracting is well described as productive agency. According to Gewirth, productive agency, in its basic form, is the ability to earn one's living and as a result be "self-sufficient" in pursuit of one's "well-being." "Insofar as all persons have rights to autonomy and to relations of mutuality, they also have a positive right to the development of their productive agency."[97] Being productive reasonably involves action that is both "voluntary and purposive action." Resulting from the free choice of the agent, it is action undertaken in pursuit of a goal intended by the agent. To the extent agency is productive, it is deemed successful in reaching the intended goal. "Productive agency is the continuing, proximate capacity or disposition for being a productive agent."[98] As such, Gewirth concluded, it was a "necessary good," constitutive of the human "rights to freedom and well-being." If we understand contracting as productive agency, we cannot underestimate how central to it is autonomy. At the same time, we have to recognize that contracting takes place under conditions of differences in the personal objectives of those party to the contract. The question then has to be asked whether and how autonomy and mutuality would survive in the face of these differences? There is after all the argument that "contract theory" is a derivative from "Game Theory" in which one of the parties, known as "the principal," enjoys all the power in the negotiations, and is in a position to make an offer that cannot, for all practical purposes, be refused.[99] Under the physical conditions of commercial baking in New York State at the beginning of the twentieth century, bakers were more likely than not, in the course of any contracting, to be faced with an offer they could not refuse. Looking at contracting from this perspective, one can see the fundamental values of autonomy and mutuality that without qualification must condition it. Ultimately, while contracting is obviously subject to law, that law, given the nature and purpose of contracting, must be grounded in ethics.

HOLMES ON LAW

Although Holmes dissented in *Lochner*, he would have disagreed with Gewirth's thinking on contracting. "Nowhere is the confusion between legal and moral ideas more manifest than in the law of contract."[100] He was correct in this one regard that ethics and law are not to be confused. Unfortunately, from that premise he drew the incorrect conclusion that there is no place for ethics in the practice of law. His misunderstanding was to be found in the belief that "the rights of man in a moral sense are equally rights in the sense of the Constitution and the law."[101] This, despite at the same time having said that "The law is the witness and external deposit of our moral life."[102] And therein lay his fundamental confusion, a confusion that persists in legal positivism. Law is external and objective, whereas ethics is internal and subjective. The source of Holmes' confusion was derived, it seems, from his understanding of law. Law was practiced because, as he put it, people want to know what the "circumstances" might be and what degree of "risk" existed of finding themselves confronted by the police powers of the state entrusted to "judges" in courts of law. Accordingly, to understand the law apart from anything else required, he maintained, coming to it from the point of view of the "bad man," not that of the "good man." To what purpose the distinction? Since the function of law was to predict what behaviors triggered the intervention of police powers, it was the bad man "who cares only for the material consequences which such knowledge enables him to predict."[103] In contrast, the good man found his reasons for acting, whether within or apart from the law, in what Holmes referred to as "the vaguer (sic) sanctions of conscience."[104]

But where does that leave any appreciation of the relation of law to ethics? Holmes asked, "What constitutes the law?" Some, he responded, would say it was a method of "reason," or something derived from "principles of ethics." All well and good, but of what interest were they to the one who counts here, the "bad man?" None. He wished only to know what the courts could be expected to do. It was this consideration that persuaded Holmes to conclude that "The prophecies of what the courts will do in fact and nothing more pretentious are what I mean by the law."[105] In his effort to avoid, correctly, any confusion of law with ethics, he had actually muddled a relation between them that was critical to a correct understanding of their respective roles in society generally and specifically, in the present discussion, in regard to contracting.

At issue is the concept of obligation. Both law and ethics, since they are concerned with human behavior, are sources of obligation. But in this capacity, law functions differently than ethics, even when they might share identical precepts, such as to honor contracts.[106] However, law functions coercively, as Holmes acknowledged. "The duty to keep a contract at common law means a prediction that you must pay damages if you do not keep it—and nothing else."[107] That the fear of punishment for violating the law motivates compliance with the law is obvious to all. That it is the sole source of compliance is far from the case. Surely, it is reasonable to think that contracts, for instance, by their very nature require to be honored, law or no law. It would be the end of contracts if they were entered into with no intention of keeping them. What then is the function of law in relation to the precept, honor contracts? If making contracts is, as a matter of principle, a good, it follows that contract law, as long as it furthers the purpose of making contracts, is also a good with which to be compliant because it is good, not because it is coercive. Put otherwise, if what motivates compliance with the law is respect for the law, then the law is functioning as a moral authority which Holmes' *good man* accepts without qualification. But if what motivates a person's compliance with the law consists in "a prophecy that if he does certain things he will be subject to disagreeable consequences by way of imprisonment or compulsory payment of money,"[108] then the law is functioning as a coercive force tailored to the disposition of Holmes' *bad man*. And since the "bad man" is no less interested than the "good" man to evade such disagreeable consequences, the only practical step to take is to draw a distinction between "morality and law." The distinction, makes clear how Holmes' good man will turn to the "vaguer (sic) sanctions of conscience" to direct their behavior in compliance with or independently of the law. The distinction is essential for Holmes. Unlike coercive law and its predictable sanctions, morality, whose sanctions are found within one's conscience, is beyond the reach of the bad man, and of no account in determining his behavior.

Already, much earlier, St. Thomas Aquinas, echoing Cicero, saw matters quite differently and more accurately by clarifying the essential relation between the good man and the law. Unlike Holmes' "bad man" who, by virtue of his behavior is under the law's scrutiny and seeks to evade its consequences, Aquinas' good man is not even "subject to the law." Why would he be with an understanding of law, grounded in reason concordant with human nature as the measure of its moral standing? Intent on avoiding the confusion of law with ethics, he did not explain their distinction in relation to the difference between the *good man* and the *bad man*, even as he used those same terms. Like others within the tradition of natural law thinking, Aquinas recognized that law as coercive compromised the possibility of moral behavior. One cannot be forced to behave ethically. But he also recognized that coercion did not completely account for compliance with the law, especially in the case of the good man. Hence the focus is less on "precepts" as such than on their "working."[109] The good man, recognizing that the law is good in what it commands or prohibits, is already disposed to act accordingly, law or no law.[110] "But the will of the good is at one with the law, whereas in the bad the will is opposed to the law."[111] That is, by virtue of its goodness, any such law is seen also to possess binding authority as a matter of conscientious affinity with human nature. Similarly, because of its badness, any such law is seen to merit resistance, but now as as a matter of conscientious incompatibility with human nature. How else might we understand Holmes' correct claim, a claim he misunderstood, that "the law is the witness and external deposit of our moral life."[112] In other words, the good person would not consider "law merely in the shape of the policeman or the law-court," even as he might feel compelled "to break laws which he deems morally indefensible."[113] For Aquinas, the identity of true law was discoverable in the human disposition to respond to it by being, due to natural affinity, obedient to it. Why should this be so? Law is the result of law-making which obviously is intentional and voluntary and therefore responsible human behavior, with other-regarding consequences, both good and bad. Consequently, in creating law, humans are subject to the exigencies of reason concordant with human nature as much as they are subject to the same exigencies in their obedience to it. When law-making meets the demands of reason concordant with human nature, obedience to the law follows naturally; when it fails to meet these demands, disobedience follows naturally.

In his insistence on law as external and ethics as internal, Holmes misrepresented both law and ethics. If his concern was to avoid turning law into ethics or ethics into law, his instincts were sound. But that can be prevented without imposing an unbridgeable chasm between law and ethics. Natural law theorists had the same concern but addressed it rather differently. They acknowledged that law was concerned with human actions in themselves, and no further, in that the act compliant with the law is action as *so ordered* simply. Ethics is no less concerned with human actions but in a manner that combines internal with external factors and secures a critical measure of objectivity as a result. In the case of law-making, this means assessing legislative initiatives tailored to mee the exigencies of particular societal conditions for their capacity for fulfilling the universal principle of social justice, in the same way we assess individual principles of behavior for their capacity to fulfill universally applicable principles of behavior.

LAW AND ANTECEDENT RIGHTS

According to Bernstein, the Lochner decision reflected almost total agreement within the Court that "due process requirements protected fundamental rights that were antecedent to government."[114] The disagreement was over how strictly to enforce these rights against New York State. There was, however, no formal procedure to identify what these rights were. Nor, to be clear, was it the practice of the Court generally to draw on these rights as though dispositive in their judicial review. Instead, the Court regarded them as a "confirmation" of the rights found in America's legal tradition of liberty. Unfortunately, this gets matters backwards and leads to muddled thinking evident in *Territory v. Ah Lim* (1890). As the Washington Supreme Court stated it the time, "It is common to indulge in a great deal of loose talk about natural rights and liberties, as though these were terms of well-defined and unchangeable meaning. There is no such thing as an absolute or unqualified right of liberty guaranteed to any member of society. Natural rights and liberties of a subject are relative expressions and have relative or changeable meanings." On its face, this is nonsense. The concept 'relative' is logically meaningless in the absence of the concept 'absolute.' It is this logical requirement which allows us to say that while, as a matter of principle, liberty is absolute, as a matter of practice it is subject to qualification. If realistically, liberty, as a natural right, is to be enjoyed in society, it will be enjoyed in common and with appropriate consideration of others in society. But it is no less the same liberty that Robinson Crusoe enjoys without qualification on his desert island. Despite his dissent, Holmes appeared to acknowledge not only the existence, but also the authority of antecedent natural rights. As he put it, unless reason and fairness conclude of necessity that the statute in question compromised these antecedent rights, the liberty enunciated in the Fourteenth Amendment would be compromised were it used to stop the "natural outcome of a dominant opinion." [115]

The mutuality and reciprocity characteristic of rights exercised within society generate a tension between two divergent forces, one centripetal and the other centrifugal. The former is a basic feature of society which seeks its own center of legitimate interests to avoid anarchy. The latter is characteristic of individuals who pursue legitimate personal interests to avoid being subsumed by society. Either outcome is unacceptable since each undermines the notion of a democratic society as an ethical construct. How then in support of this construct should members of society behave towards their fellow citizens and interact with their centers of governance? A brief review of some key points in Kantian ethics should prove enlightening.

KANTIAN CONSIDERATIONS

In ethics, "we are not concerned with accepting reasons for what happens but with accepting laws of what ought to happen even if it never happens—that is, objective practical laws."[116] More recently, Hare, no stranger to Kantian thought, made essentially the same point. "The reason why actions are in a peculiar way revelatory of moral principles is that the function of moral principles is to guide conduct."[117] It is also the case that ethics involves reason as it "deals with the grounds determining the will,"[118] which Immanuel Kant conceived as a "power" directing oneself to act according to particular "laws," constituting the essence of ethical behavior.[119] Couched in the imperative, valid "moral reasoning" must result in a command—you ought to do X.[120] And if the agreement with the command is made in earnest, one will choose, as an act of will, to do as commanded.[121] And if the reasoning is valid, it will be universalizable, applying to all rational persons. "The practically good (what ought to be done) is that which determines the will by concepts of reason, and therefore not by subjective causes (self-interest), but objectively—that is, on grounds valid for every rational being as such."[122]

Here Kant was concerned to establish what he called a genuine "supreme principle of morality" as a counterweight to the then prevailing confusion between moral principles and principles of self-interest.[123] From this concern came his formulation of the categorical imperative which was designed to provide an ultimate, objective criterion against which to assess whether the subjective counsels motivating individual behavior in particular circumstances could rise to the level of universality and therefore objectivity. Kant provided three formulations of his categorical imperative. The first grounded the necessity of a principle that has universal application, satisfying the concomitant need for objectivity and thereby rescuing ethics from subjectivity and relativism. "Act only on that maxim through which you can at the same time will that it should become a universal law."[124] Of the three formulations, the second applies most immediately to the matter of contracts. "Act in such a way that you always treat humanity, whether in your own person or in the person of any other, never simply as a means, but always at the same time as an end."[125] The third formulation gives expression to "the Idea of the will of every rational being as a will which makes universal law."[126]

This third formulation is not as obvious in its meaning as are the previous two. But the meaning emerges when the formulation is considered in relation to the other two. According to Kant, if every "rational" agent is to be regarded as an "end in himself," then as such he must also be able, with regard to any particular law governing him, to consider himself the maker of "universal law." That is to say, it is the potential of personal "maxims" of individual behavior to become universal law that renders rational agents able to be their own purpose. This entails always selecting their principles of behavior from the understanding of themselves and every other rational agent as law makers, hence meriting being called persons. The result is Kant's notion of a "kingdom of ends," with the concept of 'kingdom" representing a "systematic union of different rational beings under common laws."[127] It was, it seems reasonable to say a precursor of Gewirth's concept of a community of rights.

Kant's notion of rational agents as being self-normative, constituting, as it were, a universal society of self-normative beings, might also be a way of understanding his notion of the social contract as the one way of locating the "natural rights" of persons within the structure of the "State."[128] Working with Kant's three-part formulation of the categorical imperative, one can see how its universal kingdom of ends can answer the question Kant shared with Holmes, "what is law?" Objectively, the justification for every practical (positive) law was found in the first formulation's requirement for universality which enabled the rule to be a law. Subjectively, the justification was found in the second formulation, which in requiring all persons to be treated as ends and not as means only, established the ultimate condition constraining the freedom of action of every rational being. The combination of the first and second formulations gave rise to the third formulation which, in viewing every rational being as law maker, stipulated an identification between the two such that the making of law was essentially an expression of the freedom innate to every rational being.

Law making, in other words, results from the exercise of practical reason by the human will which gives expression to the freedom innate in every rational being. Freedom implies the capacity to act, that is, *act as one can act*, or *act as one ought to act*. Acting on the basis of a principle that already is or can be valid for every rational being results in law at once universal and objective and hence a "duty," something that ought to be fulfilled for its own sake. In relating every maxim of the will, considered universal, to the will of every other rational being, practical reason recognizes the "dignity" of "a rational being who obeys no law other than that which he, at the same time, enacts himself."[129] It is, according to d'Entreves, clear from this that Kant, in responding to the question, "what is law?" dismissed experience-based explanations, inferring as they do the concept of "law" from inductive reasoning of an increasingly broader and far-reaching form.[130] In resisting legal empiricism, Kant noted "that knowledge of what the laws actually 'say or have said' will never enable the jurist to know what law *is*, but only what *pertains to* the law . . . in a given place and at a given time."[131] To know the former, we must employ "pure reason" as the ground on which to base all "possible legislation."[132]

When one reads the words of the Fourteenth Amendment: "nor shall any state deprive any person to life, liberty or property without due process of law; nor deny to any person within its jurisdiction the equal protection of its laws," it is reasonable to see how personhood is understood in the Kantian sense of equally-enjoyed, irreducible worth. Why then, when the Lochner Court looked at the conditions under which bakers worked did it fail to see these workers for what they were in Kantian terms, mere means to their employer's ends? What liberty were they deprived of when for all practical purpose they had none? In which case, one has to ask who was deprived of what liberty when the New York State legislature authorized provisions to eliminate inhumane working conditions, including hours of work, and to reinstate employees as persons in their own right, with the possibility of equality with, and freedom from prospective employers in any contract they chose to agree to? If one assesses Lochner in this light, it is hardly difficult to see how wrongly it was decided.

NOTES

1. Pope Leo XIII, *Rerum Novarum, Encyclical of Pope Leo XIII on Capital and Labor* (1891), http://www.vatican.va/content/leo-X111/encyclicals/documents/hf_1-X111_enc_15051891_rerum-novarum (accessed December 10, 2020).

2. U.S. Supreme Court, *Jacobson v. Massachusetts*, 197 U.S. 11 (1905), https://supreme.justia.com/cases/federal/us/197/11/ (accessed October 17, 2020); and U.S. Supreme Court, *Lochner v. New York*, 198 U.S. 45 (1905), https://supreme.justia.com/cases/federal/us/198/45/ (accessed October 17, 2020).

3. Cornell Law School, "Lochner Era," *Legal Information Institute*; https://www.law.cornell.edu/wex/lochner_era (accessed October 16, 2020).

4. Cornell Law School, "Lochner Era."

5. David E. Bernstein, "*Lochner* Era Revisionism, Revised: *Lochner* and the Origins of Fundamental Rights Constitutionalism," *Georgetown Law Journal* 82, no. 1 (2003): 1–61, George Mason University Law & Economics Research Paper No. 03–18, https://papers.ssrn.com/sol3/papers.cfm?abstract_id=395620 (accessed October 17, 2020).

6. Cass R. Sunstein, "Lochner's Legacy," Columbia Law Review 87, no. 5 (1987)873–919, https://www.jstor.org/stable/1122721 (accessed October 16, 2020).

7. *Lochner v. New York* at 65.

8. *Lochner v. New York* at 61.

9. *Lochner v. New York* at 70.

10. *Lochner v. New York* at 69.

11. New York State, Supreme Court, Appellate Division, Fourth Department, *People v. Lochner*, 73 N.Y. App. Div. (1902), at 120, https://casetext.com/case/people-v-lochner-3 (accessed August 29, 2018).

12. New York State, Supreme Court, *People v. Lochner* (1902), at 127.

13. See Encyclopaedia Britannica, "Lochner v. New York," *Encyclopaedia Britannica*, https://www.britannica.com/print/article/345714 (accessed August 29, 2018).

14. See Alex McBride, *Lochner v. New York* (1905), https://www.thirteen.org/wnet/supremecourt/capitalism/landmark_lochner.html (accessed November 14, 2020).

15. New York State, Court of Appeals, *People v. Lochner*, 177 N.Y. 145 (1904), at 182, https://cite.case.law/ny/177/145/ (accessed August 29, 2018).

16. New York State, Court of Appeals, *People v. Lochner* (1904), at 174.

17. An 1896 statute of the State of Utah that restricts working hours in mines to eight hours a day and deems guilty of a misdemeanor persons, corporations, managers, and employers who have violated these provisions of the statute is "a valid exercise of the police power of the State and do not violate the provisions of the Fourteenth Amendment to the Constitution of the United States by abridging the privileges or immunities of its citizens, or by depriving them of their property, or by denying to them the equal protection of the laws." See U.S. Supreme Court, *Holden v. Hardy*, 169 U.S. 366 (1898), at 366, https://supreme.justia.com/cases/federal/us/169/366/ (accessed October 17, 2020).

18. David E. Bernstein, "Freedom of Contract," *Liberty of Contract, in Encyclopedia of the Supreme Court of the United States*, ed. David S. Tanenhaus (2008): 1–10, George Mason University Law and Economics Research Paper Series No. 08–51, http://ssrn.com/abstract id=1239749 (accessed August 31, 2018).

19. Bernstein, "Freedom of Contract."

20. *Lochner v. New York* at 52; emphasis mine.

21. H. L. A. Hart, "Positivism and the Separation of Law and Morals," *Harvard Law Review* 71, no. 4 (1958): 593–629, at 601–2, https://doi.org/10.1093/acprof:oso/9780198253884.003.0003, quoted in "Legal Positivism," *Wikipedia*, https://en.wikipedia.org/wiki/Legal_positivism#cite_note-1 (accessed August 31, 2018).

22. Crystal Schwanke, "Early 20th Century Unemployment," *Lovetoknow*, https://jobs.lovetoknow.com/Early_20th_Century_Unemployment (accessed August 31, 2018).

23. See "Notes on Labor, 1875–1900," *Georgetown Preparatory School*, http://claver.gprep.org/sjochs/labor.htm (accessed September 1, 2018).

24. *Lochner v. New York* at 54.

25. U.S. Bureau of Labor Statistics, "American Labor in the 20th Century," by Donald M. Fisk (2001; repr. 2003): 1–8, https://www.bls.gov/opub/mlr/cwc/american-labor-in-the-20th-century.pdf (accessed October 17, 2020).

26. See New York Baking Companies, "Unions: The Baking Industry in the State of New York," *Ward Baking Company* (2005): 1–3, http://www.wardbakingcompany.com/library/docs/New YorkBakingCompanies.pdf (accessed October 18, 2020).

27. *Lochner v. New York* at 54.
28. *Lochner v. New York* at 55.
29. *Lochner v. New York* at 59.
30. *Lochner v. New York* at 70.
31. *Lochner v. New York* at 70.
32. *Lochner v. New York* at 71.
33. *Lochner v. New York* at 72.
34. *Lochner v. New York* at 72.
35. *Lochner v. New York* at 73.
36. *Lochner v. New York* at 73.
37. *Lochner v. New York* at 76.

38. U.S. Supreme Court, *Northern Securities Co. v. United States*, 193 U.S. 197 (1904), https://supreme.justia.com/cases/federal/us/193/197/ (accessed October 18, 2020).

39. U.S. Supreme Court, *Otis v. Parker*, 187 U.S. 606 (1903), https://supreme.justia.com/cases/federal/us/187/606/ (accessed October 18, 2020).

40. *Lochner v. New York* at 75

41. *Lochner v. New York* at 76

42. *Lochner v. New York* at 75

43. *Lochner v. New York* at 57

44. *Lochner v. New York* at 57.

45. Ruth Mayhew, *What are the Functions of Labor Laws?* https://smallbusiness.chron.com/functions-labor-laws-61595.html

46. Otto Kahn-Freund, *Labour and the Law*, Hamlyn Lectures 24th ser. (London: Stevens, 1972), 7, https://doi.org/10.1093/iclqaj/22.1.199 (accessed October 18, 2020).

47. Kahn-Freund, *Labour and the La*w, 7.

48. Kahn-Freund, *Labour and the Law*, 7

49. *Otis v. Parker* at 69.

50. *Otis v. Parker* at 69.

51. Mortimer J. Adler, "Does the End Ever Justify the Means?" *SCI Library*, repr. February 2001, https://www.cooperative-individualism.org/adler-mortimer_does-the-end-justify-the-means-2001.htm (accessed September 8, 2018).

52. Adler, "Does the End Ever Justify the Means?"

53. *Lochner v. New York* at 75.

54. John Stuart Mill, "On Liberty" (1859), in *On Liberty. In The English Philosophers From Bacon to Mill*, ed. Edwin A. Burtt (New York: Random House, 1939), 952.

55. Mill, "On Liberty," 956.

56. Mill, "On Liberty," 957.

57. See Erwin Chemerinsky, "Substantive Due Process," *Touro Law Review* 15, no. 4 (1999): 1500–1534 (Article 15), https://digitalcommons.tourolaw.edu/lawreview/vol15/iss4/15 (accessed October 18, 2020).

58. See Harry Burrows Acton, "Herbert Spencer," *Encyclopaedia Britannica*, April 23, 2020, https://www.britannica.com/biography/Herbert-Spencer (accessed October 5, 2018).

59. Alan Gewirth, *The Community of Rights* (Chicago: University of Chicago Press, 1996), 96 ff.

60. See Albert Jay Nock, "Spencer," *Online Library of Liberty*, n.d., https://oll.libertyfund.org/pages/spencer-by-albert-jay-nock (accessed December 10, 2020).

61. See Nock, "Spencer."

62. Acton, "Herbert Spencer."

63. Acton, "Herbert Spencer."

64. Acton, "Herbert Spencer."

65. Henry James Sumner Maine, *Ancient Law, Its Connection with the Early History of Society, and Its Relation to Modern Ideas* (London: John Murray, 1861), 170.

66. Lawrence O. Gostin, *Public Health Law and Ethics: A Reader*, 2nd and rev. ed. (Berkeley: University of California Press, 2010), 73–74.
67. *Lochner v. New York* at 57.
68. U.S. Department of Labor, "Government Regulation of Workers' Safety and Health, 1877–1917," by Judson MacLaury, N.d., https://www.dol.gov/general/aboutdol/history/mono-regsafeintrotoc (accessed October 18, 2020).
69. U.S. Department of Labor, "Government Regulation."
70. *Lochner v. New York* at 59.
71. *Lochner v. New York* at 59.
72. *Lochner v. New York* at 59.
73. *Lochner v. New York* at 60.
74. *Lochner v. New York* at 60.
75. *Lochner v. New York* at 60.
76. *Lochner v. New York* at 61.
77. *Lochner v. New York* at 61.
78. *Merriam Webster Online Dictionary*, s.v. "Legal Right," (2020), https://www.merriam-webster.com/dictionary/legal%20right (accessed November 14, 2020).
79. Steve McCartney and Rick Parent, "2.9 Social Contract Theory," in *Ethics in Law Enforcement* (Victoria, BC: BC Campus, 2015), 30–32, https://opentextbc.ca/ethicsinlawenforcement/open/download?type=pdf (accessed October 18, 2020).
80. "No state shall . . . pass any Bill of Attainder, ex post facto Law, or Law impairing the Obligation of Contracts." in U.S. National Archives, The Constitution of the United States, art. 1, sec. 10, https://www.archives.gov/founding-docs/constitution-transcript (accessed October 18, 2020).
81. David E. Bernstein, "Freedom of Contract," *Liberty of Contract, in Encyclopedia of the Supreme Court of the United States*, ed. David S. Tanenhaus (2008): 1–10, George Mason University Law and Economics Research Paper Series No. 08–51, http://ssrn.com/abstract id=1239749 (accessed December 13, 2018).
82. U.S. Supreme Court, *Ogden v. Saunders*, 25 U.S. 213 (1827), https://supreme.justia.com/cases/federal/us/25/213/ (accessed October 18, 2020).
83. U.S. Supreme Court, *Allgeyer v. Louisiana*, 165 U.S. 578 (1897), https://supreme.justia.com/cases/federal/us/165/578/ (accessed October 18, 2020).
84. Bernstein, "Freedom of Contract."
85. *Holden v. Hardy* (1898).
86. Bernstein, "Freedom of Contract."
87. Bernstein, "Freedom of Contract."
88. Bernstein, "Freedom of Contract." See *Williamson v. Lee Optical, Inc.*, 348 U.S. 483 (1955), at 348. https://supreme.justia.com/cases/federal/us/348/483/ (accessed December 5, 2020).
89. A Law Dictionary, Adapted to the Constitution and Laws of the United States, by John Bouvier, s.v. "Impairing the Obligation of Contracts," n.d., https://legal-dictionary.thefreedictionary.com/Impairing+the+obligation+of+contracts (accessed December 13, 2018). *Williamson v. Lee Optical Inc.*
90. Mary Ann Glendon, *Rights Talk: The Impoverishment of Political Discourse* (New York: Free Press, 1991), 38.

91. Glendon, *Rights Talk*, 38.

92. Herbert Morris, "Persons and Punishment," in *Human Rights*, ed. A. I. Melden (Belmont, CA: Wadsworth Publishing, 1970), 111–134.

93. Morris, "Persons and Punishment," 133.

94. Richard Wasserstrom, "Rights, Human Rights, and Racial Discrimination," in *Human Rights*, ed. A. I. Melden (Belmont, CA: Wadsworth Publishing, 1970), 96–110.

95. Wasserstrom, "Rights, 98.

96. Wasserstrom, "Rights, 99.

97. Gewirth, *Community of Rights*, 132.

98. Gewirth, *Community of Rights*, 132.

99. Lars A. Stole, "Lectures on the Theory of Contracts," (1993; rev. 1999), *Yale CampusPress*, http://campuspress.yale.edu/dirkbergemann/files/2011/01/lectures.pdf (accessed December 19, 2018).

100. Oliver W. Holmes, Jr., "The Path of the Law," *Harvard Law Review* 10, no. 8 (1897): 457–78, http://moglen.law.columbia.edu/LCS/palaw.pdf (accessed October 18, 2020).

101. Holmes, "Path of the Law, 460.

102. Holmes, "Path of the Law," 459n3.

103. Holmes, "Path of the Law," 459n3.

104. Holmes, "Path of the Law," 459n3.

105. Holmes, "Path of the Law," 461n3.

106. Alessandro Passerin d'Entreves, *Natural Law: An Introduction to Legal Philosophy* (London: Hutchinson University Library, 1964).

107. Holmes, "Path of the Law," 462.

108. Holmes, "Path of the Law," 460.

109. d'Entreves, *Natural Law*. 92.

110. d'Entreves, *Natural Law*. 92.

111. St. Thomas Aquinas, T. "First Part of the Second Part," in *Summa Theologica*, 2nd and rev. ed., trans. Father of the English Dominican Province (New Advent, Online Edition, 1920), question 96, art. 5, https://www.newadvent.org/summa/2.htm (accessed October 15, 2020), as cited by d'Entreves, *Natural Law*.

112. Holmes, "Path of the Law," 459.

113. d'Entreves, *Natural Law*, 92.

114. Bernstein, "*Lochner* Era Revisionism, Revised."

115. *Lochner v. New York* at 76, Holmes dissenting.

116. Immanuel Kant, *Groundwork of the Metaphysic of Morals*, trans. and analyzed H. J. Paton (New York: Harper Torch Books/The Academy Library, 1964), 94

117. R. M. [Richard Mervyn] Hare, *The Language of Morals* (1952) (Oxford: Clarendon Press, 2003), 1.

118. Immanuel Kant, *Critique of Practical Reason*, trans. Lewis White Beck (Upper Saddle River, NJ: Prentice Hall, 1993), 15.

119. Kant, *Groundwork*, 95.

120. Hare, *Language of Morals* (2003), 39.

121. Hare, *Language of Morals* (2003), 19–20.

122. Kant, Groundwork, 81.

123. Kant, *Groundwork*, 76.
124. Kant, *Groundwork*, 88.
125. Kant, *Groundwork*, 96.
126. Kant, *Groundwork*, 98.
127. Kant, *Groundwork*, 100.
128. See d'Entreves, *Natural Law*, 57, citing Kant, *Rechtslehre* (*Science of Right* or *Doctrine of Right*), in *Die Metaphysik der Sitten* (*The Metaphysics of Morals*) (1797), *47, trans. J. W. Semple, ed. and intro. Rev. Henry Calderwood, 3rd ed. (Edinburgh: T. & T. Clark, 1886), https://oll.libertyfund.org/titles/1443 (accessed December 10, 2020).
129. Kant, *Groundwork*, 102.
130. See d'Entreves, *Natural Law*, 114–15.
131. d'Entreves, *Natural Law*, 115; emphasis in the original; citing Kant, *Rechtslehre*.
132. d'Entreves, *Natural Law*, 115, citing Kant, *Rechtslehre*.

Chapter 2

DeShaney v. Winnebago County Department of Social Services, 489 U.S. 189 (1989): Liberty and the Due Process Clause of the Fourteenth Amendment

The U.S. Supreme Court decision noted: "Today the Court purports to be the dispassionate oracle of the law, unmoved by natural sympathy. But in this pretense, the Court itself retreats into a sterile formalism."[1] Of all the decisions discussed in this book, the decision in Joshua DeShaney's case, *DeShaney v. Winnebago County* (1989), is the most controversial. One commentator was so incensed by the decision, he called it an "abomination."[2]

FACTS OF THE CASE

The case of a two-year old infant, defenseless against a brutally abusive father, called out for compassion and yet all it appeared to have received from the U.S. Supreme Court was indifference. It is remarkable that the decision in such an emotionally charged case would have hinged ultimately on two technicalities. Resting on a narrowly drawn interpretation of the substantive part of the Fourteenth Amendment's Due Process clause, the decision came down to a distinction between the words, action, and inaction that was so conceptualized as to have little bearing on human behavior in general, and none on the behavior exhibited in the circumstances of the case itself. Connected with this technicality was a second, the concept of causation, used to determine who was responsible for the physical harm that Joshua DeShaney suffered. Combined, they led the Court into what Justice Harry A. Blackmun, in his dissent, called "a sterile formalism."[3]

Joshua DeShaney was born in 1979. In 1980, after the divorce of his parents in Wyoming, the divorce court gave custody of Joshua to his father, Randy DeShaney, who then moved to Wisconsin. In 1982, the Wisconsin authorities were informed by Mr. DeShaney's second wife that Joshua might be the victim of abuse from his father. Subsequently informed of this by law enforcement, the Winnebago County Department of Social Services (DSS) interviewed the father who denied the charges. As a result, DSS decided not to pursue the matter further. However, in 1983, Joshua had to be admitted to a local hospital for treatment for a number of bruises and abrasions. The physician who examined him on this occasion suspected abuse and notified DSS to that effect. DSS then obtained a court order placing Joshua in the custody of the hospital. At the same time, DSS set up an *ad hoc* Child Protection Team which included a pediatrician, a psychologist, a police detective, a lawyer for the county, and a caseworker representing DSS. The team concluded there was insufficient evidence of abuse and consequently had no reason to keep Joshua in the custody of the court. Nevertheless, it did recommend, by way of protection for Joshua, that he be enrolled in a preschool program and that Mr. DeShaney undergo counseling. A month later, emergency room personnel called DSS to inform them that Joshua had to be treated for yet again suspicious injuries. But the social worker assigned to Joshua's case concluded that despite this latest episode there was no reason to take action. For the next six months, the social worker made monthly visits to Joshua's home and meticulously submitted reports on Joshua's condition. During this time, according to her reports, the social worker noted a number of suspicious injuries to Joshua's head and drew attention to the fact that the earlier recommendations from DSS were being ignored. In November 1983, DSS was again informed of suspected abuse of Joshua. When in December, and later in January 1984, the social worker attempted to see Joshua, she was refused with the explanation that Joshua was too ill to be seen. Despite this rebuff, DSS felt comfortable taking no action on Joshua's behalf. In March, Mr. DeShaney beat Joshua so severely that he was rendered comatose from severe brain damage. As a result, Joshua had to be placed permanently in an institution for the care of the profoundly retarded.[4]

These developments prompted Melody DeShaney, Joshua's mother, together with Joshua's guardian ad litem to sue DSS on the grounds that it had deprived Joshua of his liberty interests in the integrity of his body, a violation of his constitutionally guaranteed rights under the substantive part of the Due Process clause of the Fourteenth Amendment. Starting in the United States District Court for the District of Eastern Wisconsin where the court ruled in summary judgment for DSS, the case, on appeal, went to the U.S. Court of Appeals for the Seventh Circuit which affirmed the lower court. Judge Richard A. Posner, who wrote the decision,[5] concluded that failure on the part of the State to protect Joshua from his father's abuse did not constitute a violation of his liberty interest guaranteed in the Constitution of the United States. Judge Posner further argued that any causal relation between the conduct of DSS and the injuries Joshua suffered was inadequate to demonstrate the State's responsibility for depriving Joshua of his constitutional rights to substantive due process. Melody DeShaney appealed the decision to the U.S. Supreme Court which accepted the case *certiorari* (to be more settled)since up to this point decisions from "lower courts" in similar cases had varied.[6] The case was argued on November 2, 1988 and decided, with Chief Justice William Rehnquist writing for the Court, on February 22, 1989.

In reading the Court's decision,[7] it is evident that Chief Justice Rehnquist relied heavily on Judge Posner's thinking. Posner had argued that the purpose of the Due Process clause was to protect individuals from an overreaching government, not from the violence of private actors. Given that, Posner rejected the position of the Third Circuit[8] that stipulated a "special relationship" coupled with a positive duty to take action. Accordingly, becoming aware that a particular child might be at risk of abuse from private actors and deciding to protect the child occasioned a "special relationship" between State and child that entailed an affirmative constitutional duty to provide whatever protection might be needed.[9] Posner had also argued that any connection between the actions of DSS and the abuse suffered by Joshua was insufficient basis for an actionable claim of violation of constitutional rights under the Due Process clause. For this reason, Posner had concluded that there was no reason to address the question as to whether the actions of DSS were indicative of a "state of mind," justifying a claim of due process.[10]

THE POSNER DECISION

Since Posner's decision provided the basis for Rehnquist's decision, it is worth examining in detail since, from an ethics perspective, the inadequacies of the Posner decision will be reflected in Rehnquist's as well. Posner began with the premise that "the Constitution is a charter of negative rather than positive liberties."[11] It should, that is, be read as a declaration of freedom from government rather than an enunciation of positive duties incumbent on government on behalf of its citizens. According to Posner, the framers of the U.S. Constitution were more concerned to prevent government tyranny than to provide social services.[12] Cleverly put, but incorrect. Recognizing that tyranny was an evil, the framers concluded they ought to take steps to prevent it in the interest of individual liberty. There was nothing to suggest that they even knew what "social services" meant, let alone viewed the concept as good or bad. Their inaction on that score had no relevance here.

The inaction of government in Joshua's case is another matter. Consequently, Posner's assertion that "simple negligence" did not, in Joshua's case, amount to a violation of substantive due process merits scrutiny.[13] It was predicated on a categorical distinction between the words, action and inaction. In the abstract, that action precludes inaction as its contradictory is clear. It is anything but clear when the words refer to specific actions taken or not taken in particular circumstances by individuals. So, when Posner asserted that "if the defendants, though blameworthy, did not cause Joshua's injuries, they cannot be said to have deprived him of his liberty; deprivation implies causation," he was begging the question central to this case.[14] There was no doubt that Joshua was brutalized by his father. Nor was there any doubt that anyone, acting on behalf of DSS in Joshua's case, participated physically in the father's brutality. But with mounting evidence, generated in large measure by DSS itself, to support a reasonable suspicion of child abuse, DSS took no action as it was designed legislatively to do. It eventually withdrew Joshua from his father's custody and assumed responsibility temporarily for his care. Following a medical examination and review of Joshua's condition, DSS decided Joshua should be returned to his father. That action exposed Joshua, as the record showed, to the violence that left him irreparably injured for the remainder of his life.

What is under consideration here? Posner, and subsequently Rehnquist following his lead, reduced this sequence of actions and their reasonably predictable consequences to a rudimentary semantic difference between action and inaction, with DSS considered as non-actors. It cannot, however, be overlooked that these were actions taken by rational individuals, acting in their professional capacities, with consequences for which they must be held accountable. Posner saw matters very differently. Since the defendants did not physically cause the abuse of Joshua, they could not be held responsible for depriving him of his liberty. Since depriving is a form of causing, absent any deprivation, there can be no causation. But what if, by returning Joshua to his father, DSS was instrumental in allowing the abuse of Joshua to continue? While away from his father, Joshua experienced no violence. But as soon as DSS acted to return him, the violence resumed. It is hard, under these circumstances, to understand Posner's claim that by returning Joshua to his father's custody DSS did "not appreciably increase the probability of Joshua's injuries."[15]

The claim was predicated on a counterfactual supposition. What if the DSS had not existed, indicating that Wisconsin "has no institutional commitment to preventing child abuse."[16] Would Joshua have suffered his injuries anyway? Since, according to Posner, the answer was yes, the logical conclusion was that the abusive actions of his father were the necessary and sufficient conditions for the occurrence of Joshua's injuries. Given that inevitability, whatever DSS did was so inconsequential to causing Joshua's injuries that it would not render the Department liable under tort law.[17] The use of the counterfactual exemplified the corrosive effects of legal positivism on law and its application. Here it allowed the violence Joshua actually experienced to become an abstraction—it would have happened anyway—the causes for which became a matter of probability calculations, not specific actions undertaken by rational human beings acting deliberately. Instead of using probabilities to explain risk of actual occurrence of human behavior retrospectively, Posner mistakenly used them to excuse the actions of DSS prospectively since nothing it could have done would have prevented the inevitable. But was Joshua's abuse inevitable? After all, Justice William J. Brennan Jr. pointedly noted in his dissent that Wisconsin, presumably aware of the prevalence of child abuse, had established the DSS in the belief that it could act effectively to minimize, if not prevent entirely, children like Joshua from enduring, as a matter of right, physical and psychological abuse at the hands of parents or others.[18] The question, consequently, was not what might have happened to Joshua in the absence of the DSS, but what actually happened to him with the DSS intimately involved in the course of events that led up to his irreparable injuries. Finding cover behind an abstraction, Posner was unable to see the case of Joshua DeShaney for what it was, a matter fundamentally of ethics. Instead, having tied the law, already unmoored from ethics, to his positivist abstraction, Posner had so compromised it that when it should have served him, the law could only fail Joshua terribly.

ANN KEMMETER

Posner's counterfactual argument would in effect have rendered DSS irrelevant were it not for Ann Kemmeter's actual involvement in Joshua's case, and Posner's assessment of her involvement. Kemmeter was the case worker representing DSS. Describing her management of the case as a botched rescue attempt, Posner concluded that while she did not help Joshua, neither did she harm him, with decisions she made at critical points leading up to the culmination of Joshua's abuse. "She merely failed to protect him from his bestial father."[19] Consequently, Posner concluded that the issues were negligence on the part of Kemmeter and the status of negligence under tort law, of which there are two kinds, common law tort and constitutional law tort. Under the common law version, someone in Kemmeter's position was liable for her negligence, even though there may have been no obligation to intervene. In contrast, under the Constitutional version, the liability of the defendant was tied to actions depriving a plaintiff of some right. Consequently, under common law, there was no need for the plaintiff to show that the negligence of the defendant made it less likely that someone else might have come to her assistance. However, this was not a concern under constitutional law since negligence did not reach the threshold of actually causing harm. "A Constitutional tort requires deprivation by the defendant and not merely a failure to protect the plaintiff from a danger created by others."[20] In this case, it should be argued that since Joshua was completely dependent on Kemmeter for his protection from abuse, her failure to act in his interests contributed proportionately to the harm he suffered. Proportionate to Joshua's dependence on Kemmeter was her moral responsibility to prevent harm to Joshua. This obligation moreover took precedence over the constitutional provisions cited by Posner and should not have been invoked to cancel Kemmeter's obligations to Joshua since they too must comply with ethics as their ultimate justification.

The distinction between the two forms of tort is a good example, for its contingency and arbitrariness, of legal positivism. Posner provided no justification for the difference in the way the two tort laws regard the same behavior. Under common law tort, Kemmeter would have been liable for her involvement. Yet the very same involvement under constitutional tort law did not render her liable. The discrepancy was disturbing for two principal reasons. The first was for the way it allowed for the complete exoneration of DSS. The second was for the consequences it led to for Joshua, providing additional evidence of the harm that resulted from legal positivism's insistence on separating law from ethics. That there are two quite distinct versions of tort law with two quite distinct outcomes when applied to the same set of circumstances is predicated on the view that a law is law because it is so ordered, without any consideration for whether it is a just law grounded in ethics.

In this regard, whatever was made of Kemmeter's behavior, it was, Posner argued, to be distinguished from any that situated Joshua in circumstances of high risk which in turn added to the probability of harm occurring to him. DSS removed Joshua from his father's custody in January 1983, to place him in the care of a local hospital upon reports of suspicious injuries to the child. Posner acknowledged that DSS subsequently decided to return the infant to his father's custody. Had that been a reckless decision, it might also have been considered a decision responsible for the harm that followed. However, that would have meant going beyond the decision in *Doe v. New York City Department of Social Services* (1987), in which the city's welfare department placed a child with foster parents, while retaining custodial responsibility for the child.[21] But since Joshua, unlike Richard Doe, was not a foundling, whether DSS had reason to believe there was risk of abuse was not the legal point. Infants who happened to be foundlings were subject to protection. Infants who happened not to be, even where there was a history of abuse, were not. To be clear, the overriding issue to be considered was not risk of abuse but the infant's status under the law. Posner argued that any attempt by DSS to end the parental rights of Joshua's father, could have led to his suing the department for "unconstitutional deprivation of his rights as a father."[22] But that presumed that those parental rights were still intact under the circumstances. What is one to make of them, in light of the fact that, in 1983, DSS had obtained a court order to remove Joshua from his father's custody and placed him in a hospital where he was examined and treated for suspicious injuries? Was not this a practical step taken by DSS, with court approval, to secure Joshua's rights as a human being? It suspended the parental rights and, since Joshua was unable to secure his rights to be free from violence, acknowledged that ensuring them for Joshua was the immediate responsibility of DSS, overriding any it had to Joshua's father.

In consideration of this, it is important to note that if individuals are said to have liberty interests, it is not because of the Constitution. It is because what they are, as human beings, is the source and justification of the claim to these interests. Moreover, it is a claim made on the basis of a self-validating human right that gives moral merit to steps taken to enjoy the right. As the object of the claim made on the basis of a human right, these interests are constitutive of human being. In their absence, the integrity of a human being is compromised to its core. If they are enjoyed as a human right, then these interests are "had by all humans" and "had against all humans."[23] That is, they are shared in common and require interdependent relations of individuals for their actual enjoyment.[24] If then our liberty interests are claimed on the basis of a human right, that is also the most powerful reason for which they can be invoked. Consequently, once the claim is made, it is no longer a matter of someone's discretion whether or not to recognize it. There is now an overriding moral, as distinct from legal, obligation to honor it.[25]

For this reason, the implications of thinking of the Constitution as a contract embodying negative rather than positive liberties should give one pause. Two come immediately to mind. First, if liberty interests are so important, it is understandable why government should not take steps that interfere with them. But why is it that these same interests are not sufficiently important that government should not take positive steps to protect them? After all, is not the burden of ensuring due process, procedural and substantive, an affirmative duty incumbent on government in the interests of individual liberty. Second, it is assumed that for the protection of liberty interests, government not interfering does result in an outcome, and that constitutionally speaking is good. Why is it then in the case of DSS, that no action on their part was considered to have no outcome for Joshua and that constitutionally speaking was also good? In the first instance, not to act was to act; in the second, not to act was not to act. The inconsistency was obvious, yet it stood, to an equally obvious harm for Joshua. Were one instead to think of the Constitution as embodying a social contract between the governed and the governing, it would make plain a preferable relation between it and liberty interests. Namely, one in which liberty interests depend on the Constitution for their fulfillment and the Constitution is seen to need liberty interests to legitimize its role in the lives of members of society. In other words, as remarkable as the Constitution is, it functions as a means, serving the liberty interests of the people. It is not some end in itself. In this capacity, it could not, as it was in Joshua's case, be its own end, to the protection of which Joshua's liberty interests were sacrificed.

In light of these considerations, an assessment of DSS's decision to return Joshua to his father's custody, subsequent to taking him out of parental custody, is critical. Since DSS had then taken full responsibility for Joshua's care, any decisions it made, along with their consequences, must be considered owned by DSS. Further, since the decision was one taken by DSS but whose consequences fall on Joshua, it was fundamentally an ethics or other-regarding decision, the ethics nature of which was intensified by the inability of Joshua to speak on his own behalf. Assessing the decision then is, in the final analysis, a matter of ethics not law. Characterizing the decision, and thereby justifying it as made to avoid a lawsuit, Posner was not helpful. When DSS decided to return Joshua to his father's custody, there was, he believed, no evidence suggesting recklessness on its part.[26] "The recklessness came later when Ann Kemmeter inexplicably failed to act on mounting and eventually overwhelming evidence that Joshua was in great peril from his father. And by then Joshua was back in his father's lawful custody."[27]

Why did Posner accuse Kemmeter of inexplicably failing to act if he did not understand that action to be expected or required of her? "Inexplicably failing" is ambiguous. "Inexplicably" could mean, used descriptively, behavior for which there is no explanation. Or, used evaluatively, it could mean not behaving as expected to behave. Similarly, "failed" used descriptively, could mean that someone did not do something, as in "the fielder failed to catch the ball." But "failed" can be used evaluatively, in which case it would mean someone did not do what should have been done. Since Posner characterizes Kemmeter's inexplicable failure to act as reckless, one has to conclude that he regarded her behavior as irresponsible. The evidence, accumulated between January 1983, when Joshua was returned to parental custody and March 1984, when Joshua was so badly abused that he suffered irreparable brain injuries, should, Posner said, have led Kemmeter to act since she knew the peril that Joshua was in. But if Joshua was legally the responsibility of his father at that point, how could Kemmeter's behavior be considered reckless at all? Not, presumably, unless acting on behalf of DSS, she had a continuing responsibility to protect Joshua consequent to the fatal decision of March 1984 to reinstate parental custody?

Posner however rejected the argument that by assuming, on one occasion, custody of a child, as Wisconsin did in Joshua's case, a state was obliged under federal law to oversee the welfare of the child. That position was presumably his way to explain the baffling conclusion that despite the overwhelming evidence of ongoing abuse of Joshua, the father's custody remained lawful. That seems a questionable but not surprising conclusion that was premised on legal positivism and its refusal to attribute any moral content to law in general and to the Due Process clause in particular.

One might have hoped that when the U.S. Supreme Court took up the *DeShaney* case, it might, on careful reflection, have seen the substantial inadequacies of Posner's reasoning and the inadequacy of the decision it led to. Unfortunately it did not. With the exception of Justices Blackmun, Brennan, and Thurgood Marshall, the majority, led by Chief Justice Rehnquist, accepted the substance of the Posner decision in its entirety.

THE REHNQUIST DECISION

In his dissent, Justice Blackmun maintained that the Court had mistakenly claimed its decision was unavoidable, given prevailing legal doctrine. Instead, he viewed the question before the Court as an open one and that the Fourteenth Amendment precedents it cited might be interpreted broadly or narrowly depending on one's choice. He chose the broader, or as he put it, a sympathetic interpretation, "one which comports with dictates of fundamental justice and recognizes that compassion need not be exiled from the province of judging."[28] Blackmun was objecting to the Court's interpretation of the meaning of the language of the Due Process clause. A "sterile formalism," he claimed, rested on "a sharp and rigid line between action and inaction."[29] Of the cases discussed in this book, *DeShaney* is the one that makes it necessary to clarify "the relationship between the language that is used to make legal standards, and the law itself."[30] The language in question is that of the Due Process clause of the Fourteenth Amendment: "nor shall any State deprive any person of life, liberty, or property without due process of law." As we saw above, Posner viewed the Constitution as embodying negative rights. Since the presumption was that persons have already rights to life, liberty, and property, government had an obligation not to interfere with the enjoyment of these rights. But should it interfere, it must comply with the requirements of both substantive and procedural due process. Substantive due process consisted in the justification for government interference. Procedural due process consisted in steps, such as holding a hearing, employing legal counsel, conducting cross examination, available under the Constitution, to persons to make their case, protesting government interference. Considering due process in this light, it did not apply in circumstances where government was inactive. It was only enforceable where a government intervention was encroaching on a person's liberty interests. But was the matter as clear cut as this? Non-interference is viewed under due process as the way to protect the rights in question. But the goal is protection of these rights which is achieved affirmatively with government assuring due process. What then if non-interference degenerated into neglecting to protect them? That would be a form of inaction, but one putting at risk life, liberty, and property, and frustrating the goal of protection. Since however the overriding goal was protection, government would have to take action to counter the consequences of neglect. Consequently, inaction relative to the language of the Due Process clause would not be as Rehnquist would have it. Yet, as he viewed the facts of case of Joshua DeShaney, he believed that the task before the Court was to determine who abused Joshua, violating his rights in consequence. The evidence, Rehnquist believed, pointed clearly and exclusively to Joshua's father. Government, in the form of the Wisconsin State DSS, was not responsible in any way for the abuse inflicted on Joshua. Its involvement with Joshua, since that in no way amounted to interfering with his liberty interests, did not qualify for consideration under the terms of the due process clause. As far as the abuse of Joshua was concerned, DSS was an inactive bystander. But was it? Rather than not interfering, was it involved in a prolonged neglect or disregard of Joshua's liberty interests that resulted in not protecting them?

There was, as we saw earlier, a pivotal moment in its involvement with Joshua when DSS made the decision, after having removed him from parental custody for several days, to return him to his father's care with devastating consequences for this defenseless infant. The brain surgery had in 1984 confirmed a series of hemorrhages which were the result of head injuries suffered over an extended period of time. This was subsequent to the reckless behavior of Ann Kemmeter who, as Posner put it, had "inexplicably failed" to see the growing and eventually undeniable evidence of the threat posed to Joshua from his father's brutal abuse. However, as Rehnquist put it, "a State's failure to protect an individual against private violence,"[31] did not violate Due Process which "imposes no duty on the State to provide members of the general public with adequate protective services."[32] However, as Posner and Rehnquist described this course of events, it was far from clear that the involvement of DSS could be characterized as inaction, particularly in regard to the abuse inflicted on Joshua.

At issue then was the meaning and interpretation of the two words, action and inaction, and how they might be applied to characterize DSS's relations with Randy DeShaney. While Joshua was in the care of the hospital, he was not abused. The evidence indicated, however, that upon returning to his father's care, following the decision of DSS to that effect, the abuse resumed.

To resume, Joshua had to be in physical proximity to his father. That was achieved directly as a result of DSS's decision to return Joshua to his father. As a result, to the extent that DSS's decision enabled Randy DeShaney to resume his abusive treatment of his son, then DSS was complicit in the abuse, without actually abusing Joshua. To the extent that, despite the growing evidence of abuse subsequent to its decision, DSS neglected to protect Joshua, its complicity in the violence, if anything, deepened. The longer DSS continued neglecting Joshua's interests, the more clearly it signaled to the father that he could continue his abuse with impunity. DSS's inaction was not constitutional non-interference. It was neglect and as such was a failure to fulfill its negative duty to protect the liberty interests of Joshua.

From the perspective of legal positivism, the inconsistency evident in the Due Process clause is tolerable. As worded, this is law because it is so ordered. Rehnquist declared that the language of the clause "cannot fairly be extended to impose an affirmative obligation on the State to ensure these interests do not come to harm through other means," because "our cases have recognized that the Due Process Clause generally confer no affirmative right to government aid, even when such aid may be necessary to secure life, liberty, and property interests of which the government itself may not deprive the individual."[33] It is literally true that there is nothing in the language of the Clause obliging the state to protect the specified interests of its citizens against private actors. Logically, however, while the language may not be interpreted to impose, neither can it be interpreted to exclude an affirmative duty. There is nothing logically incompatible between the Clause, on the one hand, requiring the state to do nothing to interfere with these interests and, on the other hand, requiring it to do something to protect them. If the liberty interests are so important that they should be free from government interference, why the inconsistency of not valuing them sufficiently to merit government protection? That the clause has been restricted to a function of non-interference only is a matter of legal precedence, predicated on a positivist understanding of law as law because so written or ordered.

From the perspective of ethics, this inconsistency is unacceptable. The rights in question are human rights that do not owe their origin or validity to the Constitution. Nor are they, as human rights, subject to conditions of enjoyment originating with the Constitution. The function of the Constitution in their regard is to confirm them in a manner that respects their self-justifying authority. As a consequence these rights are not at the discretion of government, as the non-interference language of the Due Process clause implies. In the discussion of Alan Gewirth's principle of human rights, we saw how these rights are enjoyed universally by humans on the basis of their being humans. As claims to certain goods constitutive of human being, they are made by individuals entitled to such things as life, well-being, or freedom. It cannot be said too often that there are two features, essential to these rights. Since they are universal, they are shared universally. And if they are shared universally, that means they are inter-dependent for their exercise in the actual life of an individual, with their inter-dependence predicated on the universal principle of justice. This in turn is predicated on the foundation of natural law, the universality of reason concordant with nature. In practical terms, this requires not just that these rights are not interfered with, but that they are positively supported. For this reason, Rehnquist was mistaken when he said that there was "no affirmative right to government aid, even when such aid may be necessary to secure life, liberty, and property interests,"[34] despite what he claimed to be the correct understanding of the language of the Due Process clause. It is precisely because such aid is necessary that there is an affirmative duty for government to provide it. If such aid is as necessary as even Rehnquist was prepared to concede, it was all the more necessary in the case of Joshua who was otherwise completely incapable of defending his liberty interests. This, as we saw earlier, is one of the main thrusts to Gewirth's valid argument that rights are dependent on societal governance for their fulfillment. At the same time, the justification for any form of governance is found in the human rights integral to all members of society.

DEFENSELESS JOSHUA

In light of this, it becomes clear how inadequate, because of its narrowness, was Rehnquist's positivist interpretation of the language of the Due Process clause. Nothing revealed it more than the person at the center of this case, Joshua DeShaney. Completely overlooked by Rehnquist was the fact that Joshua, since he was only four years old, was unable to represent, on his own behalf, his fundamental liberty interests. Not only defenseless against his father's abuse, Joshua was voiceless in pursuit of these interests. To enjoy them would have taken more than non-interference from government. In his case, it required active agency from a third party which in normal circumstances would have been his parents. His mother was not able to provide it because she lacked custodial authority. His father, who should have done so, chose instead to abuse the child. Joshua was helpless.

Of course, matters would have been different if Joshua had been incarcerated by the state. According to Rehnquist, there was an affirmative duty under the Due Process clause but only when, by one of its affirmative actions, such as incarceration, the state rendered the individual, who now became dependent on the state, incapable of protecting their liberty interests. This, he argued, constituted a transgression of the substantive limitations placed on state action by the Due Process clause. Accordingly, "In the substantive due process analysis, it is the State's affirmative act of restraining the individual's freedom to act on his own behalf . . . which is the 'deprivation of liberty' triggering the protections of the Due Process Clause, not its failure to act to protect his liberty interests against harms inflicted by other means."[35] Why would the incarceration of a convicted criminal constitute a transgression of Due Process? A transgression is an unlawful act. Since incarcerating a convicted criminal, all things being equal, is a lawful act, why would it trigger the provisions of the Due Process clause which is concerned with unconstitutional interference with an individual's liberty interests? Due Process has already been satisfied with the trial that led to conviction and incarceration. An indicted, incarcerated individuals, despite their crime, remain human beings with their human rights intact. Were it otherwise, it would be cruel and inhumane punishment, ultimately violating natural law, from which such rights originate, well before violating any constitutional law. It is these fundamental rights that trigger the responsibilities the state has under justice for the well-being of those incarcerated within its jurisdiction, since their civil rights have for all practical purposes been suspended. If the Due Process clause was relevant here, it should have been as a constitutional confirmation, grounded however in ethics, of these fundamental rights.

In contrast, citing *Estelle v. Gamble* (1976),[36] Rehnquist had explained matters in positivist terms. "We reasoned that because the prisoner is unable 'by reason of the deprivation of his liberty [to] care for himself' it is only 'just' that the State be required to care for him."[37] He maintained that it was only in transgressing the terms of the Due Process clause that the state incurred an affirmative duty to compensate for a prisoner's deprivation of liberty by incarcerating him. And, since in the case of Joshua, the State of Wisconsin had done nothing comparable to transgress the limitations placed on its actions under the Due Process clause, it had done nothing that would trigger the protections to life, liberty, or property afforded by the Due Process clause. However, none of this would apply to Joshua in so far as he was not incarcerated by the State. But neither does it reflect Joshua's circumstances. An infant has no freedom to be deprived of to care for himself since he is no position to care for himself. Joshua was dependent on others to provide whatever care was necessary. Unlike the circumstances of someone incarcerated, under which the issue is the consequences to one's loss of freedom, in Joshua's case the circumstances were those of complete dependence on others, and under which he was incapable of providing care for himself. To be clear, the care in Joshua's case was not medical care, as it was the case in *Estelle*. More critical, it was care that would protect him from his father's relentless violence. That was care to be claimed as a human right, so essential was it to his very survival. As such, it should be claimed under the constitutional provisions afforded by the Due Process clause as an affirmative responsibility of the state. And it would be, were the language of the clause being interpreted, not in Rehnquist's narrowly positivist terms, but as a matter of law grounded in ethics. Since clearly these were not analogous cases, as Rehnquist implied they were, his argument here was misleading. But it has been throughout. To say that the language of the Due Process clause cannot fairly be extended to impose an affirmative obligation for states to secure these interests because "our cases have recognized that the Due Process Clauses generally confer no affirmative right to government aid" confuses the logic of the language of the clause with the history of its interpretation. Providing due process is itself an affirmative obligation of the state. If Rehnquist had wanted us to take his analysis of the language of the Due Process clause seriously, he should have taken the logic of the language seriously.

Instead, his argument, at its foundation, was predicated on a dichotomous use of the terms, action and inaction. Used in the abstract, they are contradictory. Used in the context of specific instances of human behavior, this absolute distinction becomes quite implausible. We noted earlier that *DeShaney* is one of those cases that makes it necessary to clarify the relationship between the language that is used to formulate and carry out a legal principle, such as the Due Process clause and the principle itself. Those who speak the "English language" well appreciate the "meaning" of the terms action and inaction. They can and do, nevertheless, differ in their application of the terms. When this occurs, "the law must find some way to ascribe to language when used as the source of legal right or obligation a certainty it inherently lacks."[38] This requires turning to the "context of use." However, "the context-dependence of the meaning of words requires an account of linguistic competence that relates it to other human capacities—capacities to judge the importance of context and to draw analogies."[39] Regrettably, Rehnquist failed on both counts, to Joshua's great injustice with the Court's decision to exonerate DSS. Instead, he proceeded with an analysis of the case that merits the rebuke of a fellow positivist, Bertrand Russell, who wrote that there are those who "say that words should never be confronted with facts but should live in a pure autonomous world where they are compared only with other words." In their view "the attempt to confront language with fact is 'metaphysics' and on this ground to be condemned."[40]

JUSTICE BRENNAN DISSENTING

In his dissent, Justice Brennan conceded that as construed by the cases cited by the Court, the Due Process clause may not create any general right to basic governmental services. That however, he insisted, is not the question before the Court here. "No one, in short, has asked the Court to proclaim that, as a general matter, the Constitution safeguards positive as well as negative liberties."[41] For Brennan, the starting point was the acknowledgment that in a constitutional setting that made a sharp distinction between action and inaction, how one perceived the behavior of the DSS was likely to be decisive for the case. The Court's starting point was to deny the presence of any positive rights in the Constitution and to consider questionable claims that might be based on such rights. From this perspective, the plaintiff's claim that when a state announced its intention to protect children in situations like those of Joshua, and was presented with them, the Constitution imposed an affirmative duty to provide those protections. That is, it becomes a claim primarily about the inaction of respondents that resulted in providing no protection for Joshua, and only secondarily about the action taken by Wisconsin to establish a program to help children like Joshua. "And from this perspective, holding these Wisconsin officials liable—where the only difference between this case and one involving a general claim to protective services is Wisconsin's establishment and operation of a program to protect children—would seem to punish an effort that we should seek to promote."[42]

Brennan however preferred to start by considering the action undertaken by Wisconsin on behalf of children like Joshua rather than any actions the State failed to take. This was the approach taken by the Court in *Estelle v. Gamble* and *Youngberg v. Romeo* and served to illustrate the real issue here that "a State's actions can be decisive in assessing the constitutional significance of subsequent inaction."[43] Brennan questioned the Court's contention that it was the affirmative action of incarceration or hospitalization, for example, that rendered the individual incapable of taking care of himself and as a result triggered the protections of the Due Process clause. This, in the case of *Youngberg v. Romeo*, he viewed as a surprising restatement of the facts in light of "our explicit observation in that case that Romeo did not challenge his commitment to the hospital, but instead argued that he had a constitutionally protected liberty interest in safety, freedom of movement, and training within the institution; and petitioners infringed these rights by failing to provide constitutionally required conditions of confinement."[44] For Brennan, it was not that the affirmative act of placing Romeo in the hospital was irrelevant. Rather, more relevant was the consideration that the State's action would not have occasioned any injury to Romeo. Consequently, it would not have prompted any action under due process of law, unless after, but not because of that, the State took no action to protect Romeo from himself or others.[45] Of considerable relevance also for Brennan was the fact that placing Romeo in the hospital did not render him incapable of caring for himself. Because of his mental status—an I.Q. of between 8 and 10, for example, he was unable to care for himself long before any state intervention.

From this analysis, Brennan drew two critical conclusions. The first was that placing Romeo in hospital was significant, not because it prevented him from taking care of himself but because it removed him from other constitutionally required sources of assistance. The second, associated with the first, was that, unlike the Court, he did not see its unambiguous divide between action and inaction. For Brennan, both *Youngberg* and *Estelle* "stand for the much more generous proposition that, if a State cuts off private sources of aid and then refuses aid itself, it cannot wash its hands of the harm that results from its inaction."[46]

In this analysis of *Youngberg* and *Estelle*, Brennan saw a direct parallel to the facts of the *DeShaney* case. In setting up its system of child welfare, Wisconsin enacted legislation that required local departments of social services to investigate instances of child abuse. Even though other government agencies, including police departments, and private citizens were responsible for reporting child abuse, all such reports went to the local department of social services for evaluation and possible action. This was what happened in Joshua's case. For example, when the second wife of Randy DeShaney reported him to the police for hitting Joshua, they, in turn, referred the complaint to DSS. Indeed, all of the evidence compiled by Kemmeter remained within DSS. More significant for Brennan was the control DSS exercised over any action to be taken for the protection of a child from suspected abuse. In Joshua's case, when he was first admitted to hospital for possible abuse, DSS withdrew him from his father's custody so as to examine all the evidence. Subsequently, it was DSS that made the decision to return the child to the care of his father. "In other words, the State of Wisconsin has relieved ordinary citizens and governmental bodies other than the Department of any sense of obligation to do anything more than report their suspicions of child abuse to DSS. If DSS ignores or dismisses these suspicions, no one will step in to fill the gap."[47]

In closing his argument, Brennan rejected the Court's assertion that the State was a bystander, doing nothing in regard to Joshua. Under the terms of its child protection program, it was actively involved in monitoring and recording the seriously harmful events affecting him while "confined . . . within the walls of Randy DeShaney's violent home."[48] Unlike Rehnquist, who, conceding that the State might have known of Joshua's perilous circumstances, insisted that it played no part in creating them and did nothing "to render him more vulnerable to them,"[49] Brennan argued that the existence of Wisconsin's program made things worse for Joshua "when the persons and entities charged with carrying it out fail to do their jobs."[50] Reduced to its simplest form, Brennan's disagreement with the Court arose from its refusal to see that inaction on the part of the State can just as easily result in abuse of power as action. As a consequence, its interpretation of the Due Process clause exonerated Wisconsin even as it removed from Joshua any alternative sources of protection, rendered him totally dependent on the State, and then walked away "from the harm it has promised to try to prevent."[51]

In joining Brennan in dissent, Blackmun characterized the Court's decision as "sterile formalism" which accounted for its failure to acknowledge the facts of the case itself, as well as the applicable legal norms. Instead, the Court conducted its review around a rigid distinction between action and inaction, with the goal of the review being to determine responsibility for Joshua's physical abuse. Seeing nothing to suggest action on the part of DSS, it therefore incorrectly concluded inaction and rejected the appeal based as it was on the Due Process clause.[52]

The Court's reliance on the concept of state inaction took two forms here. The first was that Wisconsin did nothing comparable to what happened in *Youngberg* to physically restrain Joshua so as prevent him from taking care of himself and so trigger protections under the Due Process clause. Given his age and total dependence on others for his welfare, however, it is hard to see how Joshua's liberty interests would be affected negatively in the way necessary for the Court's argument to be relevant. Whether in prison or in hospital confinement, there was no way that Joshua could be said to have been deprived of his liberty interests as a result of confinement. But the Court's argument was that since there was no such confinement in Joshua's case comparable to Romeo's, there was nothing to trigger the protections of the Due Process clause. But even if there had been a comparable confinement, there was no liberty of which to be deprived due Joshua's total dependence as an infant on others for his welfare. For this reason, Brennan felt compelled to expand the notion of restraint beyond physical restraint to include the equally real restraint that resulted from the operation of Wisconsin's child welfare program. By placing Joshua beyond the reach of alternative sources of assistance, such as the police, the only assistance available would have had to come from DSS. That that assistance was never forthcoming effectively restrained Joshua in a manner far more consequential than in any way conceivable in *Youngberg*. If nothing else, that should have argued more urgently for Joshua's claim to the constitutional protections afforded by the Due Process clause. Instead the Court relied on a clearly unrealistic distinction between action and inaction so as to argue that the State did nothing to deprive Joshua of his liberty interests. As a consequence, it failed to acknowledge that not to do anything is not to do nothing.

There is no doubt that there is a clear distinction between the words *action* and *inaction*, the logical implications of which cannot be ignored if, when applied to the complexity of human behavior around Joshua, we expect to interpret and use them accurately. In this sense, the Court's use of the logical distinction between action and inaction amounted to an abuse of a distinction that is a necessary but not a sufficient condition for a correct assessment of what actually transpired in Joshua's case. A word is said to be ambiguous if it has two or more meanings. The word, *remember*, for example, is ambiguous since it may refer to something procedural, as in *remember to call my lawyer*, or to something informative as in *remember that tomorrow is a holiday*. There is also a "conceptual" and a "contextual ambiguity." The word, inaction, certainly in relation to the word action, is not conceptually ambiguous but it is contextually ambiguous, in the way that "teaching" in the sentence, "Hitler's teaching was atrocious," is "contextually ambiguous." The Court, in its use of the word, *inaction* failed to acknowledge its contextual ambiguity, as well as the implications of that for assessing the nature of the behavior of DSS.[53]

To his credit, Brennan did sense this in a way that clearly escaped Rehnquist. As Brennan addressed the matter, it remained unknown why the DSS failed to help Joshua but, for the Court, that was of no consequence. That is, as long as it was not done to be discriminatory or, because they thought so little of him, that they could not bother to deliberately intend discrimination for some arbitrary reason. Unwittingly, the language of the Court implied the possibility that not to act was not to do nothing. On the contrary, it could be, for instance, in order to be discriminatory. But having ruled out discrimination, it falsely extended that absence to conclude that it was sufficient to show that inaction was simply that—inaction, nothing less, nothing more.

Another persuasive consideration for the Court was that since no state actor inflicted the physical harm suffered by Joshua, there was no way the State could be held accountable for deprivation of life, liberty, or property under the Due Process clause. It was true that no one in DSS involved in Joshua's case physically harmed him. But that did not exonerate DSS from any culpability in causing the harm suffered by Joshua. Our actions have consequences and our informed actions have consequences for which we may be held accountable simply because we are actors in a given situation where the qualification, state actor, is irrelevant. That the State was actively involved in Joshua's life, there can be no doubt. But whereas for Brennan that involvement was of the greatest consequence, for Rehnquist it appeared to be inconsequential. At one point he described it as taking temporary custody, and an offering of shelter, as if to suggest it was a humanitarian gesture. But it was not, as presumably DSS viewed it, taking custody of a child, who, as required under Wisconsin's child welfare program, is suspected of suffering abuse by his father. But taking temporary custody did not mean, Rehnquist contended, that the State had a permanent responsibility for securing an individual's safety.[54] However, since the individual in question was a child, the primary issue was custody rather than its duration. A physician, examining Joshua after he had been admitted to the hospital, suspected abuse and, following state law, reported his suspicions to DSS. Judging the suspicions to have merit, DSS sought custody of Joshua from a juvenile court but subsequently concluding the evidence was insufficient to prove abuse, DSS returned the custody of Joshua to his father.[55] Nevertheless, it would be reasonable to conclude that there was justification for concern for Joshua's safety when, even as it returned Joshua, DSS came to a voluntary agreement with Joshua's father to provide him with counseling, urged him to remove his then more recent girlfriend from the home and to enroll Joshua in a preschool program. There can be little doubt that while DSS might have returned custody of Joshua to his father, it nevertheless acknowledged its responsibility for Joshua in the face of a continuing concern for the child's welfare. It was a return of custody under certain conditions. Over the course of the seven months following Joshua's return to his father, there were further indications of abuse, all faithfully recorded but never acted on by DSS. Joshua was not enrolled in a preschool program and the girlfriend had not left the house. The consequences of DSS's decision to return Joshua to his father's care culminated in abuse so severe that it demonstrated Randy DeShaney's not unreasonable conclusion that he could take DSS's predictable inaction as a tacit sign that he could continue to abuse Joshua with impunity

Despite its faithful recording of what should have been considered disturbing events at the center of which lay DSS's decision to return custody of Joshua to his father, the Court concluded, "That the State once took temporary custody of Joshua does not alter the analysis, for, when it returned him to his father's custody, it placed him in no worse position than that in which he would have been had it not acted at all."[56] In light of his acknowledgement of what occurred following Joshua's return to his father, Rehnquist's description of Joshua's situation as *no worse* seemed to have justified for him the conclusion that since the result would have been the same whether DSS acted or not, that it acted made no difference. As with his assessment of custody, Rehnquist's assessment of abuse was a matter of degree. As long as its decision to return custody to the father did not make matters worse for Joshua, then DSS could not be accountable for depriving Joshua of a liberty of which he was already being deprived, and critically for Rehnquist, being deprived by a private not a state actor.

This was a curious piece of reasoning. It was as if to say that because custody by DSS was temporary, it did not, however briefly, alter Joshua's situation by securing for him some safety from abuse. As a result, the act of returning custody changed nothing. That hardly accorded with the facts. Presented with the possibility of abuse, DSS acted to prevent the possibility of abuse continuing. As long as Joshua remained in hospital custody, he was not presumably be at risk of abuse by his father. That however changed with DSS's reckless decision to return Joshua and expose him to the likely resumption of abuse. It is this decision that should have altered for the

Court, the analysis of the case since it placed Joshua in harm's way. Once there, it then deprived him irremediably of his liberty interests. The physical abuse was undoubtedly inflicted by Randy DeShaney. But that became possible only because of the recklessly enabling action of DSS, followed by its equally reckless inaction that led to a predicably tragic outcome. Contrary to Rehnquist's assertion, that decision did make things worse for Joshua by placing him precisely where abuse could occur with impunity, repeatedly and with an increasing severity to the point of irreparable brain damage. One has to ask how much worse, short of death, could it have become for Joshua? Since it refused to take action despite the mounting evidence of abuse, taking great care to record it with one hand, while equally determined to ignore it with the other hand, DSS was complicit in the harm inflicted on Joshua and should have been held accountable. Law as law because so written in the hands of Brennan and Blackmun was unable to prevent injustice. Law as law because so ordered was well able to cause injustice. Law as law because just would have insisted on justice for Joshua.

At the close of his decision, Rehnquist revealed the serious shortcomings of his legal positivism. While he acknowledged that Joshua and his mother had suffered grievous harm and justice screamed for adequate compensation, nevertheless any natural sympathy we as humans might feel for their plight was to be considered an impulse. "But before yielding to that impulse, it is well to remember once again that the harm was inflicted not by the State of Wisconsin, but by Joshua's father."[57] For Rehnquist the distinction was dispositive in concluding that no matter the harm and its severity matters were beyond the reach of remedy from the Due Process clause. What was Rehnquist really saying? In effect, the impulse of natural sympathy must, since it is misguided, yield to his distinction as correctly holding accountable the person responsible for Joshua's abuse. Might it not, however, be argued that Rehnquist had imposed an artificial distinction on the circumstances surrounding Joshua's case that conveniently coincided with the requirements of the Due Process clause even though it failed to reflect the totality of human behavior that went into the making of Joshua's fate. That behavior was far more interconnected, both in causation and in consequence, between that of DSS and Randy DeShaney than is allowed for in Rehnquist's verbal distinction between action and inaction. Nor was it permissible for the Court to deny such interconnectedness so as to impose a separateness so artificial as to misrepresent how Joshua's abuse came about. Joshua was physically abused by his father, but that sustained abuse would not have been possible had it not been for DSS's decision to return custody of Joshua to his father, a decision it refused to change despite mounting credible evidence that under Wisconsin's child welfare program required intervention. That no intervention was forthcoming on the part of DSS did not mean that nothing happened that could be laid at the doorstep of DSS, as Rehnquist argued. On the contrary, it was instrumental in giving tacit permission to Randy DeShaney to continue abusing his son.

There is something profoundly disturbing about this decision. As we saw, there was Rehnquist's incomplete analysis of the language of the Due Process clause. Also, there was the refusal to acknowledge the complexity of human behavior that may not be reduced to the simplicity of the distinction between action and inaction. However, the decision was disturbing for even more serious reasons that have to do with Rehnquist's understanding of the concept of law. It was such that it allowed him to unhinge the Due Process clause from its moorings as though it were an independent principle, sufficient unto itself and without need of relating it to a larger conceptual framework for its proper application. That, in its truest formulation, would be law understood as right reason in conformity with human nature. In other words, law understood as expressing a contract between the individual and society. The purpose of the contract is to enable that which is moral located in the freedom of individuals to be combined with that which is political located in the executive power of government so that the values of life, liberty, and property of individuals are secured through its exercise in the form of law. We can trace this approach to law to John Locke's formulation of a social contract that is fundamentally moral in purpose. As parties to the contract, human beings enjoy "rights to life, liberty, and property" originating apart from any positive legal framework prevailing in their own societies. Further, born in freedom and equality, they are in a position to choose to surrender some of their rights to government on condition that it secures by what it does and does not do a predictable enjoyment of these fundamental or natural rights.[58]

Placed in this context, the Due Process clause is not nearly as absolute and independent as Rehnquist would have us believe. Here, as an expression restraining government from unwarranted encroachment on free and equal persons, it only makes sense in relation to the state's logically prior and morally precedent duty to secure conditions conducive to the enjoyment of life, liberty, and property. The injunction that no state shall deprive any person of life, liberty, and property without due process of law only makes sense since, according to its language, it is the due process of law as the arbiter of what is owed to persons that will determine whether deprivation of what is otherwise owed, in light of that prior positive duty, is merited. It was Locke's argument that since the state governs only with the agreement of the governed, so as to secure their liberty interests, it follows that where a state is unsuccessful, the governed acting as free persons and therefore moral agents may choose to change their government.[59] The failure ultimately is moral, since it occurs by means of a misuse of law, the content of which is moral. *A fortiori*, the Due Process clause, as a subsidiary part of law, may not be used in the way

Rehnquist used it, to exonerate the State of Wisconsin when, by its treatment of Joshua, it failed in its positive duty to secure his liberty interests. It is Rehnquist's argument that only in circumstances where the action taken by the state, such as imprisoning a person, thereby rendering that person incapable of acting in his or her own best interests, does the Due Process clause trigger a positive duty for the state to protect those now compromised interests. But since those interests of life, liberty, and property are enjoyed independently of the Due Process clause, the source of the state's duty must be found elsewhere, namely the prior agreement between the governing and those freely governed. It is a curious aspect of Rehnquist's interpretation of the Due Process clause that positive duties are triggered even in regard to those whose behavior has forfeited the exercise of their interests but not in regard to persons like Joshua who have done nothing to forfeit the enjoyment of those same interests. This illustrates his mistaken view that these interests are not independent of the Due Process clause, or, for that matter, of the Constitution. As Rehnquist put it, "the Due Process Clause does not transform every tort committed by a state actor into a constitutional violation."[60] It is this same view that led Rehnquist to reduce Joshua's case to a matter of who was responsible for the physical abuse of Joshua. An insight provided by Linda Greenhouse was correct but hardly flattering. "Chief Justice Rehnquist couldn't get past the fact that the actual injuries were inflicted not by government agents but by a private person."[61] But of course physical abuse was a symptom of the larger moral abuse of the state that permits the physical abuse by choosing to choose to do nothing to prevent it. Rehnquist failed to appreciate this because of his impoverished, positivist view of the law which allowed him in this case to reduce law itself to the narrowest possible interpretation of the Due Process clause, with the result that like the Winnebago County DSS, the U.S. Supreme Court stood by and did nothing in the name of the Due Process clause but exonerate those complicit in the injustice suffered by Joshua. The fundamental moral content of law, that is law as just, was betrayed at the altar of law as bereft of moral content, that is law as so ordered. Joshua was the unfortunate sacrificial lamb. "Poor Joshua!"[62]

NOTES

1. U.S. Supreme Court, *DeShaney v. Winnebago County Department of Social Services.* 489 U.S. 189 (1989), at 212. Justice Harry Andrew Blackmun dissenting.; https://www.law.cornell.edu/supremecourt/text/489/189 (accessed October 19, 2020); https://supreme.justia.com/cases/federal/us/489/189/ (accessed October 19, 2020).

2. Aviam Soifer, "Moral Ambition, Formalism, and the 'Free World' of DeShaney," *George Washington Law Review* 57, no. 6 (1989): 1513–32, https://ssrn.com/abstract=1539685 (accessed October 19, 2020).

3. *DeShaney v. Winnebago County*, 489 U.S. 189 at 212.

4. CaseBriefs, "DeShaney v. Winnebago County," *Bloomberg Law*, 1989. https://www.casebriefs.com/blog/law/evidence/evidence-keyed-to-waltz/nonfeasance/deshaney-v-winnebago-county/ (accessed October 19, 2020).

5. U.S. Court of Appeals, *DeShaney v. Winnebago Cty. Dept. of Soc. Serv*, 812 F.2d 298 (7th Cir. 1987), https://casetext.com/case/deshaney-v-winnebago-cty-dept-of-soc-serv/ (accessed October 19, 2020); aff'd, 109 S. Ct. 998 (1989).

6. Garrett M. Smith, *"DeShaney v. Winnebago County*: The Narrowing Scope of Constitutional Torts," *Maryland Law Review* 49, no. 2 (1990): 487, https://digitalcommons.law.umaryland.edu/mlr/vol49/iss2/9 (accessed October 19, 2020).

7. *DeShaney v. Winnebago County*, 489 U.S. 189.

8. U.S. Court of Appeals, *Estate of Bailey by Oare v. County of York*, 768 F. 503, 510–511 (3rd Cir. 1985), https://casetext.com/case/estate-of-bailey-by-oare-v-county-of-york (accessed October 19, 2020).

9. *DeShaney v. Winnebago County*, 489 U.S. 189 at 194, referencing 812 F. 2d at 303–4.

10. *DeShaney v. Winnebago County*, 489 U.S. 189 at 194, referencing 812 F. 2d at 301–3.

11. *DeShaney v. Winnebago County*, 489 U.S. 189 at 194, referencing 812 F.2d 298 at 301.

12. *DeShaney v. Winnebago County*, 489 U.S. 189 at 194, referencing 812 F.2d 298 at 301.

13. *DeShaney v. Winnebago County*, 489 U.S. 189 at 194, referencing 812 F.2d 298 at 302.

14. *DeShaney v. Winnebago County*, 489 U.S. 189 at 194, referencing 812 F.2d 298 at 302.

15. *DeShaney v. Winnebago County*, 489 U.S. 189 at 194, referencing 812 F.2d 298 at 302.

16. *DeShaney v. Winnebago County*, 489 U.S. 189 at 194, referencing 812 F.2d 298 at 302.

17. *DeShaney v. Winnebago County*, 489 U.S. 189 at 194, referencing 812 F.2d 298 at 302.

18. *DeShaney v. Winnebago County*, 489 U.S. 189 at 208.

19. *DeShaney v. Winnebago County*, 489 U.S. at 194, referencing 812 F.2d 298 at 302.

20. *DeShaney v. Winnebago County*, 489 U.S. at 194, referencing 812 F.2d 298 at 302.

21. *DeShaney v. Winnebago County*, 489 U.S. at 194, referencing 812 F.2d 298 at 303. See *Doe v. New York City Department of Social Services*, 649 F. 2d 134 (2nd Cir. 1981), https://casetext.com/case/doe-v-new-york-city-dept-of-social-services-2 (accessed October 19, 2020).

22. *Doe v. New York City Department of Social Services*, 649 F. 2d 134.

23. Alan Gewirth, *The Community of Rights* (Chicago: University of Chicago Press, 1996), 6.

24. Gewirth, *Community of Rights*, 6.

25. See Richard Wasserstrom, Rights, Human Rights, and Racial Discrimination in *Human Rights*, ed. A.I. Melden (Belmont, California: Wadsworth Publishing Company, 1970), 98–99.

26. *DeShaney v. Winnebago County*, 489 U.S. 189 at 194, referencing 812 F.2d 298 at 303

27. *DeShaney v. Winnebago Cty. Dept. of Soc. Serv*, 812F2.d 298 at 15.

28. *DeShaney v. Winnebago County*, 489 U.S. 189 at 213.

29. *DeShaney v. Winnebago County*, 489 U.S. 189 at 212

30. Timothy Endicott, "Law and Language," *Stanford Encyclopedia of Philosophy*, ed. Edward N. Zalta (Summer 2016 ed.), 2.2, https://plato.stanford.edu/archives/sum2016/entries/law-language/ (accessed October 19, 2020).

31. *DeShaney v. Winnebago County*, 489 U.S. 189 at 189.

32. *DeShaney v. Winnebago County*, 489 U.S. 189 at 189.

33. *DeShaney v. Winnebago County*, 489 U.S. 189 at 196.

34. *DeShaney v. Winnebago County*, 489 U.S. 189 at 196

35. *DeShaney v. Winnebago County*, 489 U.S. 189 at 200.

36. U.S. Supreme Court, *Estelle v. Gamble*, 429 U.S. 97 (1976), https://supreme.justia.com/cases/federal/us/429/97/ (accessed October 19, 2020).

37. *DeShaney v. Winnebago County*, 489 U.S. 189 at 199.

38. Donald Nicholls, "My Kingdom for a Horse: The Meaning of Words," (2005) 121 LQR 577 at 579, as cited in fulfillment of the requirements for the degree of Doctor of Philosophy in Law, Victoria University of Wellington, 2012.

39. Endicott, "Law and Language," 2.2.

40. Bertrand Russell, *My Philosophical Development* (London: Routledge, 1995), 110.

41. *DeShaney v. Winnebago County*, 489 U.S. 189 at 204.

42. *DeShaney v. Winnebago County*, 489 U.S. 189 at 204.

43. *DeShaney v. Winnebago County*, 489 U.S. 189 at 205.

44. *DeShaney v. Winnebago County*, 489 U.S. 189 at 206.

45. *DeShaney v. Winnebago County*, 489 U.S. 189 at 206.

46. *DeShaney v. Winnebago County*, 489 U.S. 189 at 207.

47. *DeShaney v. Winnebago County*, 489 U.S. 189 at 210.

48. *DeShaney v. Winnebago County*, 489 U.S. 189 at 210.

49. *DeShaney v. Winnebago County*, 489 U.S. 189 at 201.

50. *DeShaney v. Winnebago County*, 489 U.S. 189 at 210.

51. *DeShaney v. Winnebago County*, 489 U.S. 189 at 212.

52. *DeShaney v. Winnebago County*, 489 U.S. 189 212.

53. Green, *Activities of Teaching*, 34–35.

54. *DeShaney v. Winnebago County*, 489 U.S. 189 at 201.

55. *DeShaney v. Winnebago County*, 489 U.S. 189 at 192.

56. *DeShaney v. Winnebago County*, 489 U.S. 189 at 201.

57. *DeShaney v. Winnebago County*, 489 U.S. 189 at 203.

58. See Alex Tuckness, "Locke's Political Philosophy," *Stanford Encyclopedia of Philosophy*, ed. Edward N. Zalta (2005; Winter 2020 ed.), https://plato.stanford.edu/entries/locke-political/ (accessed August 2, 2018).

59. Tuckness, "Locke's Political Philosophy."

60. *DeShaney v. Winnebago County*, 489 U.S. 189 at 190.

61. Linda Greenhouse, "The Supreme Court and a Life Barely Lived," *New York Times*, January 7, 2016, https://www.nytimes.com/2016/01/07/opinion/the-supreme-court-and-a-life-barely-lived.html (accessed October 19, 2020).

62. *DeShaney v. Winnebago County,* 489 U.S. 189 at 213.

Chapter 3

New York v. United States, 505 U.S. 144 (1992): Wither the Social Contract?

If the public has an interest in being assured of conditions under which its members can expect to be healthy, the outcome in *New York v. United States* (1992) was far from reassuring. Involved was the safe disposal, nationally, of low-level radioactive waste.

FACTS OF THE CASE

According to Justice Sandra Day O'Connor, who wrote the decision for the Court, disposal of this waste in the United States had begun in 1962 in Beatty, Nevada. Between 1962 and 1972, additional sites—Maxey Flats, Kentucky, and West Valley, New York—were opened. In 1965, a fourth site became available in Hanford, Washington, followed in 1967 with the opening of a fifth site in Sheffield, Illinois. A sixth site opened in Barnwell, South Carolina in 1971. However, within the following decade, the site in Illinois reached full capacity and was closed, with subsequent site closings in Kentucky and New York. By 1979, three sites—Nevada, Washington, and South Carolina—remained open to serve the country as it sought to dispose of low-level radioactive waste. However, in that same year, the sites in Washington and Nevada ceased operations temporarily, leaving the only remaining open site in South Carolina available to the entire country for waste disposal. This development prompted the governor of South Carolina to declare a reduction of 50% in disposal capacity at Barnwell. And when the sites in Nevada and Washington closed permanently, prospects for appropriate disposal nationally became questionable.[1]

Low-level radioactive waste includes generally "a wide range of items that have become contaminated with radioactive material or have become radioactive through exposure to neutron radiation."[2] Further, according to the Nuclear Information and Resource Services (NIRS), "so-called 'low-level' radioactive waste includes every radioactive element. In fact, radioactive elements that are high-level nuclear waste become 'low-level' when they leak out of the irradiated fuel rod cladding." NIRS concluded that low-level radioactive waste is not, as a result, low risk.[3] Given this, and the fact that disposal was increasingly becoming a problem, the need for a solution was urgent. It is noticeable, however, that, apart from acknowledging the history of low-level radioactive waste, Justice O'Connor took no account of its risk to the public as something that might be very important, if not overriding, to a constitutional assessment of the Federal Government's response to what it clearly considered an impending national crisis. The Court's assessment, we will see, was made strictly within constitutional confines and without any apparent consideration of its consequences for the public's well-being. It is instead an exercise in pure legal formalism.

In response to these alarming developments, the federal government passed the *Low-Level Radioactive Waste Policy Act* (1980).[4] Under the terms of the *Act*, each state was to be "responsible for providing for the availability of capacity either within or outside the state for the disposal of low-level radioactive waste generated within its borders."[5] And it was the opinion of the U.S. Congress that disposal would best be accomplished through state compacts, organized on a regional basis and to be approved by Congress. The 1980 *Act* also stipulated that by 1986, approved compacts would be able to confine their disposal services to member states only.[6] Since, however, Congress refrained from imposing any penalties on states reluctant to comply with the terms of the legislation, it became clear the *Act* lacked teeth. As a result, five years into the Congressional timetable for the development of regional compacts, the only compacts that had been approved were those associated with the original facilities at Nevada, Washington, and South Carolina. With only one year left of the timetable and with little prospect of further progress being made on the basis of the current legislation, Congress decided it had to revisit the issue with a noticeably different approach. This it did in 1985 with the passage of the *Low-Level Radioactive Waste Policy Amendment Act*, which, as O'Connor noted, "was again based largely on a proposal submitted by the National Governors' Association."[7]

The 1985 legislation authorized three approaches intended to encourage individual states to meet their responsibilities for the disposal of low-level radioactive waste produced within the state. The first approach was in the form of payments to be made by the Secretary of Energy to the states that, by July 1, 1986, had joined a regional compact or that intended independently within the state to establish its own disposal facility. The second approach amounted to a doubling of the surcharge to be collected by states with operating disposal sites and directed at those states that had failed to meet the July 1, 1986 deadline of the earlier legislation. For this, a deadline of January 1, 1988 was set and if not met would result in quadrupling the surcharge in the second half of 1988. The third approach took the form of a "take title" provision, requiring those individual states or regional state compacts unable to provide for disposal of their radioactive waste by January 1, 1996 to assume ownership of the waste when requested to do so by whoever produced it. In addition, those states would be held liable for direct or indirect damages incurred by radioactive waste generators or its owners in the event the state had not taken possession of the waste.

Following passage of the 1985 legislation and its implementation over a period of seven years, the State of New York, responsible for a proportionately significant production of the nation's low-level radioactive waste, passed its own legislation to site and to finance a disposal facility within its borders. Five possible sites—three in Allegany County and two in Cortland County—were identified, only to provoke opposition from residents in these counties. As a result, in 1990, the State, together with Allegany and Cortland counties, filed suit against the United States on the grounds that the 1985 federal legislation, specifically the so-called take title provision, violated: the Tenth and Eleventh Amendments to the Constitution of the United States, the Due Process clause of the Fifth Amendment, and the Guarantee clause of article 4 of the U.S. Constitution. Upon review, the District Court found against New York, but the Court of Appeals, reversing, found for the State. Eventually before the U.S. Supreme Court, New York's appeal had been modified so that it now confined itself to claims that the 1985 *Amendment Act* was in violation of the Tenth Amendment and the Guarantee clause.

The Tenth Amendment declares that "The powers not delegated to the United States by the Constitution, nor prohibited by it, are reserved to the states respectively, or to the people." As O'Connor explained, "If a power is delegated to Congress in the Constitution, the Tenth Amendment expressly disclaims any reservation of that power to the States; if a power is an attribute of state sovereignty reserved by the Tenth Amendment, it is necessarily a power the Constitution has not conferred on Congress."[8] She concluded that because of the Tenth Amendment, the need was "to determine whether an incident of state sovereignty is protected by a limitation on an Article 1 power which states that "All legislative Powers herein granted shall be vested in a Congress of the United States."[9] At issue ultimately for O'Connor, it would appear, was the matter of federalism and the implications for governance by a federal government of limited powers. In consideration of this matter, the Court had, according to O'Connor, taken one of two approaches to determine the balance of power between the Federal Government and the States. One had been to ask whether an act of Congress can be considered warranted by one of the powers delegated to Congress in article 1 of the Constitution. Alternatively, the Court had asked whether an act of Congress encroached upon state sovereignty as secured in the Tenth Amendment. The result had been a consistent assumption on the part of the Court that states enjoyed a 'significant measure of sovereign authority . . . to the extent that the Constitution has not divested them of their original powers and transferred those powers to the Federal Government.'[10] O'Connor"s inference was that like consideration of a limitation on an article 1 power, consideration of the Tenth Amendment directed the Court to assess the constitutional merits of Congress's efforts to address the disposal of low-level radioactive waste as a federal responsibility.

This brought her to a pivotal point in her decision and where the limitations of the constitutional review of the case responsible for that decision began to come under a relevant ethics scrutiny. While O'Connor conceded the acknowledged benefits of federalism, they were, she insisted, irrelevant because the task before the Court in this instance would remain the same even if there were no benefits to be had from constitutional federalism. That task was to determine what powers the federal government actually had, not what powers it ought to have had.[11] It will become clear that this premise, which amounts to declaring that federalism is an end in itself, will dictate a line of reasoning in the Court's decision allowing an individual state to exercise its sovereignty in the name of federalism even at the expense of the safety of its own residents, or those of neighboring states. The common good would take second place to the constitutional principle of federalism.

The overriding focus of O'Connor's concern was the third provision of the 1985 *Act*, the so-called take title provision which she saw as overreach from the federal government, threatening state sovereignty. Unlike the first two provisions of the *Act*, the third provision "had crossed the line distinguishing encouragement from coercion."[12] According to the provision, should States choose not to comply with the directions of Congress, they will have "the option of taking title to and possession of the low-level radioactive waste generated within their borders and becoming liable for all damages waste generators suffer as a result of the States' failure to do so promptly."[13] This provision, O'Connor argued, had no comparable precedent in any earlier federal legislation that would present a state government with no alternative but to carry out legislation passed by Congress.[14] There was nothing in this provision suggesting Congress "has held out the threat of exercising its spending powers or its commerce power; it has instead held out the threat, should the States not regulate according to one federal instruction, of simply forcing the States to submit to another federal instruction."[15] It is, to be clear, a Hobson's choice of sorts. As a result, she concluded, whether you understood the "take title" provision to be beyond the power of Congress, or saw it as an encroachment on state sovereignty, "the provision is inconsistent with the federal structure of our Government established by the Constitution."[16]

This may be true, but only very narrowly and in a manner prejudicial to a reasonable appreciation of the circumstances that led up to passage of the *Amendment Act*. It should not therefore have been the end of the discussion for the Court. Where that was depended on one's view of the nature and purpose of law. Is it law because so ordered or is it law because it is just—*lex ut jussum(as ordered)* or *lex ut justum (as just)*? For O'Connor, it was the former. But the argument to be advanced here is that it must be the latter. And that will mean that the justices of the Court, as persons before they are justices, have a moral responsibility, beyond fidelity to the letter of the Constitution, to uphold the values for which the Constitution in general, and federalism in particular, stand, and to which both the Constitution and federalism must be accountable. From this perspective, it is reasonable to ask whether the "take title" provision amounts to coercion? In what other world would congressional passage of legislation crafted by, and upon a formal request from the National Governors' Association, be considered coercive? Only in a world of legal positivism where the law is used not to assess congressional behavior with reference to context and motive, but, divorced from both, to command. As a consequence, it is in this world of legal positivism that one would declare the "take title" provision to have crossed the line distinguishing encouragement from coercion without any discussion of where this line should be drawn in relation to O'Connor's verbal boundaries. Given what is at stake in this case, such a discussion would seem critical.

CONSTITUTIONAL CONSIDERATIONS

But even if the "take title" provision was designed to encourage rather than to coerce compliance by States, it would, O'Connor insisted, be for their residents to decide whether to comply or not. Indeed, should they judge the policies of the federal government to be contrary to their interests, they were at liberty to resist any proffered inducements. "If state residents would prefer their government to devote its attention and resources to problems other than those deemed important by Congress, they may choose to have the Federal Government rather than the State bear the expense of a federally mandated regulatory program."[17] Since it was critical for state governments to remain responsive to the wishes of their residents, and for elected officials to remain accountable to the electorate, Congress might have encouraged but not compelled state regulation.[18]

Evidently, political accountability weighed heavily in O'Connor's opinion. As a result, she was prepared to argue that should the residents of New York State have concluded that the disposal of radioactive waste was not a compelling interest for them, they were at liberty to elect like-minded representatives. She went on to say that "that view can always be pre-empted under the Supremacy Clause[19] if it is contrary to the national view." Given that condition, the federal government could have made the decision as long as it did so publicly, thereby suffering any consequences had the decision proved to be harmful or unpopular. Whatever O'Connor meant by the national view, it is surely not unreasonable to consider the position of the National Governors' Association as representative of it. A second condition of O'Connor, that the decision be made publicly so as to ensure accountability to the electorate was also met. The Congressional Record shows that the bill passed unanimously in the U.S. House, with 378 members approving and 56 members simply not voting. In the U.S. Senate, the vote to approve was taken by voice vote so that there is no record of individual votes. But for any New York State resident, it would not have been difficult to discover how either Senator Daniel Patrick Moynihan or Senator Alfonse M. D'Amato voted.

But if the Supremacy Clause is relevant here, why did O'Connor invoke it, apparently as possible justification for the 1985 *Amendment Act*, only to dismiss it because the matters involved are not pre-emptible by federal regulation?[20] But arguably the appropriate disposal of low-level radioactive was pre-emptible within the enumerated powers of Congress, among which is the power to provide for the general welfare of the United States. O'Connor had, after all, observed that with the prospect of the nation being without any sites for waste disposal, Congress, in response to the National Governors' Association, had passed the *Low-Level Radioactive Waste Policy Act* to address what she described then as one of our nation's newest public policy challenges.[21] She had also acknowledged that "The Court's broad construction of Congress' power . . . has of course been guided . . . with respect to Congress' power generally, by the Constitution's Necessary and Proper Clause."[22] Nevertheless, none of this was sufficient to persuade O'Connor that at the end of the day Congress was not commandeering the States, using them "as implements of regulation."[23] Instead, she cited several cases,[24] in which the Court approved of legislation precisely because it did not "commandeer the legislative processes of the States by directly compelling them to enact and enforce a federal regulatory program."[25] It should be noted however that the cases cited are hardly comparable to the case at hand in that they do not involve matters in which the interests of one state may be dependent on the policies of another, possibly adjacent states. As the events of 1979 clearly demonstrated, and as the National Governors' Association recognized with alarm, provision for adequate facilities for the disposal of low-level radioactive waste was not a matter of the isolatable interests of this or that State, or even of this or that region, but of the interdependent interests and common good of every State in the Union.

That point seems to have gone largely unnoticed by O'Connor who seemed to discount the fact that it was because the States collectively considered this of compelling interest that they approached the federal government for its assistance. For them the issue was substantive, yet the judicial response was merely procedural. "Petitioners do not contend that Congress lacks the power to regulate the disposal of low level radioactive waste."[26] Indeed, O'Connor continued, "Petitioners likewise do not dispute that under the Supremacy Clause Congress could, if it wished, pre-empt state radioactive waste regulation," providing yet further confirmation that the matter of radioactive waste disposal was pre-emptible, just not in the way Congress had chosen.[27] That is to say, instead of directing the States to regulate disposal, Congress should have directly regulated the generators of the waste.[28] In support of this, O'Connor cites *FERC v. Mississippi* in which the State of Mississippi sought relief from two provisions in the *Public Utility Regulatory Policies Act (PURPA)* of 1978 on the grounds that, contrary to the Tenth Amendment, they amounted to an encroachment on state sovereignty.[29] According to the Court, "Titles I and III do not compel the exercise of a State's sovereign power . . .[however] If Congress may require a state administrative body to consider proposed federal regulations as a condition to its continued involvement in a pre-emptible field, it may require the use of certain procedural minima during that body's deliberations of the subject."[30] In that vein, why could not the Court have considered the three provisions of the *Amendment Act* as *procedural minima* required of States as they deliberated their response to the crisis emerging before them? As we shall see, there is sufficient evidence to think that this was the approach taken by the State of New York as it considered the implications of the *Amendment Act* and crafted its own legislation for radioactive waste disposal in response. Possibly more relevant, it was the expectation of Congress, given the unanimity and urgency of the request for assistance from the Governors' Association, that response from the States would render moot the "take title" provision.

JUDICIAL REVIEW

Having laid down what, for her, was the necessary condition of accountability, O'Connor was ready to assess the constitutional standing of the three provisions that lay at the core of the 1985 legislation. Her approach raised the reasonable question whether its focus was on the provisions as a means of solving the waste disposal challenge facing the nation, or on addressing what she deemed to be the oldest problem in constitutional law—"discerning the proper division of authority between the Federal Government and the States," as if incidentally occasioned by the matter of radioactive waste disposal.[31] It might be argued that, in this instance, the responsibility of the Court was to determine the proper balance of power between the federal government and the States. It was for Congress to fix the waste disposal problem. Put this way, this might satisfy the constitutionally required separation of powers, judicial from legislative. But would it satisfy sufficiently the purpose behind separated spheres of government influence, federal and state? Not according to O'Connor. "State sovereignty is not just an end in itself: 'Rather, federalism secures to citizens the liberties that derive from the diffusion of sovereign power."[32] But this is to state the matter incorrectly. The Constitution makes a powerful statement for human rights, not, however, as their originator but their guarantor. And federalism as a diffusion of sovereign power is merely a practical means to secure the rights embodied in the Constitution. These rights, as human rights, derive from human being as constitutive of human being, which federalism, as a constitutional construct exists to serve, not be served by. If so, this suggests that the Justices of the Court cannot be content with applying the Constitution merely to achieve technical adjustments between it and specific legislation. Theirs is an overriding responsibility to give priority to the values on which the Constitution is established, particularly when constitutional means, such as federalism, might otherwise compromise those values.

Something of this is captured in very practical terms in a 2013 *New York Times* editorial that discussed remarks on the American criminal justice system made by Justice Anthony M. Kennedy. Declaring the system to be broken, particularly its practice of total incarceration, he concluded, "This idea of total incarceration isn't working," adding that total incarceration was not humane. In response, the editorial pointed out that the Court could stop this practice by applying the Eighth Amendment which prohibits cruel and unusual punishment, noting that the four justices dissenting in such cases did so precisely on the basis of this constitutional prohibition. Yet, according to the editorial, in 2003 in two cases, Justice Kennedy was one of a 5 to 4 majority confirming sentences of twenty-five years to life and fifty years to life for stealing a few hundred dollars. His defense of both sentences was to say that fixing the problem of prison sentences was a matter for legislatures not the courts. Of course, this is the technical response based on the doctrine of separation of powers. Fortunately, ethics does not respect these artificial boundaries, anymore than human behavior does. When he said that total incarceration was inhumane, Kennedy made a moral, not a legal, judgment. Unless the term inhumane is meaningless, having used it, it brought him logically to the moral choice between acting in a manner that either embraces his judgment or abandons it. As a justice of the Court, Kennedy may not have had the power to legislate but that does not mean that he and the other members of the Court were helpless in the face of an unjustifiable law, unless you are wedded to legal positivism. If that is the case, it is likely that Kennedy believed his characterization of total incarceration was nothing more than an expression of some personal, subjective judgment. If so, he was laboring under the false notion that judgments of this kind, ethical judgments, lack objectivity. Since ethics, ultimately, is grounded in reason concordant with human nature, it is hard to see how thinking that total incarceration is inhumane cannot be considered rational and objective and tied to an understanding of what humane incarceration not only ought to stand for but as what ought also to be provided under law. To its credit, the editorial concluded that to accept Kennedy's rationale, would "too easily absolve the justices of their constitutional responsibility."[33] More to the point here, the editorial might have said that it would allow the justices to engage in a legal formalism, characteristic of the modern Court, that treats deciding constitutional law as if it were a chess game without any connection to the world.[34] The editorial did not say in what that responsibility consisted, and it did not explain what "violating" means. Nor did it consider the significance of a decision that was made by means of arbitrary numerical criteria. There is nothing about the number five as greater than the number four that allows us to conclude that a decision agreed to by five justices is truer than a dissent agreed to by four justices, a clear indication that the Constitution is unable to prevent itself from being the occasion of injustice. Indeed, had Kennedy's thinking been more informed by the values underlying the Constitution than by reliance on technical arguments, he would presumably have enabled the Court to reach a very different decision. The notion of punishment as cruel and unusual does not derive from law but from ethics. Cruel to whom? Beyond what point does punishment become a denial that a human being is suffering it? Beyond what point does punishment become punishment for the sake of punishment? Punishing is above all a moral act. Divorced from ethics, it loses its overriding force and becomes an optional or contingent consideration with, as in these two cases, some justices applying it and others not.

THE MORALITY OF PUNISHMENT UNDER LAW

While these two decisions[35] were not directly related to public health, examining them can lay bare, from an ethics perspective, the inadequacy of O'Connor's argument in *New York v. United States*. This was an argument premised incorrectly on the understanding that the Constitution is an end in itself, rather than a means to secure in very practical ways a set of values, including that of punishment, indispensable to human behavior as such. Infused with these values, the Constitution serves to retain the unconditional connection positive law ought to have with ethics. Both decisions involved California's criminal sentencing policy of "3-strikes and you're out," designed to curb criminal recidivism in the interests of public safety. Where members of the Court disagreed had, for the most part, to do with the proportionality of a sentence of twenty-five years for Mr. Gary A. Ewing for stealing three golf clubs, valued at $399 each, and a sentence of fifty years for Mr. Leandro Andrade for stealing eight children's video tapes, against a background of repeated felonies by both men. In her decision, O'Connor argued that "it is enough that the State of California has a reasonable basis for believing that dramatically enhanced sentences for habitual felons 'advances the goals of [its] criminal justice system in any substantial way.'"[36] It is enough presumably if you exclude any consideration of a significant ethics issue unambiguously begged in her argument, that is, whether the end justifies the means adopted to achieve it. A reasonable basis for dramatically enhanced sentences would presumably be the effectiveness in reducing recidivism. But does effectiveness equate with justice? Since it does not necessarily do so, what is the threshold of enhancement beyond which we ought not take it without it becoming unjust, however effective? There is no question that securing the public's safety against crime is commendable in every respect, including ethics. But does it justify dramatically enhanced sentences, even in the case of habitual felons?

It is difficult to answer that question properly without knowing what these sentences are directed against. Is it the discrete crime of stealing, for example, three golf clubs? If so, a sentence of twenty-five years to life would seem egregiously disproportionate, and therefore, laudable as the goal of the public's safety is, it would not justify penalizing to this degree someone guilty of stealing three golf clubs. If not the discrete crime, the only target remaining would be recidivism or habituation to criminal behavior, suggesting that such habituation is in itself a crime, for which the remedy for the public's safety is not so much incarceration for purposes of retribution as it is incarceration for purposes of incapacitation. Since, in the case of Mr. Ewing, he had appealed his sentence on the grounds that it violated the Eighth Amendment, the focus of the constitutional analysis was on the proportionality of the sentence relative to the crime. O'Connor argued that nothing in the Eighth Amendment prohibits California from enacting "3-Strikes" legislation. But it does not follow from that assertion that the Amendment authorizes such legislation, even if it is the case, as she added, that "States have a valid interest in deterring and segregating habitual criminals."[37]

With reference to the Eighth Amendment, Kennedy had in an earlier case advanced four principles for assessing proportionality.[38] These were primacy of the legislature, the variety of legitimate penological schemes, the nature of our federal system, the requirement that proportionality review be guided by objective factors informing the final one: the Eighth Amendment does not require strict proportionality between crime and sentence; it only forbids extreme sentences that are grossly disproportionate to the crime.[39] But in the same case, as O'Connor noted, "Justice Scalia, joined by the Chief Justice, wrote that the proportionality principle was 'an aspect of our death penalty jurisprudence rather than a generalizable aspect of Eighth Amendment law.'"[40] Consequently, he argued, if a sentence can be imposed for reasons other than retribution, say incapacitation, then an assessment of the sentence cannot consist solely in proportionality. Beyond that, it has to consider whether a State's interest in public safety justifies incapacitating recidivist criminals. That it does, he has no doubt, but what that interest has to do with proportionality is, he confesses, a mystery. It would be for anyone who thinks of law as law because so commanded. It would not for anyone who thought of law as law because just. However, in an earlier Eighth Amendment case,[41] Justice William J. Brennan Jr. had no difficulty seeing the connection.

The right to be free of cruel and unusual punishment, like the other guarantees of the Bill of Rights, "may not be submitted to votes; [it]depend[s] on the outcome of no elections." He concluded "The very purpose of a Bill of Rights was to withdraw certain subjects from the vicissitudes of political controversy, to place them beyond the reach of majorities and officials and establish them as legal principles to be applied by the courts."[42]

Unlike O'Connor, who seemed to think it dispositive in itself that several States had adopted "3-Strikes" policies, Justice Brennan drew a sharp distinction between "the generality of a law" and "what may be said of the validity of a law on the books."[43] As he put it, "The basic concept underlying the [Clause] is nothing less than the dignity of man. While the State has the power to punish, the [Clause] stands to assure that this power be exercised within the limits of civilized standards."[44] That is, "The 'essential predicate,' constitutionally, is 'that a punishment must not by its severity be degrading to human dignity.'"[45] At stake for Brennan was "the fundamental premise of the Clause that even the vilest criminal remains a human being possessed of common human dignity."[46] Is this what Kennedy meant when he declared before Congress that total incarceration is inhumane? If so, why, unlike Brennan, did he not allow this assessment to inform his constitutional thinking in *Ewing v. California*? And if the right to be free from cruel and unusual punishment is to be untouched by the vicissitudes of political disagreements, as Brennan argued, why did O'Connor think differently?

VISION OF LAW

The answer to both questions appears to lie in a differing vision of law. There is in Brennan's thinking the unmistakable imprint of Cicero's understanding that "True law is right reason in agreement with nature."[47] Accordingly, for Cicero, liberty and tyranny, justice and the common good, are ultimately not pure political categories that can be brought into being and perpetuated by constitutional forms alone. They are, rather, moral categories, descriptions of the ethos of the rulers and citizens who make up the political community. The ethical attitude of its public men is the animating spirit that vivifies and regulates the state. This animating spirit is the real foundation and criterion of public life, transcending constitutional structures.[48]

In its simplest expression, this is to say that for Cicero, "positive law is unable to tell us the last word about the real nature of legal experience."[49] By definition, law is *other-regarding*. As a societal mechanism, it is designed to secure predictably just relations among members of society, as well as between members of society and of society itself understood as the collective good. Constitutional law may be understood as a legal framework within which statutory law functions and by which it is assessed for its warrant. As such, statutory law is a practical means to meet very specific needs of varying levels of collective interest, while invariably triggering conflicts between interests. The *Low-Level Radioactive Waste Policy Amendment Act* (1985) was no exception, bringing into conflict a State's interest in its sovereignty with Congress's interest in the nation's health. As arbiter of the conflict, the Supreme Court responded with the doctrine of federalism, since, as O'Connor saw it, the task before the Court "consists, not of devising our preferred system of government, but of understanding and applying the framework set forth in the Constitution."[50] The question before the Court was what can Congress do under federalism, not what Congress ought to do, federalism notwithstanding? But since the question that is ruled out is the ethical question, one has to ask, what does this mean for those moral categories, referred to above, that vivify and regulate the state, and that transcend constitutional structures? That depends on the moral standing of federalism which in turn depends on its purpose, the complete answer to which demands, because it is other-regarding, consideration not only of what it can be made to do, but also what it ought to be made to do.

FEDERALISM

Put simply, federalism is a system of government by which governance is carried out between a central government and decentralized state-based governments. As James Madison saw it, the national government and state governments were "different agents and trustees of the people, constituted with different powers."[51] But such differences did not, according to Madison, mean that federal and state governments were not controlled by a common superior. Anyone thinking otherwise "must be told that the ultimate authority, wherever the derivative may be found, resides with the people alone . . . depend[s] on the sentiments and sanction of their common constituents."[52] As a consequence, Madison argued that while it was natural for people to favor the more familiar local, over the less familiar, federal government, they "ought not surely be precluded from giving most of their confidence where they discover it to be best due." And this presumption, Madison believed, should not cause concern for state government, since federal power could only be exercised beneficially within certain limits.[53] In his comparison of federal and state governments, Madison saw that the advantage lay with state governments because, going in, the pre-dispositions of members of the federal government were favorable to the states, whereas the attitudes of members of state governments were unlikely to favor federal government. "A local spirit will infallibly prevail much more in the members of Congress than a national spirit will prevail in the Legislatures of the particular States."[54]

Here, Madison might be thought to have spoken prophetically of New York State in the matter of low-level radioactive waste disposal. As he explained this last point, any consideration of mistakes made by state legislatures showed in many cases their members to have been prepared to "sacrifice the comprehensive and permanent interest of the State to the particular and separate views of the counties or districts in which they reside."[55] But, if it was beyond them to provide for the common good of their states, "how can it be imagined that they will make the aggregate prosperity of the Union" their concern?[56] Madison concluded his paper with the observation that whatever powers were proposed for the federal government, they posed little threat to state government but they were absolutely necessary for securing the purposes of the Union.[57] Weighed in terms of practical politics, the Constitution being proposed in 1788 was, Madison believed, to the advantage of states' interests. Furthermore, within that state-based reference, the advantage lay with local interests. "Measures will too often be decided according to their probable effect, not on the national prosperity and happiness, but on the prejudices, interests and pursuits of the governments and people of the individual

States"[58] At serious risk, as a result, were larger considerations, namely the purpose of the Union and its common good.

Madison emphasized what federal and state's government had in common in one superior union, and in this way he saw their union as a means to a common good. In contrast, O'Connor emphasized the separation between the two as an end in itself. In part, her argument appears to be based on Alexander Hamilton's observation that establishing a new government occasioned delicate questions prompted by a constitution "founded upon the total or partial incorporation of a number of distinct sovereignties."[59] But whereas O'Connor emphasized state sovereignty as a condition for the protection of individual liberties against federal encroachment, Hamilton looked to time to "mature and perfect so compound a system . . . liquidate the meaning of all the parts and . . . adjust them to each other in a harmonious and consistent whole."[60] While O'Connor conditioned the preservation of individual liberties by placing them between federal and state government, positioned in a permanent constitutional stand-off, Hamilton insisted that it was from within the confederacy that the people would be able to secure their interests. "How wise will it be in them by cherishing the union to preserve to themselves an advantage which can never be too highly prized."[61]

Relative then to appreciating the moral standing of federalism is the essential recognition that, as Madison argued, federal and state governments were not mutual rivals and enemies whose ultimate authority was proportionate to its ambition to enlarge its jurisdiction, one at the expense of the other.[62] Rather, if either functioned at all, it should do so more in virtue of its respective responsibility to what enjoys real sovereignty, namely, the interests of a shared constituency. To the extent that in their respective roles federal and state government ought to secure these sovereign interests, they could claim sovereignty. This, as seen above, was what Madison was alluding to when he said that the people ought not be prevented from giving most of their trust in government as such where they saw it is going to be most effective. Put this way, the constitutional challenge had less to do with the balance of power between federal and state government than between the merits of competing interests, the responsibility for the resolution of which ought to lie with that government best able in the judgment of the people to do that. Otherwise, given the tendency, natural politically, to prefer local over national interests, a tendency exacerbated by confederation, how ought we, to echo Madison and Hamilton, secure the good of the Union as harmonious and consistent? O'Connor's formalism in understanding and applying federalism in *New York v. United States* was such that it confirmed when it ought to have countered what generally had become known by the time she rendered the Court's decision. It was by then clear that the State of New York, in abandoning its commitments to establish a site for radioactive waste, had sacrificed not only national but even its own interests in public safety to the most local of interests. But if the Court's decision, in this case informed in large measure with a particularly narrow view of federalism, so ill-served the interests of the public's health what if any recourse is available?

There are, fortunately, other federalism constructs. But as Heather K. Gerken pointed out, "Federalism debates are best understood not as disagreements over which model to choose but as disputes over how to strike the right balance between different types of institutional arrangements."[63] The balance, she argued, will depend on the setting and which form of federalism serves a specific setting. Gerken identified three models of federalism—"sovereignty," "process," and "cooperative." Briefly, sovereignty federalism requires that states rule on the basis of two rights, the "right" to be free of external hindrance and the "right" to originate legislation and "policy."[64] Process federalism is premised on actual rather than legal "autonomy." To be successful, process federalism depends not on judges but on "politics, tradition, inertia and interdependence" as necessary conditions of "state" governance.[65] Despite their differences, both expressions prefer self-rule to centralization, self-reliance to cooperation.[66] Cooperative federalism functions under conditions where regional and national governance coincide in the execution of national "policy."[67] It is a model premised on cooperation rather than self-reliance.[68] "States do not rule separate and apart from the system and the power they wield is not their own" but "part of a complex amalgam of national, state and local actors implementing federal policy."[69]

In light of this analysis, it is clear that O'Connor, caught up in her legal positivism, misconstrued the basic state of the question before the Court by presenting it as matter of what power the federal government actually has, not what power it ought to have. But in the case of *New York v. United States*, the basic question was whether the federal government had the power it ought to have, on the principle that government, governing in justice, governs as it ought to govern. And if it ought to govern at all, then the presumption is that it can govern. It is only when one can do something that it is reasonable to ask whether one ought to do it. Almost impossible to address from the perspective of O'Connor's constricted federalism, it was necessary to reconsider federalism in the form of a mechanism for the voluntary distribution of power towards securing the common good as the legitimate goal of states' sovereignty and accountability to the electorate. That in turn would yield a rather different assessment of the "take title" provision. In his dissent, Justice Byron R. White provided the possibility for such a reconsideration based on a more comprehensive account of the negotiations between the U.S. Governor's Association and Congress in their efforts to solve an impending national crisis.

JUSTICE WHITE DISSENTING

White viewed the 1985 *Act* as "very much the product of cooperative federalism, in which the States bargained among themselves to achieve compromises for Congress to sanction."[70] This was in reference to the extensive negotiations, begun in 1979 and designed to secure a state-based solution to the waste disposal problem.[71] In that year, according to White, the Nevada and Washington waste disposal sites closed for a time because of serious problems with the transportation of waste to both sites. That led the governor of South Carolina to limit by some 50% the amount of waste to be disposed of at Barnwell, the South Carolina disposal site. Subsequently, the governor of Washington added to an emerging national crisis by declaring he was prepared to close the Hanford, Washington site by 1982 in the event there was no movement toward establishing regional arrangements for waste disposal. Earlier that same year, according to White, the National Governors' Association had established a task force to determine policy proposals on behalf of the states. And in 1980, The State Planning Council on Radioactive Waste Management presented President Jimmy Carter with the following unanimous recommendation:

> The national policy of the United States on low-level radioactive waste shall be that every state is responsible for the disposal of low-level radioactive waste generated by non-defense related activities within its boundaries and that States are authorized to enter into inter-state compacts, as necessary, for the purpose of carrying out this responsibility.[72]

White went on to note that when the National Governors' Association subsequently accepted this recommendation, it recognized that "the Federal Government could assert its preeminence in achieving a solution to this problem but requested instead that Congress oversee state-developed regional solutions."[73] White further noted that the governors wanted Congress to authorize inter-state agreements to set up regional disposal sites. To encourage participation in these agreements, regional sites would be authorized to exclude waste generated by states not party to an agreement. Thinking this sufficiently persuasive at the outset, the Governors' Task Force recommended that Congress refrain from taking steps requiring additional disposal sites for two years at least. If at that point, the states had failed to take action on their own initiative, Congress might need to consider more forceful action.[74] It was White's understanding of subsequent developments that in July 1980, when the Senate was considering legislation authorizing a federal study, oversight, and management of radioactive waste, Senator Strom Thurmond successfully proposed an amendment for the adoption and implementation of the recommendation of the State Planning Council On Radioactive Waste Management.[75]

In describing the events that led up to the 1985 amendments, White noted that efforts among states to form compacts and gain congressional approval had proved contentious. Officials from un-sited states were opposed to the approval of those compacts under formation, whereas officials from sited states were insisting on the fulfillment of the provisions of the 1980 *Act*. Concerned to see to it that states retain the initiative in formulating policy amendments, the National Governors' Association held meetings to secure consensus among states.[76] With only three disposal sites in operation and threatening to accept only waste generated with their respective compacts, the urgency to reach some sort of compromise was increasing.[77] It took the form of an agreement on the part of the sited states to continue receiving waste and in return un-sited states were expected to develop their own disposal facilities according to strict timelines. Failure to meet them would render non-compliant states liable to penalties. Citing then Representative Ed Markey, White pointedly observed that "[this] compromise became the basis for our amendments to the Low-Level Radioactive Waste Policy Act of 1980." White was careful to note that Markey represented the entire effort as concessions agreed to by all sides in their attempt to arrive at a bill acceptable to all involved.[78] Or, in White's words, it represented "cooperative federalism."[79] Further, White thought it critical to understand that in all of the steps undertaken by it, Congress saw itself as mediating in a serious dispute among the states. Whereas O'Connor saw the 1985 *Act*, specifically its "take title" provision as an instrument of congressional commandeering, White saw it as the result of congressional refereeing of an agreement arrived at among the states. "The distinction," he insisted, "is key and the Court's failure properly to characterize this legislation ultimately affects its analysis of the take title provision's constitutionality."[80]

The issue was larger than a failure to describe the legislation accurately, however consequential from a constitutional perspective that failure may have been. Larger still was the failure to prescribe appropriately the Court's task. That failure can be traced back to two things. The first was O'Connor's seriously inadequate representation of how Congress came to enact the 1985 amendments. The second was her apparent acquiescence to circumstances under which little or no attention was paid to the consequences of the states having failed to reach an agreement. But O'Connor must have been aware of the deep concern in Congress over the prospect of failing to address the waste disposal problem. On December 19, 1985, during the debate on the *Amendment Act*, Representative Don Bonker, of Washington State, declared "If we fail to act on this bill in a timely manner, Congress will have lost an opportunity to avert a potential crisis." Describing the then current situation as intolerable, he pointed to the injustice of a disposal system where the states of Washington, South Carolina, and Nevada provided the entire country's only disposal sites. "My State of Washington took 52 percent of this waste last year."[81] The potential crisis lay in part, according to Bonker, in the possibility that "the three receiving States could decide to make good on their threat to close their sites to all outside waste."[82]

The injustice of the situation was not lost on members of the House. It informed their assessment of the constitutional viability of the "take title" provision. Members of the House had accepted the Senate's insistence that states begin in 1996 to take ownership of low-level waste generated in their territory. But they did so in the not unreasonable expectation that, as Representative Mo Udall of Arizona put it, "all States will have developed management ability by that time." If so, the "take title" provision would not be an issue because states would have acted responsibly before the 1996 deadline, while meeting any obligations under the *Atomic Energy Act*.[83] Regarding the provision itself, Udall insisted that "Although States are also liable for damages consequential to taking title to the waste, we intend this [to be] a very limited liability, limited to situations in which State actions are directly involved."[84] Overall, it had to be understood that the bill was intended to meet the needs of the three states which were bearing a disproportionate burden since they were the only states with commercial disposal sites. To redress the injustice of the burden, these states could have imposed additional costs on those states generating waste but which had not established their own disposal sites as scheduled under terms of the bill. Congress was, in effect, stating the obvious. Since this potential crisis was of the states' own making, they were responsible for taking steps to avert it in the interests of the public's health.

For O'Connor, the "take title" provision amounted to commandeering to the detriment of federalism, and as such, was unconstitutional. Consequently, the Court was unable to approve of the provision. For White, it was a matter of refereeing intended to ensure cooperative federalism and so was constitutional. As a result, the Court was able approve of the provision. It is not the purpose of this analysis to mediate between O'Connor and White. There is nothing to suggest that despite his differing conclusion, it was not different because it derived from the necessity to uphold the values for which the Constitution in particular and federalism in general stand, and to which both must be accountable.[85] From this perspective, since federalism, cooperative or otherwise, was the focus of their disagreement, we have to ask of both how they saw, from their respective positions, federalism being accountable to and thereby justified by these values? From this perspective, the critical question is what is the moral standing of, or justification for federalism, since, as a mechanism of governance it has significant consequences for state residents.

O'Connor's constricted view of federalism as a division of authority resulted in an equally narrow view of accountability. She had earlier in her partial dissent in *FERC v. Mississippi* (1982) laid out her argument for federalism as a constitutional arrangement designed to allow citizens to be actively engaged in representative government. In *New York v. United States*, she expressed this as occurring where "a State whose citizens do not wish to attain the Act's milestone may devote its attention and its resources to issues the citizens deem more worthy; the choice remains at all times with the residents of the State, not with Congress."[86] As a statement of the sovereignty of the citizen, this formulation takes us so far but not far enough unless it includes criteria of worthiness which inform the choices made by citizens as citizens and not private persons pursuing exclusively personal interests. The distinction is critical to ensuring that choices made by citizens are informed by their social responsibilities, both to their state of residence and to the federation of which their state is a member, enjoying the benefits of membership, in this case the ability to dump its waste in another member state. The goal of federalism, according to O'Connor, was the division of "authority between federal and state governments for the protection of individuals". . . from. . . "the risk of tyranny and abuse from either front."[87] But what if her version of federalism were to trigger another tyranny lurking there? That is, the tyranny of private interests superseding the common good? What would be the point of insisting on a federalism, which was, even on her terms, only a means to an end, if it results in substituting one tyranny for another? By the time O'Connor wrote her decision, private interests had brought the efforts of New York State to manage its own waste disposal to a complete halt.

There were three goals or ends at play here whose inextricable relations require precise understanding if federalism, as the means, selected to secure them, is to be considered justified. There was the goal of the *sovereignty* of the citizen, that of the *accountability* of public officials to those whose interests, in a representative democracy, they served to secure, and finally the goal of the *common good*. But as a matter of ethics, there is necessarily a priority of values represented by these three goals. The sovereignty of citizens, however much a good it may be, is not and cannot be unrestricted, any more than the accountability of public officials to those they represent is limitless because both are subject in their exercise to the common good. It follows logically that if the sovereignty of citizens is subject to the common good then so too is accountability of public officials as a condition of the sovereignty of citizens. As Justice John Marshall Harlan II noted, "the liberty secured by the Constitution of the United States to every person within its jurisdiction does not import an absolute right in each person to be, at all times and in all circumstances, wholly freed from restraint. There are manifold restraints to which every person is necessarily subject for the common good."[88] Echoing John Stuart Mill, Justice Harlan II argued that "Real liberty for all could not exist under the operation of a principle which recognizes the right of each individual person to use his own, whether in respect of his person or his property, regardless of the injury that may be done to others."[89] But as if anticipating the terms of O'Connor's constitutional recipe, when the State of New York took the matter of waste disposal into its own hands, the outcome represented everything that Harlan II had warned against.

NEW YORK STATE

Following the passage of the *Low-Level Radioactive Waste Policy Amendment Act* (1985), the State of New York, along with other states, began negotiations to form a northeast regional compact. The negotiations collapsed over the fact that the states involved individually generated different levels of low-level radioactive waste, with New York generating the highest levels. At that point, New York decided it would establish its own disposal site. The *New York State Low-Level Radioactive Waste Disposal Act* (*LLRW*) of 1986 was indicative of the State's intention to take ownership of the problem of disposal of low-level radioactive waste generated within its borders, just as Congress had anticipated. Under the *LLRW*, a siting commission, proceeding in phases, began its work by identifying areas that had to be excluded due to state or federal regulation. The second phase consisted in identifying so-called candidate areas and was followed by a third phase during which potential sites were identified. As it worked its way through these phases, "the Siting Commission evolved from an obscure public body holding sparsely attended public meetings to the focus of fervent public protests involving hundreds of citizens."[90]

In its report on the work of the Siting Commission, a Review Committee found that the Siting Commission ultimately failed because in adhering conscientiously to an unrealistic time table, it was unable to involve the general public sufficiently so as to assuage the anxiety its work caused. A difficult task under these circumstances, made even more difficult because there were those who were determined not to agree to any site no matter what technical criteria justified its selection, while others would have no part in the siting process itself.[91] The opposition was intractable despite the fact that no actions, such as allowing a study team onto a site, with tangible consequences for potential sites or their residents, were undertaken.[92] Rather, opposition was the result, largely of a psychological reaction to the mention of the disposal of nuclear waste and associated socioeconomic side effects.[93] For example, responses to a questionnaire assessing residents' feelings towards disposal sites for "nuclear waste" indicated unambiguously sentiments of "dread, revulsion, and anger" across communities.[94]

For New York, the depth of these sentiments was such that incentives, like the conservation of "open spaces" and the creation of "local" employment, for agreeing to host a disposal site proved unpersuasive.[95] Was such opposition justified? If so, did it in turn justify the termination of efforts to identify a disposal site? If this was an exercise in what O'Connor called the sovereignty of citizens, holding members of the New York State legislature accountable, presumably it was justified since it comported with her constitutional understanding of one of the purposes of federalism's diffusion of political power. Diffusion of power in a democratic system is assumed. But it should amount to a balance of power between the governing and the governed acting as partners, and mutually responsible by means of the legislative process in the pursuit of the common good. As other-regarding behavior, governance in a democracy depends upon a mutual and reciprocal relationship between the governing and the governed. From the outset, this consists in an array of options as far as what can be done in the course of governance. But because of the other-regarding consequences of governance, none of the options among what can be done may be undertaken before deciding that it ought to be done. In the absence of an appreciation of law as law because it is just, governance is more likely than not to be held hostage to the pursuit of narrow vested interests rather than a common good. If, as appeared to be O'Connor's position, the only law we have recourse to is law as law because so ordered, we should not be surprised by what resulted when it was combined with *accountability*. The outcome had little to do with accountability and almost everything to do with irresponsibility both on the part of members of the New York State Legislature and the residents of the State.

In the case of New York State, accountability found expression in a *not-in-my-backyard* (NIMBY) posture. As a public posture it was "particularly vitriolic towards hazardous and radioactive waste."[96] That may be understandable in itself. It is, however, critical in this discussion of the serious limitations of the legal formalism of O'Connor's decision to understand fully the nature of the NIMBY disposition. It is not so much an expression of opposition to what is being proposed, such as a disposal site, as it is an expression of opposition to the location of the proposed site. If there is a need for a site for the disposal of low-level radioactive waste, then so be it, as long as it is elsewhere and not in this community. This public disposition was evident in the first phase of the Siting Committee's work when it was excluding communities from consideration as a possible site. Within those communities, no voice was raised in opposition to having a site as such for the disposal of low-level radioactive waste.

For those of the NIMBY disposition, they justified it with the argument that what was being proposed was simply unfair. "Developing a low-level radioactive waste disposal site creates a burden on one community for the benefit of another."[97] Is this claim entirely accurate? It seemed to assume that there was only burden and no benefit for the community chosen to be the disposal site. It was certainly the case that those communities not chosen enjoyed an unqualified benefit in the fact that elsewhere there was a site for appropriate disposal of radioactive waste. To be appropriate, a site must exhibit specific geologic and hydrologic features that prevent the release of radionuclides since it is ground surface and a shallow subsurface that ultimately determines the level of risk of such a release. Assuming a site meets the required standards, a community adjacent to the disposal site will also enjoy the benefits of safe disposal. In the absence of a regulated disposal site anywhere in a state, all communities are at risk. That there are burdens associated with hosting a disposal site is undeniable. The ethics question will be whether they are undue burdens so that they outweigh any of the benefits associated with hosting the disposal site.

The primary and enduring burden is exposure to the risk of leakage and of any subsequent harm to human health and environmental safety. Low-level radioactive waste is disposed of in "containers approved" by the "Nuclear Regulatory Commission" (NRC). Disposal is achieved by depositing them in specifically designed "trenches" covered with requisite levels of "soil." Once buried, "containers" remain untouched for some "thirty years," by which time the risks from "radioactivity" is minimal.[98] Technological developments, together with current environmental regulation, have greatly reduced the risk of containers leaking. By comparison, the risks associated with the system of disposal now in place, which consists in many hundreds of unnamed, improvised disposal sites around a state, are far greater.[99] Not accepting the burden of the proposed system because of its limited but known risk while expecting to benefit in all other respects from residence in the state seems irresponsible if the interests of the state overall call for properly managed disposal sites. Consequently, accepting a system that consisted in innumerable stop-gap disposal sites as if adequate was to ignore a problem that could only get worse, since sites of this kind did not benefit from the appropriate supervision that secured safe operation. Regrettably, 16 years after the Court's decision, "191 generators of low-level-radioactive waste in New York stored approximately 319,803 cubic feet of low-level-radioactive waste in undisclosed locations."[100]

Compounding this irresponsibility was that refusal to serve as a site also involved acting on the basis of a double standard. While it was deemed unacceptable by members of one community to serve as a disposal site, despite meeting the selection criteria, the members would presumably not have refused the disposal services of another community had its members agreed to their selection on the basis of the identical criteria and with a comparable ratio of benefit to burden. It may be argued that if members of this other community agree to serve as a disposal site, it is their decision. That is correct.

But for the community, whose members refused to serve as a disposal site, to use the disposal services of another community would be exploitative. As one commentator put it, all exploitation consists in the exploiter gaining something by benefiting from some personal trait of the one exploited, even when the "interests" of the one exploited are unharmed and the one exploited agrees to the exploitation.[101] Speaking out of a constitutional positivism, O'Connor opted for federalism as diffusion of power in the liberty interests of individuals *simpliciter*. "Where Congress encourages state regulation rather than compelling it, state governments remain responsive to the local electorate's preference; state officials remain accountable to the people."[102] However, the exercise of this power by the people in the pursuit of their interests is far from being fair, with the consequence that any outcome, including exploitation, is also far from being fair. The State of New York enacted, without federal coercion, its own legislation for the disposal of low-level radioactive waste. It then went to the electorate in a sophisticated exercise in accountability. But in the face of intractable opposition from the most local, narrow self-interests, insisted upon without regard for the common good of the State, the legislature abandoned its responsibilities for the safe disposal of its own low-level radioactive waste and sought cover in legal action against the federal government.

Unlike O'Connor, White viewed the actions of New York State as a breach of faith. Alluding to the statements made by members of Congress when debating the 1985 legislation, they reveal, he noted, that it was the preference of the states to assume the leadership in their efforts to solve the waste disposal problem. To this effect, the states, including New York, "had agreed among themselves to the various incentives and penalties implemented by Congress to ensure adherence to the various deadlines and goals."[103] This explains why New York State enacted its own waste disposal legislation and why, by 1988, it had identified possible sites to be used for disposal purposes. But even as it challenged the "take title" provision which it had accepted earlier, New York State "continued to take full advantage of the import concession made by the sited states, by exporting its low-level radioactive waste for the full 7-year extension period provided in the 1985 Act."[104] What concerned White was that since New York State had decided not to set up its own waste storage site, the consequence of this failure to meet its obligations was that states with storage sites were required under the agreement to accept waste from New York. The operative word is "obligation" and the question is whether we are speaking of a legal obligation or of a prior moral obligation that stands, law or no law?

There is nothing to suggest that White is not talking about New York State's legal obligation, which, according to his understanding of the Constitution could be enforced by the Court. Using the same Constitution, O'Connor concluded the opposite. Which position was correct? For purposes of the Court's decision that depended on something ultimately arbitrary—where a majority of justices was to be found reading the letter of positive law as though it were, to recall Cicero, the final comment on our experience of law. Clearly it was not when, as in this case, six justices concluded there is no obligation to be enforced, while three conclude the opposite. Whether consciously or not, White captured the moral dilemma that would, predictably, remain unresolved by the Court's decision resting, as it did, on the inadequacy of law understood as law because so ordered. "The Court's refusal to force New York to accept responsibility for its own problem inevitably means that some other State's sovereignty will be impinged by its being forced, for public health reasons, to accept New York's low-level radioactive waste."[105] For White then, his disagreement with O'Connor was over what he described as her "formalistically rigid obeisance to 'federalism.'"[106] However, the disagreement outlined in this chapter goes much deeper. What could explain why O'Connor would not have seen the moral presuppositions of White's statement? Very simply, this had to do with her failure to see that the "take title" provision had considerably less to do with her notion of federalism and everything to do with that animating spirit that Cicero insisted is the real foundation of public life, transcending even as it grounded constitutional structures in pursuit of the common good.

It is worth recalling that in the 20 years following *New York v. United States*, the Court's decision had made the low-level radioactive waste disposal problem considerably worse throughout the country by misreading the take-title provisions. What after all does take-title mean? It means quite simply to take ownership. What then could be questionable in a state taking ownership of something for which it was responsible for producing? That was the premise of the federal legislation in its original and amended iterations, the premise for stipulating state responsibility for dealing with the consequences of producing radioactive waste within state boundaries. That is to say, Congress was stating the obvious. But the Court said something rather different, transforming a matter of hazardous waste threatening the entire country into a matter of state sovereignty as something to be preferred even at the risk of national well being. In its preoccupation to use the Constitution as an end in itself, the Court chose to ignore a simple fact. New York State as a member of the of the United States, and enjoying very considerable benefits from interdependent membership owed to all other member states, as a matter of ethics or of law as just, that it deal effectively with the disposal of its low-level radioactive waste. However, instead of interpreting the 10th Amendment in the context of state interdependence, the Court insisted unnecessarily on applying it in a context of state independence only. The notion of state sovereignty in a matter of such national consequence is ethically out of the question. As a consequence, the Court released New York State from its moral obligations to the rest of the country and was complicit in the continuation of the nationwide impasse bedeviling the disposal of low-level radioactive waste. The Court may not hide behind the Constitution as if it released them from its moral obligation to secure the wellbeing of the nation. Like the Constitution, members of the Court are accountable to normative ethics already given expression in law as law because just. If nothing else, this outcome should illustrate how bad a decision the Court made in *New York v. United States*.

NOTES

1. U.S. Supreme Court, *New York v. United States*, 505 U.S. 144 (1992), at 150, https://supreme.justia.com/cases/federal/us/505/144/ (accessed October 15, 2020).

2. U.S. Nuclear Regulatory Commission (U.S. NRC), "Low-Level Radioactive Waste (LLW)," April 10, 2017; last updated June 29, 2020, https://www.nrc.gov/reading-rm/basic-ref/glossary/low-level-radioactive-waste-llw.html (accessed October 20, 2020).

3. Nuclear Information and Resource Services (NIRS), "'Low-Level' Radioactive Waste Is Not Low Risk," *NIRS*, April 2009, https://www.nirs.org/wp-content/uploads/factsheets/llwnolowrisk.pdf (accessed October 20, 2020).

4. U.S. Congress, *The Low-Level Radioactive Waste Policy Act*, Pub. L. 96–573 (1980), 94 Stat. 3347, 94 Stat. 3348; 94 Stat. 3349 (96th Cong. 2nd sess.) (December 22, 1980), https://www.govinfo.gov/link/statute/94/3347 (accessed October 20, 2020).

5. *Low-Level Radioactive Waste Policy Act*, 94 Stat. 3348 at 4(a)(1).

6. *Low-Level Radioactive Waste Policy Act*, 94 Stat. 3348 at at 4(a)(2)(B).

7. U.S. Congress, *The Low-Level Radioactive Waste Policy Amendments Act*, Pub. L. 99–240 (1985) H.R. 1083 (99th Cong. 1st sess.) (January 15, 1996), https://www.congress.gov/bill/99th-congress/house-bill/1083 (accessed October 21, 2020), noted in *New York v. United States* at 151.

8. *New York v. United States* at 156.

9. According the Constitution of the United States, art. 1, sect. 1, "All legislative Powers herein granted shall be vested in a Congress of the United States, which shall consist in a Senate and House of Representatives." See U.S. National Archives, The Constitution of the United States, https://www.archives.gov/founding-docs/constitution-transcript (accessed October 18, 2020).

10. *New York v. United States* at 156.
11. *New York v. United States* at 156.
12. *New York v. United States* at 175.
13. *New York v. United States* at 175.
14. *New York v. United States* at 177.
15. *New York v. United States* at 176.
16. *New York v. United States* at 177.
17. *New York v. United States* at 168.

18. *New York v. United States* at 168.

19. The U.S. Constitution, art. 6, sec. 2, declares that "This Constitution, and the laws of the United States which shall be made in Pursuance thereof; and all Treaties made, or which shall be made, under the Authority of the United States, shall be the supreme Law of the Land; and the Judges in every State shall be bound thereby, anything in the Constitution or the laws of any State to the Contrary notwithstanding."

20. *New York v. United States* at 169.

21. U.S. Constitution, art. 6, sec. 2, of *New York v. United States* at 149.

22. *New York v. United States* at 159. U.S. Constitution, art. 1, sec. 8, clause 18 declares, "The Congress shall have the Power . . . To make all Laws which shall be necessary and proper for carrying into Execution the foregoing Powers, and all other Powers vested by this Constitution in the Government of the United States, or in any Department or Office thereof."

23. *New York v. United States* at 161.

24. See U.S. Supreme Court, *Hodel v. Virginia Surface Mining and Reclamation Assn., Inc.*, 452 U.S. 264 (1981), 288, https://supreme.justia.com/cases/federal/us/452/264/ (accessed October 20, 2020); U.S. Supreme Court, *FERC v. Mississippi*, 456 U.S. 742 (1982), 758–59, https://supreme.justia.com/cases/federal/us/456/742/ (accessed October 20, 2020).

25. *New York v. United States* at 145.

26. *New York v. United States* at 159.

27. *New York v. United States* at 160.

28. *New York v. United States* at 160.

29. *FERC v. Mississippi*, cited in *New York v. United States* at 161.

30. *FERC v. Mississippi* at 743, referencing 770–71.

31. *New York v. United States* at 149.

32. *New York v. United States* at 182, citing *Coleman v. Thomson*, 501 U.S. 722, 759 (1991).

33. New York Times Editorial Board, "Justice Kennedy's Plea to Congress," *New York Times*, April 4, 2015, SR 10, https://www.nytimes.com/2015/04/05/opinion/sunday/justice-kennedys-plea-to-congress.html (accessed October 20, 2020).

34. The analogy between playing chess and deciding constitutional law is borrowed from Alan Turing's analogy between playing chess, which involves only the state of the chessboard and that of the player's brains, and the formalist understanding of mathematics, or "any purely symbolic system involving anything technical, as something to be used without considering any connection with the world. "That question was, as it were, always left for someone else to tackle." See Andrew Hodges, *Alan Turing: The Enigma* (Princeton, NJ: Princeton University Press, 2014), 530–35.

35. U.S. Supreme Court, *Ewing v California*, 538 U.S. 11 (2003), https://supreme.justia.com/cases/federal/us/538/11/ (accessed October 20, 2020); U.S. Supreme Court, *Lockyer v Andrade*, 538 U.S. 63 (2003), https://supreme.justia.com/cases/federal/us/538/63/ (accessed October 20, 2020).

36. *Ewing v California*; and see U.S. Supreme Court, *Solem v. Helm*, 463 U.S. 277 (1983), at 297n22, https://supreme.justia.com/cases/federal/us/463/277/ (accessed October 20, 2020).

37. U.S. Supreme Court, *Parke v. Raley*, 506 U.S. 20 (1992), at 27, https://supreme.justia.com/cases/federal/us/506/20/ (accessed October 20, 2020).
38.. U.S. Supreme Court, *Harmelin v. Michigan*, 501 U.S. 957 (1991), https://supreme.justia.com/cases/federal/us/501/957/ (accessed October 20, 2020).
39. *Harmelin v. Michigan* at 1001.
40. *Harmelin v. Michigan* at 997.
41. U.S. Supreme Court, *Furman v. Georgia*, 408 U.S. 238 (1972), https://supreme.justia.com/cases/federal/us/408/238/ (accessed October 20, 2020).
42. *Furman v. Georgia* at 268, citing West Virginia State, *Board of Education v. Barnette*, 319 U.S. 624, 638 (1943), https://supreme.justia.com/cases/federal/us/319/624/ (accessed October 20, 2020), at 269.
43. *Furman v. Georgia* at 292.
44. *Furman v. Georgia* at 270, citing U.S. Supreme Court, *Trop v. Dulles*, 356 U.S. 86 (1958), https://supreme.justia.com/cases/federal/us/356/86/ (accessed October 20, 2020), at 100.
45. *Furman v. Georgia* at 281.
46. *Furman v. Georgia* at 273.
47. Marcus Tullius Cicero, *De Republica*, in *On the Republic*, trans.Clinton W. Keyes (Cambridge, MA: Harvard University Press, 1928), http://www.attalus.org/translate/republic3.html (accessed September 5, 2020), bk., 3, sec. 22/33.
48. Marcia L. Colish, *The Stoic Tradition from Antiquity to the Early Middle Ages*. Vol. 1. *Stoicism in Classical Latin Literature* (New York: E. J. Brill, 1990), 91.
49. d'Entreves, A.P. Natural Law: An Introduction to Legal Philosophy. London: Hutchinson University Library, Eighth impression, 1964; p 65
50. *New York v. United States* at 157.
51. James Madison, "The Federalist No. 46," in *The Debate on the Constitution, Federalist and Antifederalist Speeches, Articles, and Letters During the Struggle over Ratification: Part One, September 1787-February 1788*, ed. Bernard Bailyn (New York: Library of America, 1993), part 2, 109.
52. Madison, "The Federalist No. 46," part 2, 109.
53. Madison, "The Federalist No. 46," part 2, 110.
54. Madison, "The Federalist No. 46," part 2, 111.
55. Madison, "The Federalist No. 46," part 2, 111.
56. Madison, "The Federalist No. 46," part 2, 111.
57. Madison, "The Federalist No. 46," part 2, 115.
58. Madison, "The Federalist No. 46," part 2, 111.
59. Alexander Hamilton, "The Federalist No. 82," in *The Debate on the Constitution, Federalist and Antifederalist Speeches, Articles, and Letters During the Struggle over Ratification: Part One, September 1787-February 1788*, ed. Bernard Bailyn (New York: Library of America, 1993), part 2, 493.
60. Hamilton, "The Federalist No. 82," part 2, 493.
61. Alexander Hamilton, "The Federalist No. 28," *Yale Law School*, https://avalon.law.yale.edu/18th_century/fed28.asp (accessed August 1, 2016).
62. Madison, "The Federalist No. 46," part 2, 109.

63. Heather K. Gerken, "Our Federalism(s)," *William & Mary Law Review* 53, no. 5 (2012): 1549–73, https://scholarship.law.wm.edu/wmlr/vol53/iss5/3 (accessed August 4, 2016).

64. Gerken, "Our Federalism(s)," 1553n8.

65. Gerken, "Our Federalism(s)," 1554.

66. Gerken, "Our Federalism(s)," 1556.

67. Gerken, "Our Federalism(s),"1556.

68. Gerken, "Our Federalism(s)," 1557.

69. Gerken, "Our Federalism(s)," 1557.

70. *New York v. United States* at 194.

71. *New York v. United States* at 190.

72. *New York v. United States* at 191.

73. *New York v. United States* at 191.

74. *New York v. United States* at 192.

75. *New York v. United States* at 192.

76. *New York v. United States* at 193.

77. *New York v. United States* at 193.

78. *New York v. United States* at 194.

79. *New York v. United States* at 194.

80. *New York v. United States* at 194.

81. U.S. Congress, Congressional Record-House (99th Cong., 1st sess.), vol. 131, pt. 27, December 19, 1985, 38115, https://www.congress.gov/bound-congressional-record/1985/12/19 or https://www.congress.gov/99/crecb/1985/12/19/GPO-CRECB-1985-pt27-2.pdf (accessed October 21, 2020).

82. U.S. Congress, Congressional Record, December 19, 1985, 38115.

83. U.S. Congress, Congressional Record, December 19, 1985, 38115.

84. U.S. Congress, Congressional Record, December 19, 1985, 38115.

85. See Ronald Dworkin, *Freedom's Law: The Moral Reading of the American Constitution* (Oxford: Oxford University Press, 1996; 2005), 7ff.

86. *New York v. United States* at 174.

87. *New York v. United States* at 182.

88. U.S. Supreme Court, *Jacobson v. Massachusetts*, 197 U.S. 11 (1905), at 26, https://supreme.justia.com/cases/federal/us/197/11/ (accessed October 17, 2020).

89. *Jacobson v. Massachusetts* at 26.

90. National Research Council, Commission on Geosciences, and Committee to Review New York State's Siting and Methodology Selection for Low-Level Radioactive Waste Disposal, *Review of New York State Low-Level Radioactive Waste Siting Process* (Washington, DC: National Academy Press, 1996), 10, https://www.nap.edu/catalog/5325/review-of-new-york-state-low-level-radioactive-waste-siting-process (accessed November 19, 2016).

91. National Research Council et al., *Review of New York State*, 6.

92. National Research Council et al., *Review of New York State*, 139.

93. National Research Council et al., *Review of New York State*, 140.

94. William F. Newberry, "The Rise and Fall and Rise and Fall of American Public Policy on Disposal of Low-Level Radioactive Waste," *South Carolina*

Environmental Law Journal 3, no. 1 (1993): 43–73, cited in Samantha Dreilinger, "Fall-Out: *New York v. United States* and the Low-Level Radioactive Waste Problem," *Northwestern Journal of Law and Social Policy* 5, no. 1 (2010): 192, https://paperity.org/p/83996251/fall-out-new-york-v-united-states-and-the-low-level-radioactive-waste-problem (accessed November 19, 2016).

95. Dreilinger, "Fall-Out," 192.

96. Richard C. Kearney, "Low-Level Radioactive Waste Management: Environmental Policy, Federalism, and New York," *Publius* 23, no. 3 (1993): 62, https://www.jstor.org/stable/3330842 (accessed October 21, 2020), cited in Dreilinger, "Fall-Out," 192.

97. Jane Chuang, "Who Should Win the Garbage Wars? Lessons from the Low-Level Radioactive Waste Policy Act," *Fordham Law Review* 72, no. 6 (2004): 2433, 2456, https://ir.lawnet.fordham.edu/flr/vol72/iss6/5 (accessed October 21, 2020), cited in Dreilinger, "Fall-Out," 192.

98. Dreilinger, "Fall-Out," 186

99. Dreilinger, "Fall-Out," 198

100. Dreilinger, "Fall-Out," 198, citing New York State Energy Research and Development Agency, N.Y. State Low-Level Radioactive Waste Status Report for 2008, at 17, 18 (2009)

101. Joel Feinberg, *Harmless Wrongdoing* (Oxford: Oxford University Press, 1988), cited in Stanford Encyclopedia of Philosophy, "Exploitation," http://plato.stanford.edu/entries/exploitation/#3 (accessed September 3, 2015).

102. *New York v. United States* at 168.

103. *New York v. United States* at 196.

104. *New York v. United States* at 198.

105. *New York v. United States* at 199.

106. *New York v. United States* at 210

Chapter 4

FDA v. Brown & Williamson Tobacco Corporation, 529 U.S 98 (2000): FDA Uses the *Food, Drug, and Cosmetics Act (FDCA) of 1938* to Claim Regulatory Authority Over Tobacco Products

The focus of this case is the reach of the Food and Drug Administration's (FDA) regulatory authority under its enabling legislation, the *Food, Drug, and Cosmetics Act* (*FDCA*) (1938).[1]

FACTS OF THE CASE

In 1996, the FDA claimed that since *FDCA* authorizes it to regulate drugs and devices, it has the authority to regulate cigarettes which function as a device to deliver a drug, nicotine, into the human body. On the strength of this, the FDA had taken measures to protect children and adolescents from tobacco products by imposing requirements on how they are promoted, labeled, and made available. Two developments were responsible for this intervention. First, the evidence was that cigarette smoking led to some 400,000 deaths in the United States each year. Second, the evidence was that a majority of adult smokers had begun to smoke when they were minors. Together, they suggested that by preventing an early start to smoking, the threat of addiction in future generations could be minimized. That in turn could reduce the rate of death and smoking-related disease.

The respondents in this case, members of the tobacco industry, including manufacturers, retailers, and advertisers, challenged the measures, seeking summary judgment that the FDA had no regulatory authority over tobacco products that were marketed without manufacturers attaching claims of medicinal benefit to consumers. The decision of the District Court found for the FDA but, on appeal to the Fourth Circuit, that decision was reversed on the grounds that the FDA lacked authorization from the U.S. Congress to regulate tobacco. At the government's request, the U.S. Supreme Court took up the case for *certiorari* (to be made certain) in order to determine whether, under *FDCA*, the FDA did have regulatory authority over tobacco products when marketed without claims to medicinal benefit.

Justice Sandra Day O'Connor, joined by Justices William Rehnquist, Antonin Scalia, Anthony Kennedy, and Clarence Thomas, wrote the decision for the Court; Justice Stephen Breyer, joined by Justices John Stevens, David Souter, and Ruth Bader Ginsburg, filed the dissent.

JUDICIAL REVIEW

In her introduction to the decision of *FDA v. Brown & Williamson Tobacco Corporation* (2000), Justice O'Connor made two remarkable statements. The first recognized the problem of the appalling frequency—in the hundreds of thousands—of premature death occasioned by the use of tobacco. The second, seriously questionable as worded, was that "in 1996, the Food and Drug Administration (FDA), after having expressly disavowed any such authority since its inception, asserted jurisdiction to regulate tobacco products."[2]

Despite the unacceptable number of fatalities from smoking, which the FDA was proposing to stop, O'Connor declared "it may not exercise its authority 'in a manner that is inconsistent with the administrative structure that Congress enacted into law.'"[3] That is to say, the law that prevents the FDA from protecting people against the fatal harm caused by smoking is the same law that, as written, allows the tobacco industry to continue exposing people to the risk of the very same harm! This is law deprived of its ethical foundations.

To be clear, O'Connor was making two claims. Notwithstanding the appalling loss of life and the need to prevent what is preventable, the status of the controlling law prevented addressing the problem as proposed by the FDA. By implication then, if the problem was to be addressed, it would be by means of the law, but the law, presumably, amended. Solving the problem then required, ultimately, legal authorization. And since nothing *could* be done without that, the preventable loss of life would go on unabated.

Despite the fact that Justice Breyer asked the same question of the same law, he arrived at the opposite conclusion. Under the law as it stood, the FDA could intervene as it proposed to do. What remains the same about these two contradictory conclusions is that both depend upon the authority of law as so ordered, or as originating from a legitimate source of law-making, in this case Congress. It is legal positivism which does not recognize anything apart from law to rescue it from contradictory conclusions. And that will depend upon the contingency of being able to secure the support of a majority of the Court's members. In a world of law, by definition contingent, there is nothing to say that this decision might have been made otherwise. And had it, that too would have been a contingent outcome. When confronting absolute alternatives, such as life or death, jurisprudence needs something more than the contingency inherent in legal positivism. Jurisprudence, like any other-regarding human behavior, must be grounded in ethics so that those practicing it have to ask, what *ought* I do to meet the demands of justice before asking, what *can* I do to meet the demands of the law. This is a jurisprudence based on an understanding of law as just, not merely as so ordered—*lex ut justum* (law as just) in contrast to *lex ut jussum* (law as so ordered). This is an understanding of law as law with a necessary connection to ethics.

However, law with a necessary connection with ethics is not meant to imply that ethics and law are interchangeable or that ethics should replace law. As observed in the earlier discussion of the natural law, the relationship is designed to anchor law to the irreducible principles of both speculative and practical reason. Natural law theory always recognized the need for positive law to deal with the emerging and changing circumstances of the human condition. But at some point, law must do this from St. Thomas Aquinas' universal perspective in accord with the principle of universal justice predicated on the equality of all human beings as such. Since this largely depends on the substance of the law in question, we need to review the pertinent provisions in *FDCA* based on which the FDA claimed regulatory authority over tobacco products.

FOOD, DRUG, AND COSMETICS ACT (FDCA)

The Court acknowledged that the 1938 *FDCA*[4] authorized the FDA, as the designee of the Secretary of Health and Human Services (HHS), to regulate what were referred to as "drugs" and "devices." In its own 1996 jurisdictional determination,[5] the FDA had made the critical claims that "cigarettes and smokeless tobacco are combination products consisting of nicotine, a drug that causes addiction and other significant pharmacological effects on the human body, and device components that deliver nicotine to the body."[6]

Further, according to the FDA, it was in the late 1970s when the Agency had last questioned whether cigarettes and smokeless tobacco could be considered drugs and devices as defined in *FDCA*. However, new evidence had become available confirming this. There was the scientific consensus that smoking cigarettes results in an addiction to nicotine. Also, there was voluminous documentation revealing that cigarette manufacturers intended the use of their cigarettes to affect both structurally and functionally the human body. If so, then the FDA concluded it had good reason to regard cigarettes and smokeless tobacco as a means designed for the delivery of nicotine to the human body.[7] The FDA found further confirmation, according to *FDCA*, that something was a drug or a device was correct, if it was "intended to affect the structure or any function of the body." The FDA had also noted that the statutory definition is intended to define "drug" much more broadly than the medical profession. Finally, whether cigarettes and smokeless tobacco were subject to FDA jurisdiction would be a matter the FDA itself was authorized to determine dispositively.[8]

The FDA was equally clear about having continuously exercised regulatory authority under the provisions of *FDCA* with regard to tobacco products when it had evidence of the intention to use them for medical purposes or to affect the structure or function of the body. On previous occasions, when it considered its regulatory authority over tobacco products, the evidence for such intentions available was insufficient. But that was no longer the case. For example, it was now well established that nicotine in cigarettes caused addiction. Knowing that, cigarette manufacturers, the FDA concluded, had intended addiction when they included nicotine in the design of their cigarettes. It was also the case that smokers were intent on experiencing the pharmacological effects of nicotine. In addition, now known but previously unavailable was clear evidence, in the form of the tobacco industry's statements, actions, and research, of its intentions to use cigarettes as a device to deliver nicotine to the human body. As a consequence, the FDA declared that it had brought its policy into line with the evidence so as to conclude that since all cigarettes, as currently designed, were marketed for the purpose of affecting the structure and functioning of the human body, they came within the regulatory authority of the FDA.[9]

In light of this, it is hard to understand why O'Connor asserted without qualification that the FDA's claim in 1996 to regulatory authority over tobacco contrasted with its denial from the very outset of any such authority.[10] But in the FDA's jurisdictional determination, which O'Connor cited, it stated quite clearly that, going back to 1914, the Agency was claiming regulatory authority over tobacco products being used intentionally for medicinal purposes. Subsequently, the Agency was responsible for successful interventions against cigarettes for which claims for therapeutic benefit were being made. In the absence of such evidence, the FDA refrained from claiming jurisdiction. For example, in the 1970s there was some evidence of the pharmacological effects of nicotine, along with preliminary data on the addictive nature of nicotine. Also insufficient was the evidence that cigarette manufacturers knew of the addictive nature of nicotine or were intentionally experimenting with varying levels of nicotine relative to the need to determine corresponding levels of consumer desire for nicotine. "It is nevertheless indisputable that the Agency has consistently claimed jurisdiction over tobacco products when it has determined that they are intended to affect the structure or function of the body or to treat or prevent disease."[11]

A refusal to exercise jurisdiction implies that one has it but chooses not to exercise it. In its response to requests from Action on Smoking and Health (ASH) to regulate filtered cigarettes as devices intended to limit the risk of disease, the FDA agreed with the ASH that a determination of what was the intended use of filters could be made on the basis of objective evidence apart from the claims of manufacturers. However, the FDA noted that in *National Nutritional Foods Association v. Food and Drug Administration* (1974), the Court had insisted that vendors' intention was integral to its statutory definition. Moreover, whatever the objective evidence provided, it must be able to override any subjective evidence offered by manufacturers.[12]

Two additional cases supported the FDA's position that objective evidence included, in addition to the intention of manufacturers and vendors, the intentions of consumers for the use of tobacco products. In this regard, the FDA had concluded that the ASH had not demonstrated that consumers use filters as a medicinal means, for example, to prevent disease, with enough evidence to justify linking the *intended use* criterion of tobacco products with their manufacturers. It merits noting that after the ASH appealed the decision of the FDA in 1980,[13] the U.S. Court of Appeals chose to defer to the FDA., adding that the FDA could change its position, a change that would be acceptable to the courts. "Nothing in this opinion should suggest that the Administration is irrevocably bound by any long-standing interpretation and representations thereof to the legislative branch. An administrative agency is clearly free to revise its interpretation."[14]

It is clear from the behavior of the ASH, the language of the courts, and the reasoning of the FDA, that it was understood that the FDA did enjoy regulatory authority over tobacco products. That the ASH would appeal the FDA's decision only confirmed this understanding. Everything about the FDA's concern to have sufficient objective evidence of intended use as defined in *FDCA* in order to regulate clearly implies an understanding that it possessed regulatory authority and wished to exercise it legitimately. Its refusal to regulate in the case of filtered cigarettes should not have been construed as a disavowal of authority to regulate, since refusal to regulate implies the ability to regulate and the choice not to.

Consistent with this position, the FDA rejected claims made by the tobacco industry that Congress has denied it authority to regulate tobacco products. In this regard, the FDA insisted that any such regulatory authority was compatible with preemptive provisions of Congress' *Federal Cigarette Labeling and Advertising Act* (*FCLAA*) (1966), as well as its *Comprehensive Smokeless Tobacco Health Education Act* (1986),[15] In support of this assertion, the FDA invoked the operative language of *FDCA*'s definition of *drugs* and *devices*, which at no point could be said to exclude tobacco products in the way, for example, that it excluded *soap* from its definition of *cosmetic*. Additional examples of Congressional exclusion of tobacco products could, the FDA observed, be found in its definition of *consumer products* in the *Consumer Products Safety Act* (*CPSA*) (1972).[16] And while tobacco is excluded in *FDCA*'s definition of dietary supplement, nothing comparable is found in its definition of *drugs* and *devices*.[17]

Another line of argument that Congress denied the FDA regulatory authority over tobacco relied on the questionable premise of the FDA's disavowal of authority and Congress' acquiescence to it. The result, the argument went, was that Congress failed to consider legislation that, had it been enacted, would have expressly authorized the FDA's jurisdiction over tobacco products. And such failure could only mean that Congress had no intention of allowing the FDA to regulate tobacco products.

In response, the FDA observed that even if Congress had not explicitly authorized the FDA to regulate tobacco products, that should not in itself have negated its claim to regulatory authority over them. It advanced three reasons for this position. One, Congress was well aware of the FDA's claim to jurisdiction and had taken no steps to refute it. Such were the interventions of the FDA in regard to claims made for cigarettes as means of weight reduction and for the prevention of respiratory disease. As it observed, "FDA has repeatedly told Congress that a tobacco product that falls within the definition of a drug or device because it was promoted to treat disease or affect the structure or function of the body would be within the Agency's jurisdiction."[18] Two, were it a matter of congressional acquiescence to the FDA's lack of jurisdiction, it was the position of the Supreme Court that such acquiescence would not prevent the FDA from changing its appreciation of the reach of its authority under *FDCA*. Third, it was also the position of the Supreme Court that congressional decisions not to enact legislation or amend an existing statute could not be the basis for understanding and applying law passed by Congress earlier.[19] As the FDA emphasized, the adoption of official policy depended on the approval of a bill in both houses of Congress, a subsequent approval from the president, and in the event of a presidential veto, a vote to override. But neither Congress nor the President had taken these steps to exclude cigarettes from *FDCA*'s definition of *drugs* and *devices*.[20] And while bills to exclude tobacco products from *FDCA*'s control had been proposed, they had not, significantly, been approved. Implicitly, at least, that would suggest a congressional preference for FDA jurisdiction over tobacco products.

That Congress passed the *Cigarette Act* (1996) and earlier the *Smokeless Act* (1986) was seen by some as an explicit preemption of the FDA's role in tobacco consumer safety. The FDA refused to accept this view, arguing that such an interpretation would result in misrepresenting both *Acts*. While true that there were preemptive provisions for the FDA regulating tobacco in both statutes, the provisions were clearly so circumscribed as to not override the FDA's authority to regulate tobacco where its use was intended to affect the structure or function of the body. Of the two preemptions in the *Cigarette Act*, for example, the first applied to language regarding smoking and health found on cigarette packaging. The second preemption, regarding cigarette advertising, was specific to State law. For good measure, the FDA noted that while Congress considered, it then declined, preempting Federal regulation in the *Cigarette Act*'s preemption provisions for advertising.[21]

Since Congress had considered Federal preemption in the *Cigarette Act*, the FDA made clear its obligation to comply with congressional provisions. But it had no reason to see what it called a blanket preemption of its jurisdiction over tobacco products when the *Act*'s actual preemption was clearly circumscribed. It concluded, as a result, that it was exercising its regulatory authority without stipulating conditions that might be at odds with the preemptions of the *Act*.[22]

It was also the FDA's position that the existence of other tobacco regulations did not justify seeing that to be something to preempt its authority to regulate tobacco products as included in its authority to regulate drugs and devices. "It is, of course, a cardinal principle of statutory construction that repeals by implication are not favored."[23] Furthermore, the FDA argued that where there was no intended provision for preemption, "One Federal statute precludes giving effect to another Federal statute only where there is an irreconcilable conflict between the two laws."[24] More to a point to be seen later, "The courts are not at liberty to pick and choose among congressional enactments, and when two statutes are capable of co-existence, it is the duty of the courts to regard each as effective."[25]

What are we to make of this sustained effort by the FDA to confirm its authority to regulate tobacco products? As the Agency reviewed consistently emerging evidence that cigarettes and smokeless tobacco were intended by both their manufacturers and consumers to be used to affect the structure and function of the human body, it confirmed the FDA's jurisdiction as articulated in *FDCA*. Since cigarettes were designed by the manufacturer and received by the consumer as a device to deliver the addictive-causing drug, nicotine, to the body, they met the criteria within the definition of device and drug stipulated in *FDCA*. And since this was new evidence, it justified an adjustment on the part of the FDA to its appreciation of its already exercised, albeit limitedly, jurisdiction over tobacco products when used with the intention of affecting the structure and function of the body.

In addition to confirming FDA's jurisdiction, the new evidence was bringing to light that nicotine addiction was a pediatric disease warranting urgent and effective regulatory intervention by the FDA. Two key points had been made clear from the emerging evidence. The first was that most of the people who suffer negative health outcomes from using tobacco products had begun their use while children and adolescents. The second was that those who had not begun to smoke from an early age were unlikely to begin smoking at all.[26] It is not hard to see why, in light of this evidence, the FDA would wish to take advantage of what it considered a unique opportunity to reverse smoking trends that were resulting in some 400,000 deaths each year in the United States. Stopping children and adolescents from starting to use tobacco products and eventually become addicted to cigarettes would make it unlikely that, as adults, they would take up smoking at all. If so, tobacco-related disease and the incidence of premature death associated with smoking could be curtailed.

In keeping with this line of thinking, the FDA took encouragement from reports indicating, at that time, that legislative and regulatory interventions were proving successful in limiting the access children had to tobacco products. At the same time, limited access to cigarettes was serving to reduce the appeal smoking might have had to them.[27]

Here was additional proof for the FDA that significant changes were called for in its appreciation of the urgency of the problem, requiring adjustments to its jurisdiction under *FDCA* over tobacco products. Now that the need for youth-centered interventions had become apparent, the earlier belief that interventions under *FDCA*, such as withdrawing tobacco products from the market were unrealistic, was beginning to change. Dawning was the realization that the FDA's regulatory authority to limit the sale to, and the use of cigarettes by persons under eighteen years old could lessen the harmful health outcomes associated with smoking. "Thus, asserting jurisdiction over cigarettes and smokeless tobacco now presents an opportunity to use the Agency's resources effectively for substantial public health gains."[28]

Data available in the 1990s could not, the FDA contended, be ignored. Tobacco use more often than not began among children and adolescents, and was beginning even earlier within this population. Citing the 1994 Surgeon General's report, the FDA noted that the average age for the first-time smoking was 14.5 years old. "Nearly all first use of tobacco occurs before high school graduation; this finding suggests that if adolescents can be kept tobacco-free, most will never start using tobacco."[29] The FDA also noted that while smoking rates among adults in the United States were in decline, they were on the rise among children and adolescents. For example, in 1995, 19% of eighth graders and 29% of tenth graders confirmed having smoked in the last thirty days, which represented an increase of one-third when compared to data from four years earlier.[30]

What appears to have concerned the FDA, because of its implications for public health, was nicotine addiction among young smokers. Of those between 12 and 17 years old, 70% admitted regretting ever having started to smoke, while 60% expressed their wish to stop smoking.[31] Those who did stop also experienced, in the same manner as adults, withdrawal symptoms. Noticeably, relapse rates among young smokers mirrored those of adults.[32]

In light of these disturbing data, the FDA issued its proposed rules to restrict the sale and distribution of cigarettes and smokeless tobacco products for the protection of children and adolescents.[33] There were two goals in mind. The first was to make access to cigarettes and smokeless tobacco less easy for children and adolescents. The second was to counter the positive imagery associated with smoking that contributed to the appeal it was making to children and adolescents. What was not a goal was a restriction on adult use of tobacco products.[34]

Specifically, the FDA proposed to establish 18 years of age as the Federal minimum age permitting the purchase of cigarettes and smokeless tobacco products. Cigarette vending machines, free samples, mail-order sales, and self-service displays were also to be prohibited. The FDA also proposed that retailers should comply with certain conditions for the sale of tobacco products, in particular, requiring them to verify that the purchaser was 18 years old. Regarding advertising and labeling, the FDA was intent on restricting both to text-only versions. Along with this, the FDA proposed a ban on the sale and distribution of non-tobacco items, like hats and tee-shirts, used to promote smoking. A major proposal was that manufacturers should establish and maintain a national public education campaign, designed for children and adolescents, as a corrective to the customary positive imagery enjoyed by smoking. The corrective was intended to undermine any appeal the years of pro-tobacco advertising might have for children and adolescents.[35]

Ultimately, these goals could be traced back to an overarching goal of the report, *Healthy People 2000*,[36] to cut the number of children and adolescents using tobacco products by 50%. The emphasis was very much on prevention so as to bring down the incidence of death and disease as a direct result of the use of tobacco products. There was no intention in this intervention of banning tobacco products for the millions of Americans already addicted from using them. Now that the connection between smoking and addiction had been established, the FDA had determined that the goal was to prevent future generations from becoming addicted at all.[37]

The FDA was not alone in its focus on preventing an early start to the use of tobacco products. In preparing these proposals, it had considered recommendations from the World Health Organization (WHO), the Office of the Surgeon General (OSG), the Centers for Disease Control and Prevention (CDC), the National Cancer Institute, and the Institute of Medicine (IOM). Two reports, the Surgeon General's 1994 report, *Preventing Tobacco Use Among Young People*, and that of the IOM, *Growing Up Tobacco Free: Preventing Nicotine Addiction in Children and Youths* (1994), had exerted considerable influence in shaping the FDA's thinking.[38]

One additional set of data cannot go unnoticed. According to the FDA, the number of smokers in the United States dropped annually by 1.7 million. There were, annually, some 400,000 deaths caused by smoking and those who managed to stop smoking each year numbered around 1.3 million. To compensate for this smoker's attrition, the tobacco industry had been turning to young people as its primary source of replenishment, with 3,000 young people joining the ranks of regular smokers each day.[39] However, when adolescent smoking became adult smoking, the risk of dying from cancer, cardiovascular disease, or lung disease increased for adolescents.[40]

It was this alarming prospect that prompted the FDA to undertake its extensive investigation and detailed legal assessment of its jurisdiction over tobacco products. Since both resulted in determining that nicotine was a drug and that tobacco products were drug delivery devices under the terms of *FDCA*, the FDA concluded it had jurisdiction over tobacco products and was justified constitutionally in promulgating its regulations.[41]

APPEALS

Upon promulgation, the regulations were challenged. A group of tobacco manufacturers, retailers, and advertisers filed suit in United States District Court for the Middle District of North Carolina on the grounds that the FDA lacked jurisdiction to regulate tobacco products. The District Court granted respondents' motion in part and denied it in part. The Court of Appeals for the Fourth Circuit reversed, deciding that Congress had not granted the FDA jurisdiction over tobacco products.[42] The Court concluded that the regulation of tobacco products by the FDA would result in some inconsistencies internal to *FDCA*, which required the FDA to determine whether regulated products are safe before they can be sold or allowed to continue in the market. However, the Court insisted, since it is the position of the FDA that tobacco products were dangerous, the Agency would under *FDCA* have to ban them, something Congress would never allow. From this, the Court inferred that Congress had never countenanced FDA regulatory authority over tobacco products. Other considerations for the Court included what it claimed as the FDA's consistent denial of jurisdiction over tobacco as recently as 1995. There was also the fact that Congress had passed its own tobacco-related legislation, while aware of the FDA's position. The Court also noted how Congress, on a number of occasions, had contemplated and subsequently rejected bills that would have authorized for the FDA regulatory authority over tobacco. This the Court interpreted as a clear sign of congressional resistance to FDA jurisdiction over tobacco. On appeal, the Supreme Court granted the Government's request for *certiorari* to determine whether the FDA had authority under *FDCA* to regulate tobacco products as customarily marketed.

In affirming the decision of the Appeals Court, the Supreme Court was clearly influenced by the terms of that Court's review. For O'Connor, relying on *Chevron U.S.A. Inc. v. Natural Resources Defense Council*,[43] the starting point for the court's review of the FDA's claim to jurisdiction over tobacco products, was whether Congress had already settled the matter of jurisdiction. If it had, then the review was complete and the court was obliged to recognize congressional intention. If this was not the case, the Court must respect the Agency's interpretation of the statute it was administering, as long as this was permissible. The Court's deference to the Agency was warranted since it was presumed to be more knowledgeable about the subjects regulated, along with the factual and circumstantial changes to which they were constantly subject.

Furthermore, in its review, the Court should avoid considering a specific statutory provision on its own, without reference to legislative context. This clearly was an acknowledgment of the ambiguity noticeably present in *FDCA*. The review had to also allow for the meaning of a statute being qualified by other subsequent statutes, such as those enacted to address the same subject matter in more specific terms. Finally, there was the need for deference to common sense so as to account for how Congress might likely have wanted to delegate jurisdiction to an agency over matters of such considerable economic and political import. Since, however. it was the conclusion of the Court that Congress had expressed its intention to deny the FDA regulatory authority over tobacco products, deference to the Agency was not warranted.[44]

According to O'Connor, the overriding concern for *FDCA* was the safety and effectiveness of the intended use of the products regulated under the statute. Citing *FDCA*,[45] she noted that the statute defined the role of the FDA to involve the protection of the public's health by guaranteeing the safety and effectiveness of drugs and devices intended for use by humans. For this, pre-market approval was a requirement. Should the FDA have determined that a new drug was not safe, it was to withhold approval. And if, having granted approval, it was discovered that a drug or device was unsafe, the statute provided for a hearing, followed by a determination to withdraw approval. Ultimately, under *FDCA*, the FDA was responsible for prohibiting the promotion of any drug or device likely to cause death or physical injury unless their use was balanced by a reasonable expectation of therapeutic outcome.[46]

The FDA's findings left no doubt about how unsafe tobacco products were. They would, consequently, qualify, according to O'Connor, as misbranded since under *FDCA*, a drug or device was misbranded "unless its labeling bears . . . adequate directions for use . . . in such a manner and form as are necessary for the protection of the user."[47] Since no such labeling was conceivable, the FDA would have no choice, had it jurisdiction, but to ban them, according to O'Connor.

JUSTICE BREYER DISSENTING

Breyer, in his dissent, saw matters differently. He noted that *FDCA*, under its provisions for devices, allowed the FDA to regulate a combination product or device, an example of which, Breyer suggested, might be a cigarette, which contained the drug, nicotine.[48] The same provisions afforded the FDA considerable discretion when it came to choosing remedies when appropriate. In situations, for example, where the agency was unable by other means to secure reasonable assurance of the safety and effectiveness of a device, it could have regulated so as to limit its sale, distribution, and use upon "such conditions as the Secretary may prescribe."[49] Furthermore, in detailing the FDA's power to ban, *FDCA* provided that when a device occasioned "an unreasonable and substantial risk of illness or injury," the Secretary may, not must, ban the device.[50]

Breyer also questioned the Court's understanding of other sections of *FDCA* as requiring the FDA to ban a drug or device outright even when the ban might have caused greater harm than available alternative regulatory interventions. He agreed with the Court that *FDCA* required the FDA to identify all devices under one of three classifications. Devices identified within the third classification were required to receive pre-market approval. But he disagreed that the FDA had to place cigarettes in Class 111 because tobacco "presents a potential unreasonable risk of illness and injury."[51] This, for Breyer, was to misunderstand the purpose of Class 111, which was relevant only when conditions prevented regulation from securing a reasonable assurance of safety. In other words, according to Breyer, *FDCA* permitted the FDA to measure the relative safety of a device against alternative regulatory interventions. Consequently, the selection of what it considered the least dangerous intervention as the safest choice would be satisfactory under *FDCA*'s terms, for the requirement for reasonable assurances of safety.[52]

This precisely was what the FDA had done by concluding that an outright ban on tobacco products, given the incidence of nicotine addiction among smokers, would have risked greater harm than any reasonable alternative short of a ban. If nothing else, common sense, one of the Court's criteria in addressing this matter, would have dictated recognizing the presence of two populations, needing two different approaches. The first was those already smoking, and the second was those who had not yet begun smoking. However reluctant the FDA might have been to see tobacco products continue to be available, so as to avoid particular consequences of a ban, such as widespread withdrawal symptoms that would test severely the ability of the health-care system to address, it could not ignore the urgent need to prevent those who had not yet started to smoke from beginning to smoke. Its dilemma should have been obvious to anyone intent on addressing the problem, instead of holding it hostage to the Court's Hobson's choice of banning or doing nothing. But if tobacco products were to remain available for smokers, then they were also available to those not yet smoking. In which case, the only means of protecting the latter was regulation.

SMOKING IN DECLINE

The decline in adult smoking supported the FDA's approach of balancing a-not-banning-policy with a regulatory policy. In 1965, 42.4% of the adult population in the United States were smokers. By 1990, smoking in the United States had declined to 25.5%, the greatest drop occurring between 1987 and 1990, which represented an annual drop of 1.1%, while doubling that occurring in the previous twenty years. Adult smoking reached a plateau of 25.6% in 1991 and 26.5% in 1992. Under an amended definition of smoking that included less than daily or infrequent smoking, adult smoking stood at 25%. This significant decline in adult smoking was in strong contrast with the smoking trends asserting themselves among the young population at the same time.[53]

The Court however was not persuaded, and they viewed this intervention as a departure by the FDA from what it, the Court, considered to be the FDA's persistent disavowal of jurisdiction. In light of the record provided by the FDA in its *jurisdictional determination*, the Court's assertion remains questionable and at the time revealed a failure to acknowledge the history of the cigarette in relation to *FDCA*. Until science had demonstrated incontrovertibly that the cigarette qualified under the statute as a device, designed by the manufacturer and understood by the consumer, to be used to convey nicotine to the body so as to alter its structure or function, the FDA's claim to regulatory authority remained unavoidably vague in the sense that the word *remember* is vague. We can say, for example, "I hardly remember the incident," or "I clearly remember the incident," and both, as statements of *remembering* are either true or false, despite the vagueness of the term 'remember.' Similarly, the term *authority*. We can say, "I have absolute authority," or "I have conditional authority," and both, as statements of *authority*, are either true or false. Vagueness, as Aristotle observed, is not a deficit. "It is the mark of the educated man and a proof of his culture that in every subject he looks for only so much precision as its nature permits."[54]

The concept of vagueness is particularly relevant here because it is seemingly irreconcilable with the position that any proposition is either true or false.[55] The identity of the nature of a cigarette, as well as the real intention for its use, had remained elusive, as we saw, until after the late 1970s. It was these circumstances that made the FDA hesitant to exercise regulatory authority, which it would have been authorized to do, were both identity as a drug-delivery device, and intention for use for pharmacological stimulation, clearly demonstrated. That had finally occurred in the 1990s, resulting in the FDA's exhaustive review of its authority to regulate tobacco products and the promulgation of regulations themselves. Inexcusably, the Court discounted the relevance of vagueness to the FDA's hesitation to exercise its jurisdiction over tobacco products. In so doing, it misrepresented the FDA's position entirely.

It should be noted that at no point did the Court deny that cigarettes qualified as a combination of drug and device under the terms of *FDCA*. Indeed, it argued that had it jurisdiction over tobacco products, the FDA would, under *FDCA*, have had to ban them as irremediably unsafe. But the Court's conclusion that the FDA lacked jurisdiction over tobacco products was grounded in other considerations. It focused on the agency's reasons for not considering a ban since that could have serious medical consequences, such as withdrawal symptoms for current smokers. The Court appeared to ignore what equally influenced the FDA, which was the fact that cigarettes had been lawfully marketed to millions of adult Americans over time.[56] The Court conceded that a serious issue like addiction deserved consideration in formulating regulation with a view to good public health outcomes. Nevertheless, the decision to leave tobacco products on the market as preferable to, because more effective than, a ban was, according to the Court, "no substitute for the specific safety determinations required by the FDCA's various operative provisions."[57]

Instead, the Court argued that *FDCA* required of the FDA the determination that the product itself was safe as used by the customer, with benefits from its use outweighing any accompanying harm. But the Court also noted how the statute included as part of the FDA's mission, protecting the public's health from drugs that were deemed unsafe for use as intended. Combining the two goals in the case of cigarettes presents a distinct challenge which the Court failed to address adequately. It is, however, one thing to determine the safety of drugs not yet marketed and another to determine the safety of drugs already marketed and used by millions of Americans since they were first introduced early in the nineteenth century. Precisely because of this long history of use, associated as it is with widespread nicotine addiction, a realistic determination of the safety of cigarettes themselves is not possible without assessing the safety of removing them from the market altogether when that is likely to be more harmful than allowing continued use, certainly in the short-term. If the goal, however, is the long-term safety of the public's health, the decline in adult smoking noted above will be insufficient for achieving this unless it is reinforced by preventing young people from beginning to smoke at all. Here the regulations proposed for young people by the FDA amounted, for all practical purposes, to a ban on access to tobacco products for young people in compliance with its jurisdiction under *FDCA*. If then the goal of *FDCA* is, ultimately, the safety of the public's health, a ban across the board of tobacco products, given the consequences for millions of addicted smokers, would be ill-advised, while compromising the statute into the bargain. Untying this Gordian knot called for something more nuanced than that advanced by the Court's interpretation of *FDCA*.

TOBACCO INTERESTS

To be clear, there is no neat and tidy resolution here, as the Court mistakenly thought, in its a-historical reading of *FDCA* and in its mistaken deference to a Congress so intent on protecting the economic importance of the tobacco industry, that it consistently had overlooked the impossible position in which this placed the FDA. Here, the Court had in mind the fact that Congress had "directly addressed the problem of tobacco and health, through legislation on six occasions since 1965," of which the latest was enacted in 1992.[58] Underpinning these legislative initiatives, the Court argued, was a provision in the 1997 United States' Code, preventing a ban on tobacco products, because "the marketing of tobacco constitutes one of the greatest industries of the United States with ramifying activities which directly affect interstate and foreign commerce at every point, and stable conditions therein are necessary to the general welfare."[59]

For quite different reasons, the FDA did not want to ban tobacco products, but it did want to regulate them for that second population of not-yet-smokers. But the Court, with a strained line of reasoning, prevented that. Its premise was to insist, mistakenly as Breyer pointed out, that should the FDA intervene, its only course of action under *FDCA* would be to ban tobacco products. That however would put it on a collision course with Congress. Faced with this dilemma, the FDA, as the Court characterized it, "concluded, somewhat ironically, that tobacco products are actually 'safe' within the meaning of the FDCA."[60] Having made that claim, the Court then argued that the regulations promulgated by the FDA for the protection of adolescents amounted to declaring the opposite for tobacco products. But it failed to see the real dilemma confronting the FDA as it sought to balance broadly under *FDCA* the health interests of those already smoking with the health interests of those not yet smoking. Specifically, it appeared to discount the consequences of banning, not something being considered for use, but already commonly in use. Given the high levels of addiction accompanying smoking, did not the FDA's concern over the capacity of the health-care system to deal with widespread withdrawal symptoms, following a ban, merit the Court's serious attention? And why was not the FDA's concern over the emergence of a black market for cigarettes as a response to a ban taken more seriously by the Court?

These questions, it might be argued, opened up for the Court, what it called a qualitatively different inquiry. As it put it, "although the FDA has concluded that a ban would be 'dangerous,' it has not concluded that tobacco products are 'safe' as that term is used throughout the Act."[61] For the Court, this was the sticking point. A drug is safe when the benefits of use as intended outweigh any accompanying deficits. Instead, it argued, the FDA's assessment of safety consists in a comparison of aggregate health outcomes yielded through alternative agency interventions. What then did the Court make of this language in the statute: "If the Secretary determines that the risk of recalling ... presents a greater health risk than the health risk of not recalling the device," no recall is required.[62] It is of course a qualitatively different inquiry because, unlike the Court, the FDA, as the expert in the field, recognized the need to determine whether not recalling tobacco products under conditions of widespread addictive use would pose less risk of harm than that posed by recalling them. Despite the obvious common sense of *FDCA*'s language here, one has to ask what reason had the Court for thinking that the statute required the FDA to ignore the prevalence of smoking when assessing safety and choosing an intervention in light of that assessment?

The answer lies in the Court's, again strained, argument that, in 1965, Congress had moved to place tobacco products within the *FCLAA* (1966) which prohibited the regulation of tobacco advertising. Instead, cigarette packages were to carry a warning that smoking may be dangerous for one's health. The warning, Congress maintained, would accomplish two goals, an informed consumer of tobacco products and the protection of the tobacco industry and its role in the national economy. In acknowledging that regulating labeling was central to *FDCA*, the Court had also to acknowledge that *FDCA* required the FDA to regulate the labeling of drugs and devices in the interests of consumers. That prompted the Court to declare that *FCLAA* and the FDA regulation of tobacco products were irreconcilable, followed by its declaration that *FCLAA*'s preemption provision ruled out FDA jurisdiction. That, as we saw above, would, in the judgment of the FDA, have been a misreading of the statute. It included two preemption provisions, both narrowly drawn. The first applied only to statements concerning smoking and health on cigarette packages. In its final rule, however, the FDA had made no such requirements for cigarette packaging. The second provision concerned State not Federal law. As the FDA noted, "if Congress had intended to preempt other Federal initiatives by the provision, it would have done so by adding the words, 'or Federal' between 'State' and 'law.'" The history of *FCLAA*, however, showed that Congress considered but then rejected preemption of Federal regulation in its advertising provision, when in conference the U.S. Senate bill which included no Federal preemption, prevailed over the U.S. House bill which did.[63]

The position of the Court, simply stated, was that "Congress has created a distinct regulatory scheme to address the problem of tobacco and health, and that scheme as presently constructed, precludes any role for the FDA."[64] Confirming this, according to the Court, was the legislative history concerning tobacco products between 1965 and 1989. Breyer took exception to this reading of history with a series of questions. Did the laws in question actually contain language explicitly excluding the FDA? There were none. Were there provisions incompatible with claims to jurisdiction by the FDA? "With one exception... the majority points to no such provision."[65] Did those same laws suspend the principles of law that, left in place, would allow the conclusion that the FDA does have jurisdiction here?[66]

It is possible, Breyer conceded, that later laws give shape and focus to the meaning of the statute enacted in 1938. However, he also noted that the Supreme Court had counseled against permitting the views of a subsequent Congress to interpret legislation enacted at an earlier time.[67] But this, he lamented, appeared to be what the majority was doing in this case. Yet it was clear that these statutes failed to confirm the conclusion drawn from them by the majority because they did not suggest the presence of any assumptions denying jurisdiction to the FDA. Indeed, these later statutes could be viewed as consistent with Congress' preference to proceed in a way that did not interfere with the FDA's regulatory authority.[68]

Critically, Breyer was drawing attention to the ambivalent nature of the statutes enacted after 1965, since he believed they could be interpreted as confirming assumptions of no jurisdiction, or simply allowing the question of jurisdiction to remain precisely where Congress found it. And since both conclusions were equally reasonable, the majority is not at liberty to argue as it did, relying on the relevant legislative history.[69] All that this history has shown is an inability of Congress to muster votes sufficient either to grant or to deny the FDA jurisdiction over tobacco products.[70] After all, as Breyer concluded, Congress had on one occasion only considered expressly the FDA's regulatory authority. In doing so, it had declared the statute was not intended to imply anything for that authority. Given this, "the proper inference to be drawn from all of the post-1965 statutes, then, is one that interprets Congress' general legislative silence consistently with this statement."[71]

Since *FDCA* was the controlling legislation here, Breyer's recommendation that it be interpreted in the larger context of Congressional goals for the public's health was reasonably pragmatic. That, he insisted, called for flexibility, something, one might add, noticeably absent from the majority's interpretation. With this flexibility, the FDA would have been able to intervene, in a way that it considered appropriate under prevailing conditions, to address the accumulated realities of a nation of addicted smokers[72]: 75% of adults who were smoking because it reduced nervous irritation, and 73% of young people (10 to 22 years old) who were smoking to relax. But, at the same time, while 70% of that smoking population wanted to stop smoking, less than 3% were able to do so.[73]

FDA MISREPRESENTED

This brings us to examine more closely one of the more disturbing aspects of O'Connor's decision, the persistent mischaracterization of the FDA's disavowal of its regulatory authority over tobacco products. As noted earlier, she wrote, "in 1996, the Food and Drug Administration (FDA), after having expressly disavowed any such authority since its inception, asserted jurisdiction to regulate tobacco products."[74] The impression conveyed by this characterization is that the disavowal was unconditional. But as Breyer noted, it was not. "When it denied jurisdiction to regulate cigarettes, the FDA consistently stated why that was so."[75] In 1963, the FDA had concluded that cigarettes did not meet *FDCA*'s requirement concerning manufacturers' "intent" in marketing them, since no therapeutic claims for their use by consumers were being made.[76] And in testimony before Congress, one FDA Commissioner underscored, for purposes of asserting jurisdiction, the importance of demonstrating manufacturer intent.[77] But this assertion in itself clearly implies the presence of jurisdiction. Why otherwise draw attention to the absence of a condition to which jurisdiction is subject for its exercise? It also implies that once the condition is met, jurisdiction can be exercised. By 1996, the FDA had reached that point with the acquisition of solid evidence robust enough to reveal manufacturer intent, distinct from any *claims* manufacturers might be making for their product.

Both Breyer and the majority agreed that the FDA's change in policy was a matter of constitutional indifference.[78] But unlike Breyer, the majority took the agency's history of denial to reinforce its conclusion that Congress' own regulatory scheme for tobacco was based on an understanding that the FDA had no regulatory authority at all. This conclusion, however, stands only if this history is an unconditional repudiation of jurisdiction. It is not. A more accurate characterization would be drawn from *FDCA*'s definitions for "drug" and "device" respectively which, since the 1990s, undeniably included tobacco products. Given these definitions, it was only a matter of time before the evidence confirmed that nicotine is a drug and that cigarettes are a device intended by cigarette manufacturers to convey nicotine into the human body so as to affect its function and structure. Such evidence for tobacco products was not available in 1938, developing only incrementally over the following fifty years. At several points in her decision, O'Connor made the point that the evidence for the addictive nature of nicotine and the serious health risks of smoking was well known publicly, failing however, to mention that it was also accompanied by controversy. As a result, it lacked the level of scientific certainty needed to justify a claim to jurisdiction. That was to come eventually in the 1990s, and to be instrumental in revealing what had been in *FDCA* all along, only in latent form, the FDA's jurisdiction over tobacco products. It is one thing for a judge to deny jurisdiction, *simpliciter*; it is another to deny the ability to exercise it in the absence of the appropriate evidence. It appears O'Connor failed to see the critical distinction. In contrast, Breyer did, concluding that a reasonable appreciation of this history of denying jurisdiction had to acknowledge the enormous difficulty the FDA had had in demonstrating manufacturer intent.[79]

Nevertheless, Breyer entertained the idea that the FDA's history of denials might have engendered within Congress a disposition to enact after 1965 the several statutes it did. If so, it might be reasonable to interpret those statutes in light of that history. But suppose an agency were to declare that it lacked jurisdiction over a particular substance unless it was treated as a food. Subsequently, it determined that the substance was intended to be eaten. Surely, that would not rule out at that point beginning to exercise jurisdiction. Since this was so similar to the earlier posture of the FDA, it was reasonable to conclude that that posture should not inform our interpretation of the statutes in question.[80]

Along with this, Breyer pursued another hypothetical line of analysis. When courts were interpreting statutes, particularly in close cases, the assumption should be that decisions of enormous social consequence were to be made by elected members of Congress and not unelected administrators. But even if there were such an underlying assumption, Breyer was prepared to deny it any authority to dispose of the decision in this case. Since any decision to regulate tobacco was indicative of the policy of an administration, it would be a decision for which the administration would be held politically accountable. *A fortiori* (more so) here. It would, he concluded, be hard to think that an FDA decision of this social and economic import would escape public scrutiny and eventual accountability at the hands of the electorate.[81]

Breyer closed his dissent with a statement whose moral implications go predictably unexamined because they lack any relevance to the Court's positivist jurisprudence. He judged the decision itself a contradiction, holding as it did that a statute intended for unsafe drugs and devices did not authorize the regulation of nicotine and cigarettes. He also underscored the fact that those making this decision acknowledged how unsafe was the use of both, placing health and life at the serious risk the FDA was intent on curtailing. "The majority's conclusion is counterintuitive."[82] It is more than that. It is unethical because it is borne of the denial, inherent to legal positivism, of a necessary connection between law and ethics.

It was noted above how O'Connor, in the opening words of her decision, had agreed with the FDA that the frequency of premature death from the use of tobacco, some 400,000 annually, was "one of the most troubling public health problems facing the Nation today." In so doing, she had rendered, within the official text of the Court's decision, an ethics judgment. Like the FDA, she was saying that this is a bad state of affairs. Their judgment is identical. Their response to it is quite different. The FDA, proposed a remedy for the problem in acknowledgment of an obligation to act embedded in the term "bad." O'Connor, citing an earlier decision of the Court, declared "'it may not exercise its authority in a manner that is inconsistent with the administrative structure that Congress enacted into law.'"[83] What might explain the discrepancy?

At first glance, the statement that "smoking causes 400,000 deaths annually is one of the most troubling public health problems facing the Nation today," might be understood simply as a statement of fact. To be precise however, it is a statement evaluating smoking, which is a fatal behavior, as bad. Now what is being said here? Typically, we would understand the question to be asking what the meaning of bad is when applied to smoking in the same way that one might ask what the meaning of blue is when applied to sky, as though bad, like blue, denoted some applicable property and suggesting that their meaning is the same. Were we, however, to ask to what use either word is being put, we would see a difference in their logical function. In the case of blue, its use is to describe, but in the case of bad, its use is to condemn. To condemn, like its opposite to commend, is to make a judgment. And either is made for the purpose of directing what we choose to do.[84] To think of something as bad is "already to 'react to it.'"[85] This would appear to be the way the FDA is using its language because, in proposing interventions designed to stop smoking, it was complying logically with the prescriptive sense of the use of the word, bad. In other words, observe the FDA and it becomes quite clear that words are better regarded as tools we use, much like carpenters use their tools, to do things with. "Talking is not always naming or reporting; it is sometimes doing."[86] Doing something, that is, that should be done, rather than, as in this case, doing what should not be done.

As noted in the Introduction, this point was drawn very clearly by R. M. Hare when he observed that the most reliable way to know the "moral principles" of someone is to study their behavior. Principles are readily invoked and readily overlooked. By working backward from what someone chooses to do in response to the question, "what should I do?" it is possible to discern with what norms the choice was made since they exist to direct our behavior.[87] Hare went on to note that since we live in conditions where concerns over our behavior pose increasingly challenging moral questions, the need to appreciate the "language" used to express and to respond to them is ever more urgent. Where there is little or no awareness of the language used in moral discourse, the risk of misunderstanding the nature of ethics and how it is applied in assessing human behavior is great.[88] It would be a mistake to think that O'Connor's use of the word, 'troubling' was merely descriptive in purpose. 'Troubling' is a value-term, synonyms for which might be 'disturbing' or 'bad.' When we use value-terms like these, or in the case of a judge, 'guilty' or 'not guilty' it is to render a judgement of either commendation or condemnation,which then becomes the justification, assuming the judgement is sincere, for taking action consonant with the nature of the judgement. In the case of someone 'guilty,' it would be to sentence to punishment. In the case of someone 'not-guilty,' it would be to declare them free. In the case of something 'troubling,' it would be to stop it or at least restrain it. In all three cases, the action taken would be taken, not as a matter of discretionary use of power but as a matter of fulfilling a moral obligation born of justice or what is owed to those guilty, not guilty, or those troubled. Judgements of guilt or innocence by a judge are judgements made according to legal norms. O'Connor's judgement of troubling is not, obviously, a legal judgement. It is a moral judgement, but a judgement nonetheless and made according to ethical norms. And since, as Nowell-Smith and Hare have demonstrated, the language used in making ethical judgement is equally normative, O'Connor having made her moral judgement of troubling is obliged to act on it in a manner concordant with the judgement. Despite its condemnation of smoking, the Court found the FDA guilty of seeking to violate the Constitution by acting beyond *FDCA* in its efforts to safeguard the health and lives of the nation's youth against smoking, while exonerating both Congress and the tobacco industry in their defense of tobacco's centrality to the nation's economy. In justification, the Court may counter with the observation that it is not authorized to amend or make law. But it does unmake or confirm law by holding legislation like *FDCA* accountable to the Constitution as the supreme law of the land in the course of its judicial review. Nevertheless, the judicial review, with all of its other-regarding consequences, may not be undertaken in some kind of legal vacuum, divorced from ethics, particularly given the moral judgement of troubling. Justices, as individuals and members constituting the Court, may not ignore their obligation to universal moral norms, even if done at the expense of the Constitution. After all, the Constitution itself is to be interpreted in terms accountable to these same norms, emanating as they do from the natural law of reason concordant with human nature. Assessed in this light, it is hard to see how protecting the centrality—falsely claimed, as we shall see—of tobacco to the nation's national and international economy justifies tolerating an appalling mortality rate associated with the use of tobacco.

Unfortunately, O'Connor's showed no awareness of the normative import of her moral judgement. Even as she condemned smoking, O'Connor contradicted herself when she invoked the law to prevent the FDA from pursuing steps to prevent young children and adolescents from starting to smoke. These steps, she argued, would be inconsistent with the administrative structure that Congress enacted into law for the regulation of tobacco, oblivious apparently to the logical inconsistency of the argument, given her condemnation of smoking.

TOBACCO AND THE ECONOMY

By the time O'Connor came to write her decision, she would have been well aware of the seriousness of the threat starting to smoke posed for both individuals and society. Despite this, she chose in favor of Congress' assessment of the importance of the tobacco industry to the strength of the United States' economy. The tobacco industry was too big to fail, even if its success cost hundreds of thousands of lives. However, the findings of a report funded by the Robert Wood Johnson Foundation and published also in 2000, could, with reason, be considered to question this assessment.[89]

According to the report, the argument of the tobacco industry had been that to stop growing tobacco and manufacturing and marketing tobacco products would be disastrous for the U.S. economy, domestic and international, with undesirable outcomes for employment, income, "tax revenues," and "trade surpluses." But in the case of the "six southeastern" states of the so-called

U.S. "tobacco bloc," the key "tobacco sectors" accounted only for "1.6%" of employment, while 50% of U.S. tobacco counties generated under "1%" of their revenues "from tobacco." "Tobacco plays a minor economic role in most local economies where it is grown."[90] Nevertheless, the tobacco industry liked to pretend that should economic activity in tobacco-related industry contract, it would be accompanied proportionately by a contraction in the "economy" overall. Here, the tobacco industry was falsely insinuating that when someone stopped buying cigarettes, the expenditures associated with tobacco use would no longer be in play at all in the economy. But as the report observed, the reality was that the money was reallocated and became available for expenditures in other areas of the economy where it contributed to the expansion of commercial enterprises other than tobacco. As the report noted, economic experts with no ties to the tobacco industry had shown how the diversion of money resulting from people stopping smoking did not have a negative effect on the nation's labor market or economy overall.

In its extensive lobbying, the tobacco industry also liked to raise the specter of employment contractions due to fewer and fewer people smoking. While true, according to the report, that any acceleration could occasion outbreaks of job loss of short duration among those working in the tobacco industry until alternative employment was secured, those alternative employment opportunities would likely have come from the expansion of industries benefiting from changes in consumers purchasing. "However, the types of declines in tobacco consumption witnessed in the major industrialized nations are so gradual that they create few transitional problems of any consequence."[91] According to the report, compared with the transitory difficulties experienced in the contraction of economic activity in the "steel industry," those in the tobacco industry were negligible. It concluded that there was little of concern for national economies in robust attempts undertaken to regulate tobacco.

One of the steps taken in government initiatives to control the use of tobacco was to impose a tax surcharge. The report noted that the tobacco industry had objected to this on the grounds that the resulting increase in the cost of smoking cigarettes was borne by the poor. Fairness, the industry argued, called for "progressive" not "regressive" taxation policies. As the report noted, in the majority of countries the smoking rate was higher among those at the poverty level rather than among the wealthier in their populations. As a consequence, any additional levies on tobacco simply exacerbated matters for the poor.

On its face, this argument seemed persuasive, but at the same time it was troubling to those seeking to control and lessen the harm associated with tobacco use. Persuasive though it appeared, however, the argument was not without its inaccuracies. But even to the extent it might have been, the regressive consequences of additional levies were not as burdensome as usually thought. Here, according to the report, it was important to draw a distinction between the fact that an existing tax on tobacco would have to be apportioned "regressively" and the fact that a "tax increase on that" might not in its effect have been "regressive" in effect. The validity of the distinction derived from a third fact that in the face of a tax increase, the less well-off were more likely than the well-off to react by limiting their smoking or stopping it altogether. On this point, a different study conducted in the United States found that those earning less were inclined to react to increases in the pricing of cigarettes that was "70%" higher than those earning more.[92] In this light, concerns over the potential for regressive consequences in the use of tax increases to control tobacco consumption were probably much less urgent. However, the cynicism evident in that the tobacco industry would exploit them to prevent tobacco control should not have been lost on members of Congress.

In closing, the report discussed the larger context within which for present purposes it is useful to assess Congress' administrative structure for the regulation of tobacco. This is the "U.S. tobacco agriculture support system" which, according to the report, was a combination of subsidies and production limits. Here, consideration of subsidies is particularly relevant since it occasioned, predictably because of the money involved, a powerful interest group active politically advocating for the industry. As the report put it, "the political power of the tobacco bloc in the US Congress is legendary."[93] It should have surprised no one how that power was deployed effectively as a constant restraint on Congressional "tobacco control policies." It would also have been hard, as a result, to argue with the report when it declared that had there been no "tobacco bloc," it was quite likely that members of Congress would have been more disposed to increase "tobacco taxes," and to insist on federal controls for "smoking" in restaurants and bars, for example. along with more robust restraints on the industry's agenda for encouraging cigarette use.

Since the data for this report, if not the report itself, were already generally available while judicial review was underway, one has to ask why the data played no part in the Court's proceedings in this case? In very large measure, the majority relied for its rejection of the FDA's proposed interventions as unconstitutional on the administrative structure for tobacco control enacted into law by Congress. Were that structure, in any reasonable sense, to be construed in the interests of the public's health, the Court's reliance might be considered justified. But if the report just discussed was to be believed, the structure was based on Congress's assessment of the central importance of the tobacco industry to the national economy. But that assessment, which the majority appeared to have accepted without qualification, was driven by a powerful political constituency acting in the interests of tobacco. What attention was paid to the public's health interests by Congress consisted in an exclusive reliance on a campaign informing the public of the dangers of tobacco use. Once made fully aware, Congress reasoned, people would become informed consumers and knowing the risks to their health would be in a position to make an informed choice about smoking. But, once more, one has to ask how realistic was the likelihood of choice in relation to the use of cigarettes when their use is deliberately designed by cigarette manufactures to be addictive?

In the case of tobacco use, the relation between informed choice and nicotine finds its most compelling expression in the universal difficulty smokers encounter when they attempt to stop smoking. According to the National Academy of Sciences, "the typical case of tobacco addiction involves a person who began smoking as a teenager; rapidly escalated to daily use and to nicotine addiction; and eventually has a 'smoking career' of 15–20 years of frequent daily use characterized by heavy regret and punctuated by unsuccessful efforts to quit."[94] In light of this portrait of a typical case, it becomes quite clear what a thin reed, in the form of signs warning of the dangers of smoking on cigarette packaging, Congress chose to ensure that tobacco consumers were freely choosing to be smokers when "addiction surrenders later freedom to choose."[95]

If O'Connor found that the FDA's proposals for regulating tobacco use by adolescents were unconstitutional, then she had also concluded that the administrative structure for tobacco regulation enacted into law by Congress, with which these proposals were inconsistent, was constitutional. However, if the basis for this structure was an erroneous assessment of the importance of tobacco to the national economy, adopted by Congress under pressure from the tobacco industry, to what degree, if at all, can the structure be considered constitutional? And if, as key to the durability of tobacco's alleged economic importance, the same structure allowed cigarette manufacturers to manipulate the highly addictive nature of nicotine in their design of cigarettes, should that not have been a serious concern for O'Connor in assessing the constitutionality of the administrative structure?

What then is meant by *being constitutional*? In its simplest form, the answer is to be in conformity with the language in which the Constitution of the United States is written. This, however, barely does justice to the question. Its presence nevertheless is evident throughout O'Connor's decision which reflected nothing of the fact that the U.S. Constitution is fundamentally a moral document, in the pre-moral sense advanced by John Locke,[96] providing a normative framework within which the mutual and reciprocal behaviors of the governing and the governed are responsibly undertaken. Nowhere is this more urgently to be recognized than in the matter of tobacco marketing and use under government supervision, the consequence of which at the time of this decision was a mortality rate of 400,000 smokers annually.

The data on smoking and its negative impact on life expectancy show how important it is to stop smoking, despite the difficulty due to addiction. A study examining "government data on more than 200,000 Americans," starting in 1997, showed that people who stopped smoking between the ages of "25–34 gained around 10 years of life" expectancy, while those who stopped between the ages of "35–44" saved some "9 years" of life expectancy. Those who quit later, between the ages of "45–59" saved between "4–6 years of life" expectancy.[97] Given the centrality of addiction to smoking, one would have expected O'Connor to make use of such data, available at the time, in her assessment of the constitutionality of the administrative structure. There is no evidence in her decision that she did.

The Constitution, as we know, opens with the words, "We the people of the United States, in order to . . . promote the general Welfare, and secure the Blessings of Liberty to ourselves and our Posterity, do ordain and establish this Constitution for the United States of America." Unmistakably, the words, *in order to*, demonstrate that in the mind of those writing the document, the Constitution was understood to be a means to secure collectively specific political, economic, and societal values, such as justice, domestic peace, and national defense. The Constitution, however important, is not an end in itself. It is a means. Unfortunately, it has not always been a reliable instrument to secure these values. This is because they stand apart from but are available to the Constitution which did not generate them, but serves to confirm them as identified with human nature and rationally constitutive of it.

In the Introduction, we discussed how the Constitution was formulated as the practical application of the principles informing the Declaration of Independence. We also saw how the principles invoked to justify the Declaration were derived from natural law. Now, while the Declaration is derived immediately from natural law, the Constitution, given its relation to the Declaration is derived, but one step removed, from natural law. As a consequence, to say of something, such as the FDA's proposals for the regulation of tobacco, that it is unconstitutional is ambiguous. Viewing the Constitution as something self-contained or self-sufficient while declaring something unconstitutional means one thing. But viewing the Constitution as a derivative, while declaring the same thing unconstitutional, means something else.

To view the Constitution as self-contained is to interpret and apply it from the perspective of legal positivism in which law stands, as long as it is enacted by those authorized to enact it. It is law because it is so ordered. Anything deemed inconsistent with the law as it stands is unconstitutional. And since, according to O'Connor's reading of the terms of *FDCA*, tobacco regulation was restricted exclusively to Congress, any proposals to this end by the FDA would have to be regarded as inconsistent with Congressional intentions and therefore unconstitutional. But this would be true only if the

Constitution incorrectly is regarded as self-sufficient, with judicial review serving, in the final analysis, to confirm this self-sufficiency, regardless of the consequences, which in this case was the continuation of the protection of tobacco use as intended by Congress. It is true that Breyer's review, using the same means, brought him to a quite different conclusion. This suggests that the Constitution occasions contradictory outcomes. And despite the declared victorious decision, the underlying contradiction remains in place as long as judicial review is denied, in the final analysis, recourse to ethics. Since it took Congress nine years to change matters with the passage of the *Family Smoking Prevention and Tobacco Control Act* (2009),[98] the Court was, with this decision, complicit in the harm inflicted in the meantime by an insufficiently regulated tobacco industry.

Had O'Connor placed the Constitution at its ultimate source, natural law, her review of this case would have had a rather different and preferable outcome. With the understanding of law as law because just, Congress' administrative structure would have been judged correctly as unethical, based as it was on false economic premises and because of the fatal harm to people its constitutional protection permitted to continue.

Enacting law, like conducting judicial review is unavoidably morally conditioned behavior in that whatever results from either activity is other-regarding, with very specific consequences for other persons. And since members of Congress and the Court are responsible for these consequences, before taking any action, their overriding responsibility to the people affected requires them to ask the fundamental ethics question, should I, or should I not, do this? For the reasons just discussed, the Justices, for example, cannot assume that their obligations to the Constitution are equivalent to those they have to the people affected by judgments made in any given case. The Constitution is there as a means for the benefit of the people. It should not be considered the other way around. Yet the history of judicial review, conducted without regard for the Constitution's ethical origins in objective, universal reason in conformity with nature is replete with evidence of this assumption, and the wrongly decided cases, including this case, resulting from it.

NOTES

1. U.S. Congress, *Food, Drug, and Cosmetics Act* (*FDCA*), 21 U.S.C. 301 (1938), https://www.loc.gov/item/uscode1934-006021009/ (accessed October 22, 2020).

2. U.S. Supreme Court, *FDA v. Brown & Williamson Tobacco Corporation*, 529 U.S. 120 (2000), at 125 https://supreme.justia.com/cases/federal/us/529/120/case.html (accessed October 22, 2020).

3. *FDA v. Brown* at 125.

4. U.S. Congress, *FDCA*, 21 U.S.C. Sect. 301 ff.

5. U.S. Congress, *Annex Nicotine in Cigarettes and Smokeless Tobacco Is a Drug and These Products Are Nicotine Delivery Devices Under the Federal Food, Drug, and Cosmetic Act:* Jurisdictional Determination, 61 FR 44619 (August 28, 1996), https://www.govinfo.gov/content/pkg/FR-1996-08-28/pdf/X96-20828.pdf (accessed October 22, 2020).

6. U.S. Congress, *Annex Nicotine*, ix.

7. U.S. Congress, *Annex Nicotine*, 10.

8. U.S. Congress, *Annex Nicotine*, 10.

9. U.S. Congress, *Annex Nicotine*, 563 ff.

10. *FDA v. Brown* at 125.

11. U.S. Congress, *Annex Nicotine*, 567.

12. U.S. Court of Appeals, *National Nutritional Foods Ass'n v. FDA*, 504 F.2d 761 (2d Cir. 1974), https://openjurist.org/504/f2d/761/national-nutritional-foods-association-v-food-and-drug-administration (accessed October 22, 2020), cited in U.S. Congress, *Annex Nicotine*, 568.

13. U.S. Court of Appeals, *Action on Smoking and Health ASH v. Harris*, 655 F.2d 236 (D.C. Cir. 1980), https://law.justia.com/cases/federal/appellate-courts/F2/655/236/65200/ (accessed October 20, 2020).

14. U.S. Court of Appeals, *Action on Smoking v. Harris* at 242n10.

15. U.S. Congress, *Federal Cigarette Labeling and Advertising Act*, 15 U.S.C. 1331–1340, 21 U.S.C. 387c (1966), https://www.ftc.gov/enforcement/statutes/federal-cigarette-labeling-advertising-act (accessed October 22, 2020); and U.S. Congress, *Comprehensive Smokeless Tobacco Health Education Act*, 15 U.SC. 4401–4408 (1986), https://www.ftc.gov/enforcement/statutes/comprehensive-smokeless-tobacco-health-education-act-1986 (accessed October 22, 2020).

16. U.S. Congress, *Consumer Products Safety Act* (*CPSA*), 15 U.S.C 2051–2089, PL 92–573, 86 Stat. 1207 (1972), https://www.cpsc.gov/PageFiles/105435/cpsa.pdf?epslanguage=en (accessed October 22, 2020).

17. U.S. Congress, *Annex Nicotine*, 597ff.

18. U.S. Congress, *Annex Nicotine*, 601; see Hearings Before the Consumer Subcommittee of the Senate Committee On Commerce, S. 1454 (92nd Cong., 2nd sess.), 239 (1972)

19. U.S. Congress, *Annex Nicotine*, 600.

20. U.S. Congress, *Annex Nicotine*, 602.

21. U.S. Congress, *Annex Nicotine*, 607; see Conf. Rep. 897 (91st. Cong., 2nd sess.), 2 (1970)

22. U.S. Congress, *Annex Nicotine*, 608.

23. U.S. Congress, *Annex Nicotine*, 608.

24. U.S. Congress, *Annex Nicotine*, 609; see *Connecticut National Bank v. Germain*, 503 U.S. 249, 253 (1992)

25. U.S. Congress, *Annex Nicotine*, 609; see *Morton v. Mancari*, 417 U.S. 535, 551 (1974).

26. U.S. Congress, *Annex Nicotine*, 582.

27. U.S. Congress, *Annex Nicotine*, 582; see U.S. Department of Health and Human Services (HHS), Office on Smoking and Health, *Preventing Tobacco Use Among Young People: A Report of the Surgeon General*, vol. 43, no. RR-4 (Atlanta: CDC, 1994), https://www.cdc.gov/mmwr/PDF/rr/rr4304.pdf (accessed October 22, 2020).

28. U.S. Congress, *Annex Nicotine*, 583.

29. U.S. Congress, *Annex Nicotine*, 584; see HHS, *Preventing Tobacco*, 5.

30. U.S. Congress, *Annex Nicotine*, 584; see J. Price, "Teen Smoking, Marijuana Use Increase Sharply, Study Shows," *Washington Times*, December 16, 1995.

31. U.S. Congress, *Annex Nicotine*, 585; see Robert Bezilla and George H. Gallup International Institute, "Teenage Attitudes and Behavior Concerning Tobacco-Report of the Findings," ICPSR 6252 (1992), https://doi.org/10.3886/ICPSR06252.v1 (accessed October 22, 2020).

32. U.S. Congress, *Annex Nicotine*, 585; see Centers for Disease Control and Prevention (CDC), "Reasons for Tobacco Use and Symptoms of Nicotine Withdrawal Among Adolescent and Young Adult Tobacco Users-United States, 1993," *Morbidity and Mortality Weekly* 43, no. 41 (1994): 745–50.

33. U.S. Congress, *Regulations Restricting the Sale and Distribution of Cigarettes and Smokeless Tobacco Products To Protect Children and Adolescents*, 60 FR 155, 41321–41338 (August 11, 1995), https://www.govinfo.gov/content/pkg/FR-1995-08-11/pdf/95-20051.pdf (accessed October 22, 2020).

34. U.S. Congress, *Regulations Restricting the Sale* (1995), Summary at 41314.

35. U.S. Congress, *Regulations Restricting the Sale* (1995), Summary at 41314.

36. See U.S. Department of Health and Human Services, *Healthy People 2000: National health Promotion and Disease Prevention Objectives, A Strategy for Improving the Health of Americans by the End of the Century* (Atlanta: CDC, 1990), https://www.cdc.gov/nchs/healthy_people/hp2000.htm (accessed October 22, 2020).

37. U.S. Congress, *Regulations Restricting the Sale* (1995), Summary at 41314.

38. U.S. Congress, *Regulations Restricting the Sale* (1995), Summary at 41315; and see the Institute of Medicine (IOM), *Growing Up Tobacco Free: Preventing Nicotine Addiction in Children and Youths*, ed. Barbara S. Lynch and Richard J. Bonnie (Washington, DC: National Academies Press, 1994); and previously noted U.S. Department of HHS, *Preventing Tobacco Use Among Young People*.

39. U.S. Congress, *Regulations Restricting the Sale* (1995), Summary at 41317; see IOM, *Growing Up Tobacco Free*, 115; Centers for Disease Control and Prevention (CDC), "Cigarette Smoking-Attributable Mortality and Years of Potential Life Lost-United States, 1990," *Morbidity and Mortality Weekly Report* 42, no. 33 (August 27, 1993): 645–49, https://www.jstor.org/stable/41965095 (accessed October 22, 2020).

40. U.S. Congress, *Regulations Restricting the Sale* (1995), Summary at 41315.

41. U.S. Congress, *Regulations Restricting the Sale* (1995), Summary at 41314.

42. *FDA v. Brown* at 130.

43. *FDA v. Brown* at 132. See U.S. Supreme Court, *Chevron U.S.A., Inc. v. Natural Resources Defense Council, Inc.*, 467 U.S. 837 (1984), https://supreme.justia.com/cases/federal/us/467/837/ (accessed October 22, 2020).

44. *FDA v. Brown* at 133.

45. *FDA v. Brown* at 134; see U.S. Congress, *FDCA*, 21 U.S.C., sec. 360j(e)

46. *FDA v. Brown* at 134; see U.S. Supreme Court, *United States v. Rutherford*, 442 U.S. 544, 556 (1979), https://supreme.justia.com/cases/federal/us/442/544/ (accessed October 22, 2020).

47. U.S. Congress, *FDCA*, 21 U.S.C., sec. 352(f)(1)

48. *FDA v. Brown* at 175; Breyer dissenting

49. U.S. Congress, *FDCA*, 21 U.S.C., sec. 360j(e)(1)

50. U.S. Congress, *FDCA*, 21 U.S.C., sec. 360f(a)

51. U.S. Congress, *FDCA*, 21 U.S.C., sec. 360c(a)(1)(C)

52. *FDA v. Brown* at 176.

53. U.S. Congress, *Regulations Restricting the Sale* (1995), at 41317

54. Aristotle, *The Nicomachean Ethics*, trans. J. A. K. Thomson (New York: Penguin Books, 1965), 27.

55. *Penguin Dictionary of Philosophy*, ed. Thomas Mautner (London: Penguin Books, 1997), 585.

56. U.S. Congress, *Regulations Restricting the Sale and Distribution of Cigarettes and Smokeless Tobacco Products To Protect Children and Adolescents*, 61 FR 168, 44396–44618 (August 28, 1996), at 44398, https://www.govinfo.gov/content/pkg/FR-1996-08-28/pdf/X96-10828.pdf (accessed October 22, 2020).

57. *FDA v. Brown* at 140.

58. *FDA v. Brown* at 137.

59. *FDA v. Brown* at 137; see 7 U.S.C. sec. 1311(a).

60. *FDA v. Brown* at 139.

61. *FDA v. Brown* at 139.

62. U.S. Congress, *FDCA*, 21 U.S.C., sec. 360h(e)(2)(B)(i)(II).

63. U.S. Congress, *Regulations Restricting the Sale* (1996), at 45263.

64. *FDA v. Brown* at 144.

65. *FDA v. Brown* at 144; Breyer dissenting, at 181.

66. *FDA v. Brown* at 144.

67. *FDA v. Brown* at 144.

68. *FDA v. Brown* at 182.

69. *FDA v. Brown* at 182.

70. *FDA v. Brown* at 183.

71. *FDA v. Brown* at 186.

72. *FDA v. Brown* at 168.

73. *FDA v. Brown* at 169.

74. *FDA v. Brown* at 125.

75. *FDA v. Brown* at 186, dissent.

76. *FDA v. Brown* at 186.

77. *FDA v. Brown* at 187.

78. *FDA v. Brown* at 186.

79. *FDA v. Brown* at 187.

80. *FDA v. Brown* at 189.

81. *FDA v. Brown* at 190.

82. *FDA v. Brown* at 192.

83. See U.S. Supreme Court, *ETSI Pipeline Project v. Missouri*, 484 U.S. 495 (1988), at 517, https://supreme.justia.com/cases/federal/us/484/495/ (accessed October 22, 2020).

84. R. M. [Richard Mervyn] Hare, *The Language of Morals* (Oxford: Clarendon Press, 2003), 127.

85. P. H. Nowell-Smith, *Ethics* (Baltimore, MD: Penguin Books, 1961), 74.

86. Nowell-Smith, *Ethics*, 69

87. Hare, *Language of Morals*, 1.

88. Hare, *Language of Morals*, 1.

89. Kenneth E. Warner, "The Economics of Tobacco: Myths and Realities," *Tobacco Control Journal* 9, no. 1 (2000): 78–89, http://dx.doi.org/10.1136/tc.9.1.78 (accessed October 22, 2020).

90. See Fred Gale, "Economic Structure of Tobacco-Growing Regions," *Tobacco Situation and Outlook*, U.S. Department of Agriculture, Economic Research Service, TBS-241 (April 1998): 40–47.

91. Warner, "The Economics of Tobacco."

92. See Centers for Disease Control and Prevention (CDC), M. C. Farrelly, J. W. Bray, and Research Triangle Institute, "Response to Increases in Cigarette Prices by Race/Ethnicity, Income, and Age Groups—United States, 1976–1993," *Morbidity and Mortality Weekly Report* 47, no. 29 (July 31, 1998): 605–28, https://www.cdc.gov/mmwr/PDF/wk/mm4729.pdf (accessed October 22, 2020).

93. Warner, "The Economics of Tobacco."

94. Institute of Medicine (IOM), *Ending the Tobacco Problem: A Blueprint for the Nation*, ed. Richard J. Bonnie, Kathleen Stratton, and Robert B. Wallace. Washington, DC: National Academies Press, 2007.

95. Russell M. Nelson, "Addiction or Freedom," *Church of Jesus Christ of Latter-Day Saints*, From a conference address delivered October 1988, https://www.churchofjesuschrist.org/study/new-era/1989/09/addiction-or-freedom?lang=eng (accessed October 22, 2020).

96. `See John Locke, *The Two Treatises of Civil Government* (1689; 1764), in *Classics of Liberty: The Enhanced Editions*, https://oll.libertyfund.org/page/john-locke-two-treatises-1689 (accessed December 10, 2020).

97. Anahad O'Connor, "Putting a Number on Smoking's Toll," *New York Times* (New York), January 29, 2013, D4, and online January 23, 2013, https://well.blogs.nytimes.com/2013/01/23/putting-a-number-to-smokings-toll/ (accessed October 22, 2020). See also Prabhat Jha, Chinthanie Ramasundarahettige, Victoria Landsman, Brian Rostron, et al., "21st-Century Hazards of Smoking and Benefits of Cessation in the United States," *New England Journal of Medicine* 368 (2013): 341–50, https://www.nejm.org/doi/10.1056/NEJMsa1211128 (accessed October 22, 2020).

98. U.S. Congress, *Family Smoking Prevention and Tobacco Control Act*, PL 111-13 (111th Cong., 1st sess.) (2009), https://www.congress.gov/bill/111th-congress/house-bill/1256 (accessed October 23, 2020).

Chapter 5

United States v. Morrison, 529 U.S. 598 (2000): Legal Formalism versus Human Rights, Federal Civil Remedies and the Victims of Gender-Motivated Violence

The U.S. Supreme Court (2000) stated: "If the allegations here are true, no civilized system of justice could fail to provide her a remedy."[1] The case concerned Christy Brzonkala who, in 1994, was a student at Virginia Polytechnic Institute, and her allegation that two other students, Antonio Morrison and James Crawford had raped her repeatedly.

FACTS OF THE CASE

The following year, she filed a complaint against Morrison and Crawford under the sexual assault policy of the Institute. Morrison was found guilty of sexual assault, following a hearing, and suspended immediately for two semesters. Crawford, due to lack of sufficient evidence, avoided any punishment. In July 1995, Brzonkala was informed that Morrison was going to pursue a court challenge to his conviction under the Institute's sexual assault policy. A second hearing was conducted on the grounds that the first hearing was mistakenly conducted under a policy at the time not well known to the student body. Accordingly, the second hearing was conducted under the University's earlier Abusive Conduct Policy. Morrison was again found guilty and suspended for two semesters. However, the description of the offense was changed from "sexual assault" to "using abusive language." Morrison then appealed the outcome of the second hearing through the Institute's administrative system.[2] On August 21, 1995, the Institute's senior vice president and provost set aside the suspension as excessive compared to other cases heard under the Abusive Conduct Policy. The Institute did not inform Brzonkala of this decision. When, however, she learned from a press report that Morrison would be returning to the Institute for the fall semester, she withdrew from the school. Subsequently Brzonkala sued Morrison, Crawford, and Virginia Polytechnic Institute in Federal District Court, alleging that the rape by Morrison and Crawford violated section 13981 of the *Violence Against Women Act* (*VAWA*) (1994) which afforded federal civil redress to victims of gender-motivated violence.[3] Both Morrison and Crawford moved to dismiss Brzonkala's suit, arguing that the civil redress provision of section 13981 was unconstitutional. The District Court agreed, finding that U.S. Congress lacked authority to enact section 13981 under either the Commerce Clause or the Fourteenth Amendment. Subsequently, the U.S. Court of Appeals, in a divided opinion, affirmed the District Court's ruling. The case finally went to the U.S. Supreme Court on writs of *certiorari* (to be made certain) because the Court of Appeals had invalidated federal legislation.[4]

JUDICIAL REVIEW

According to Chief Justice William Rehnquist, who delivered the opinion of the Court, the central constitutional question was the legitimacy of section 13981 of *VAWA*, 42 U.S.C. which provided federal civil redress to victims of gender-motivated violence on the grounds that every person in the United States has a right to be free from violence of this nature.[5] The statute declared that anyone committing such a crime, thereby denying another of the right stipulated, was answerable to the injured person for damages and any additional relief the Court might find owing.[6] The crime of violence intended in the statute was one that was committed specifically because of the gender of the victim. The statute defined a crime of violence, whether against a person or against property that resulted in harm to persons, as a felony and was punishable by imprisonment for more than a year. Furthermore, litigants under section 13981 could turn to either federal or state courts for redress since both had concurrent jurisdiction over complaints brought under this section. The statute was also clear that it excluded, among other things, random acts of violence unrelated to gender.

Having identified the intent and reach of section 13981, Justice Rehnquist noted that any law enacted by Congress must emanate from any one or a combination of its enumerated powers under the U.S. Constitution. In this case, he pointed out, U.S. Congress had justified its legislation based on the provisions of section 5 of the Fourteenth Amendment to the Constitution, in addition to those of section 8 of article 1 of the Constitution. Accordingly, the Court would assess the authority of Congress to authorize redress under these constitutional provisions.[7] And, it would do so with due deference to a coequal branch of Government and a presumption of constitutionality, unless it was clear that Congress had acted beyond its constitutional limits.[8]

The petitioners, the United States and Brzonkala, based their case on the provision found in the third clause of article 1, section 8 of the Constitution which gave Congress authority to regulate commerce internationally and domestically. With regard to the history of the Commerce Clause, Rehnquist noted that since 1937, Congress had enjoyed greater regulatory latitude than earlier case law sanctioned. Nevertheless, citing his earlier decision in *United States v. Lopez* (1995),[9] he added that this expansion of regulatory power did have its limits. In *Lopez*, the concern was for the federal-state system of government lest further regulatory expansion would in effect amount to a completely centralized government.[10] In *Lopez*, the Court recognized three broad categories within which Congress could regulate commerce. The first involved the use of the channels of interstate commerce. The second involved the instrumentalities of interstate commerce. The third involved activities related to interstate commerce in such a way as to affect it substantially.[11] It is under this third category that Petitioners sought redress, contending that crimes of violence motivated by gender bias had a negative effect on interstate commerce. Of the three categories available, Rehnquist was in agreement that this was the appropriate one to pursue. Further, since *Lopez* had served to clarify the Court's understanding of this third category, it now provided an appropriate frame of reference for reviewing this case.[12]

In *Lopez*, the Court had ruled that the *Gun-Free School Zones Act* (*GFSZA*) (1990),[13] making possession of a gun in a school zone a federal crime was an overreach under the Commerce Clause. As a criminal statute, the *Act* had nothing to do with commerce, unlike the "wide variety of congressional acts regulating intrastate economic activity where we have concluded that the activity substantially affected interstate commerce."[14] As Rehnquist saw it, there is an obvious consistency in the Court's analysis, one accurately reflected in *Lopez*: "Where economic activity substantially affects interstate commerce, legislation regulating that activity will be sustained."[15] In contrast with Petitioners and with Justice David Souter's dissent, Rehnquist was not prepared to dilute the economic nature of the activity being regulated under the Commerce Clause. As he put it, "a fair reading of *Lopez* shows that the noneconomic, criminal nature of the conduct at issue was central to our decision in that case."[16] While Rehnquist admitted that "any conduct in our interdependent world" may in the final analysis have some origin or outcome in commerce, the Court has not been prepared to say that the regulating power under the Commerce Clause may reach that far.[17]

There were two additional issues of concern that influenced the decision in *Lopez*. The first was the absence in the statute of an explicit jurisdictional provision limiting its reach to the possession of a discrete set of firearms that clearly affected interstate commerce. The second concern was the absence of any empirical evidence advanced by Congress to demonstrate the effects on "interstate commerce of gun possession in a school zone."[18] Rehnquist conceded there was no requirement for Congress to provide data of this kind. Nevertheless, having the data could have been helpful in measuring the soundness of its judgment that gun possession in a school zone did have a negative effect on interstate commerce even though the effect may not have been readily apparent.[19] The Court, however, was not persuaded by the argument that possession of guns might have led to violent crime which in turn led to significant costs to the national economy. No more persuasive was the argument that violent crime inhibited travel to areas of the country thought to be dangerous. Finally, the argument that gun possession at schools compromised educational activities, thus resulting in a less well-prepared work force which would be detrimental to interstate commerce was also rejected.[20] As Rehnquist, citing *Lopez* put it, to concede these arguments would allow Congress to "regulate not only all violent crime, but all activities that might lead to violent crime, regardless of how tenuously they relate to interstate commerce."[21] Having taken his cue from *Lopez*, Rehnquist had no hesitation in concluding that gender-based crimes of violence "are not, in any sense of the phrase, economic activity."[22] There might be something to this emphatic assertion, were it true that we could equate as an economic activity gender-based violence with possession of a gun in a school zone. The former, is an extremely complex societal reality that calls for a far more nuanced review than Rehnquist's decision provided. As a result, it failed to deliver what was owed to women [and men] who have been, or will be, the victims of gender-based crimes of violence. In violating the fundamental principle of justice, the decision was unethical.

GENDER-BASED VIOLENCE CAUSES ECONOMIC ACTIVITY

The injustice began with the refusal to recognize, despite the overwhelming evidence provided by Congress, that, at its core, gender-based violence was economic in nature and by design. "Traditionally, primary economic activity involves production, distribution and consumption of goods and services at all levels in any given society."[23] In contrast, "non-economic activity consists in activities that have no monetary measurement and is performed without regard to monetary gain."[24] As a way of conceptually distinguishing between economic and non-economic activity, this was reasonable. Applied to gender-based violence, if Rehnquist was correct, it would mean that there was no way to measure this violence in economic terms. Was that the case? There were two ways to answer this question. The first way was to show a causal connection between the act of violence and economic activity as a direct consequence specific to the violence itself, in the absence of which this economic activity would not have occurred without affecting commerce significantly.

For example, in 2005, the United Nations issued an expert brief on the economic costs of violence against women.[25] The brief noted that economic costing studies have the ability to consider different cost categories, and might use different methods of data collection and employ different calculations for reaching estimated costs. "A common component is their use of a basic accounting model to aggregate costs."[26] According to the brief, the model should be thought of as a matrix of effects across many aspects of society. It added that each entry in the matrix stood for a cost to an individual or an organization in society and was assessed in a unique manner. Summing all the entries resulted in the total cost while still identifying the variety of specific costs involved. However, calculating costs within each category of cost was the same. As the brief explained it, each consequence of violence represented "goods or services used by the victims, their family, friends, or co-workers or the perpetrator."[27] The quantity of the service used was then multiplied by the cost of the service for each consequence in every category of costs. With all of the costs calculated separately, they could be combined to provide an aggregate cost.

To illustrate how this methodology was applied in practice, the brief presented the case of women who phone the police or go to the emergency room after falling victim to violence.[28] As the brief explained, phoning the police involved officer hours and administrative overheads. Since going to the emergency ward involved staff time, technical assessments of victims were necessary to calculate the number of victims using specific goods and services, as well as the level of use involved. Data on the cost of each of the goods and services were required in addition. Also needed was to know how many women phoned the police, and how many women went to emergency wards as a result of violence. When they did, what was the average amount of time spent with victims while providing the service. What were the materials used when servicing the needs of a victim. The hourly rate of police services and the in-hospital costs of x-rays, staff salaries, or over-night hospital stays had also to be accounted for.

In sum, the total cost of violence against women was to measured against categories of costs, percent of violence victims using services, percent of population not affected by violence but using services, the total number of violence victims eligible to use service, and the per-person cost of service.[29]

As a result, the level of service was measured by taking the differential usage rate of victims of violence and multiplying it by the number of victims so as to get the number of victims using service as a result of violence. The costs resulting from violence were then found by multiplying that figure by the per person cost of providing the service. It is important to note that the use of the same services for reasons other than gender-based violence can and must be subtracted otherwise the true costs of this violence will be overstated.

Among the several national studies on violence against women, the brief listed the 2003 study undertaken by the Institute for Women of Andalusia, Spain.[30] The study was based on a national survey on violence against women and a survey of 300 women victims undertaken to assess information about their service usage over the lifetime of their suffering. Compiling more than one hundred indicators of the effects of violence on women and on their children, the study estimated the costs in 2002 at $2.9 billion in US dollars for health, judicial, social, educational, employment, and psychological components, in addition to pain and suffering.

GENDER-BASED VIOLENCE IS ECONOMIC ACTIVITY

The second, more significant but overlooked way to understand how gender-based violence relates to economic activity was to demonstrate that it actually constituted, in itself, an economic activity. This became quite clear when this particular violence was examined from the perspective of women's economic empowerment. Ultimately, the origins of violence against women could be found in what OXFAM America called, in its 2015 report, unequal gender relations, or gender-based expressions of economic power.[31] Describing women's economic empowerment as the enjoyment of "their rights to control and benefit from resources, assets, income, and their own time, and . . . have the ability to manage risk and improve their economic status and well-being,"[32] the report focused on understanding why economic empowerment increased or decreased the risk of domestic violence. Ultimately, that depended on acknowledging gender-based violence, as distinct from other expressions of violence against women, for what it was, a denial of a woman's human right to exist as person, equal in every respect of personhood with a man. Although *United States v. Morrison* did not involve a case of domestic violence, it is critical to recognize its violence as traceable to the unequal gender relations long institutionalized in the conjugal setting where what is called domestic gender-based violence is common. Three years after the *Morrison* decision, the Centers for Disease Control and Prevention (CDC), citing its National Violence Against Women Survey, had found that about 3.5 million women, ages 18 years and older, experienced intimate partner violence (IPV) each year. This violence resulted, according to the survey, in 2 million injuries, more than 550,000 of which called for medical care. In addition, victims of IPV lost a total of nearly 8 million days of paid work, the equivalent of more than 32,000 full-time jobs and around 5.6 million days of household productivity as a consequence of this violence. The survey also reported that the costs of intimate partner rape, physical assault, and stalking amounted annually to $4.1 billion for direct medical and mental health care.[33] That violence of this frequency, unchecked by the inevitability of its severe consequences, occurred every year within the very intimacy of the conjugal setting, and illustrated as nothing else could how the identity of women as unequal to men had been institutionalized. And if there, where intimacy might be expected to generate mutual respect based on equality, should it have been surprising to find gender inequality expressed in settings considerably less intimate, such as a university, where there were no immediate forces conducive to men's appreciation of women as their equals? As if to confirm this, the Court's summary of the case included Brzonkala's claim that within thiry minutes of meeting Morrison and Crawford, they assaulted and repeatedly raped her. Following the violence, Morrison allegedly said to his victim, "You better not have any . . . diseases." The summary also included reports that, in the months after the rape, Morrison was allegedly heard saying publicly how "he liked to get girls drunk and. . .." The summary refrained from completing verbatim what was said but indicated that what was omitted could be found in the briefs filed with the Court. Paraphrased, it consisted of "debased remarks about what Morrison would do to women, vulgar remarks that cannot fail to shock and offend."[34] Nothing pointed to gender inequality as clearly as this kind of language did.

ECONOMIC POWER, GENDER INEQUALITY, AND GENDER-BASED VIOLENCE

The OXFAM Report, cited above, was designed around the concept of intersectionality. A feminist theory and analytical tool for understanding how gender interacted with an individual's other identities, such as race or class, it enabled seeing that the experience, whether of marginalization or privilege, was defined by gender. From there it led to the conclusion that whatever the resulting identity might be, whether it was marginalized or privileged, it would have been "determined, shaped by, and imbedded in social systems of power."[35]

Given its intersectional approach, the OXFAM Report positioned itself "between economic and gender-based expressions of power, between economic rights and the right to be free of violence."[36] From there, the report was quite clear that violence against women was an expression of unequal gender relations. Further, a woman's economic status in relation to this underlying gender inequality conditioned the risk of violence against her. Significantly, however, the report found nothing to suggest a correlation between a woman's economic improvement and a lower risk of violence. That was because the connections between women's economic empowerment and an increase or decrease in their risk of violence were conditioned by additional forces in their circumstances and environments.[37]

According to the report, understanding these connections was essential for securing what it called a more holistic empowerment of women as outlined above.[38] Three economic explanations, referring to the impact made by economic resources, were advanced to this end. The first had to do with bargaining occasioned by the conjugal relationship as a setting for negotiations around resources. If one started with the assumption that women depended economically on men and accepted some level of violence as part of the price for economic support, then had a woman increased her income, it might have lessened her risk of violence in proportion as her economic dependence lessened. The second economic explanation saw violence as an instrument employed for the purpose of controlling behavior or allocating resources. "As women become increasingly economically empowered, the risk of DV (domestic violence) may increase because men may use violence as an instrument to disrupt women's market-oriented behavior, seize women's income, or exert authority over managing it."[39] The third economic explanation of domestic violence indicated that as women's income increases, the risk of domestic violence might have lessened with the overall economic improvement of their households which, in turn, lessened the economic stress that men might have felt as the main bread winner in the family. It was, however, no less likely that men regarded women's economic empowerment as a threat to their status and responded by resorting to domestic violence.[40] All three explanations left no doubt that gender-based violence was inherently economic in nature and in purpose.

The report was clear that while women's economic dependence on men occasions violence, other forces of a social and cultural nature also contribute. For example, in a society where the relations between men and women are relations of un-equals, domestic violence is more likely than not. An example of this would be the South African IMAGE project designed to reduce the risk of gender-based HIV resulting from sexual violence and women's economic dependency on men. The project involved a microfinance institution enabling women to participate in financial enterprises and providing a forum for participants to consider steps they could take against gender-based violence. Results from the project showed women improving their control within the household and reducing their experience of gender-based violence as their economic power developed and dependency on men lessened.[41]

That IMAGE was a response to circumstances in South Africa, arguably not entirely comparable to those in the United States, this should not detract from its relevance to the present discussion. It remains the case that IMAGE saw fit to address the societal and cultural forces directly associated with gender inequality, for the preservation of which gender-based violence was the chosen means since, in the final analysis, it was economic in nature and in purpose. If it was the case that economic empowerment resulted in either an increase or a decrease in violence, one could have drawn the reasonable conclusion that gender-based violence was a factor inherent to the economic status of women and their experience of economic power.

In light of this broadly-based evidence, the inescapable conclusion is that violence against women is itself an economic activity. Consequently, when Rehnquist rejected the position "that Congress may regulate non-economic, violent criminal conduct based solely on the conduct's aggregate effect on interstate commerce," he was working with an incomplete understanding of gender-based violence, seeing only the criminal aspect, and failing to see, as he ought, in the interests of a just decision, the essentially economic character of this violence. It was injustice inflicted violently, born of an institutionalized gender inequality. And that is what justifies the claim that gender-based violence is, in the final analysis, legitimately to be considered economic in nature and in purpose. That is why the evidence consistently shows that the underlying antidote to gender-based violence is not criminal justice that addresses symptoms so much as it is social justice that by de-institutionalizing gender inequality replaces it with women's economic empowerment. With gender inequality removed, and economic empowerment in place, gender-based violence is more likely to cease, or at least lessen. It was ironic that Rehnquist criticized Petitioners and Justice Souter's dissent for minimizing "the role that the economic nature of the regulated activity plays in our Commerce Clause analysis,"[42] when he had ruled out the inherently economic nature of gender-based violence as a result of incorrectly equating it with the possession of a firearm. It may be the case that gun possession in a school zone should not have been considered "an essential part of a larger regulation of economic activity."[43] It may be the case there was nothing commercial about the actors or their behavior. It may be there was nothing commercial in the design and purpose of the *GFSZA*.[44] "The Act neither regulates a commercial activity nor contains a requirement that the possession be connected in any way to interstate commerce."[45] That was hardly true of the statute at the center of this case.

THE COMMERCE CLAUSE

Rehnquist conceded that determining the commercial or non-commercial nature of any intrastate activity may result in legal uncertainty. In *Lopez*,[46] he imported Chief Justice John Marshall's definition of Congress' commerce power in which commerce as intercourse between nations and parts of nations was regulated in its conduct.[47] As something complete in itself, this power was exercised, Chief Justice Marshall asserted, without limitations other than those enumerated in the Constitution.[48] They included commercial activities that were purely internal, such as that conducted between persons in a state or different regions within the same state, without affecting other States. "The enumeration presupposes something not enumerated; and that something, if we regard the language, or the subject of the sentence, must be the exclusively internal commerce of a state."[49] Conditioned by this presupposition, it was not surprising, as Marshall concluded that "the question respecting the extent of the powers actually granted is perpetually arising, and will probably continue to arise as long as our system shall exist."[50]

Rehnquist's rehearsal of the history of the Court's commerce decisions bore this out. For a century following *Gibbons v. Ogden* (1824), the Court's decisions were less concerned with the reach of Congress' powers than with the limits the Commerce Clause placed on state legislation that was biased against interstate commerce. In 1887, the *Interstate Commerce Act* became law, followed in 1899 by the *Sherman Anti-Trust Act*. Subsequently, in cases connected to this legislation, the Court found that Congress could not regulate activities of production, manufacturing and mining because they were sources of commerce but not commerce itself. Nevertheless, the Court could not overlook those circumstances under which intrastate and interstate commercial activities intermingled to such a degree that the direct regulation of interstate commerce unavoidably necessitated indirect regulation of intrastate commerce. Here the Court acted on the belief that the distinction between "direct" and "indirect" was required if our constitutional system was to survive as intended. The distinction meant that activities affecting interstate commerce directly were within Congress' jurisdiction, while activities affecting intrastate commerce, having only an indirect impact, lay beyond its authority. Without it, there would be little possibility of limiting Congress' power and preventing a completely centralized government. But when the Court, in 1937, found for the *National Labor Relations Act*, it abandoned the "direct-indirect" distinction on the grounds that the reach of Congressional power was a matter of degree. Where intrastate activities were substantially related to interstate commercial activities, their control by Congress was required in the interests of interstate commerce. That is to say, there were circumstances where its control of intrastate commerce was a necessary means to ensure the exercise of Congress' granted power to regulate interstate commerce. For Rehnquist, a pivotal moment in this history came with *Wickard v. Filburn* (1942)[51] because it rejected previous "direct-indirect" effects on interstate commerce.[52] According to the *Wickard* Court, however local the activity, even non-commercial activity, "it may still, whatever its nature, be reached by Congress, if it exerts a substantial economic effect on inter-state commerce."[53]

According to Rehnquist, *Wickard* reflected a markedly expanded understanding of Congressional authority under the Commerce Clause. He interpreted this to be, in part, a recognition of the significant changes occurring in the way commerce was being conducted in the United States. What had been local or regional activities were becoming national in reach. It also reflected a philosophical change resulting from the view that earlier Commerce Clause decisions amounted to an artificial limitation on the federal government's authority to regulate interstate commerce. Despite *Wickard*, the Court, according to Rehnquist, remained alert against so expanded an authority that it threatened to replace our dual system of government with one wholly centralized.[54] Accordingly, the Court had, in its decisions, sought a rational basis on which to determine whether "a regulated activity sufficiently affected interstate commerce."[55]

RATIONAL BASIS FOR DETERMINING INTER-STATE COMMERCE

The key question now became what constituted a *rational basis*. Citing *Maryland v. Wirtz* (1968), Rehnquist noted that there the Court acknowledged that Congressional power to regulate commerce, though broad, was subject to limits which the Court had power to enforce.[56] As Justice John Marshall Harlan II, who wrote the decision put it, citing *Katzenbach v. McClung* (1964), "Of course the mere fact that Congress has said when a particular activity shall be deemed to affect commerce does not preclude further examination by this Court."[57] In a footnote in *Lopez*,[58] Rehnquist appeared to borrow Justice Harlan's language but not in its entirety. As Rehnquist transcribed it, "Simply because Congress may find that a particular activity substantially affects interstate commerce does not necessarily make it so."[59] His language, "does not make it so," is not quite the same as Harlan's "does not preclude further examination by this Court." Unlike Harlan, who believed the question must remain open, pending that examination, Rehnquist did not. In the same footnote, by way of elaboration, he cited Justice Hugo Black, concurring in *Heart of Atlanta Motel v. United States* (1964). "Whether particular operations affect interstate commerce sufficiently to come under the constitutional power of Congress to regulate them is ultimately a judicial rather than a legislative question and can only be settled finally by this Court."[60] Determining what amounted to sufficiently affecting commerce was for both Harlan and Rehnquist a necessary condition for establishing a rational basis by which to justify congressional power to regulate interstate commerce. "But when we find that the legislators . . . have a rational basis for finding a chosen regulatory scheme necessary to the protection of commerce, our investigation is at an end."[61] For Harlan, that meant assessing the validity of the empirical evidence provided as the rational basis for the conclusion that a particular activity did affect commerce. In *Maryland*, the Court found there was a rational basis "for the logical inference that the pay and hours of production employees affect a company's competitive position." But the logical inference reached further. Accordingly, for a company doing interstate business, its competition with companies elsewhere was affected by a constellation of its accompanying labor costs beyond those of employees having physical contact with goods and services under consideration.[62] It was important for Harlan to note that in *Katzenbach v. McClung,* it was evident that to justify the legislation involved there, Congress had completed an extensive investigation of the available evidence. However, a major objection to the extensions of the *Fair Labor Standards Act (FLSA)* (1938) was that the legislative history of the amendments before the Court provided no factual rationale for extending the original *Act*.[63] Even if this were true to whatever extent, Harlan declared it irrelevant. The original *Act*, he argued, provided, in its justification for the amendments, Congress' empirical evidence as of 1938. Any subsequent extensions of coverage were, he felt safe to presume, based on evidence similarly sufficient. Given that Congress' conclusions were factual, the Court was not concerned with how they were reached.[64]

But we cannot leave *Maryland* without considering what Harlan referred to as a wholly different kind of analysis in support of the extension of coverage under consideration. As he understood it, the original *Act* advanced findings that substandard labor conditions were likely to occasion disputes and strikes. When they disrupted companies engaged in interstate commerce, commercial activities themselves were affected. To address this, Congress pursued the regulation of hours, wages, and commerce for purposes of securing labor peace, not unlike in other cases, such as that of the *National Labor Relations Act*, where the Court found a rational basis for statutes regulating labor conditions in order to protect interstate commerce from labor unrest.[65] As Harlan noted, the *Fair Labor Standards Act* was extended to cover certain hospitals, institutions, and schools, while modifying the definition of employer so as to remove the exemption of the States and their subdivisions as it related to employees of hospitals, institutions, and schools.[66] Appellants had objected to this extension as unconstitutional under the Commerce Clause. However, the Court found that labor conditions in schools and hospitals can affect commerce. Harlan wrote, "the facts stipulated in this case indicate that such institutions are major users of goods imported from other States." As an example, he pointed to *Maryland* where, in fiscal year 1965, 87% of the $8 million spent for supplies and equipment represented direct interstate commerce.[67]

Throughout the history of the Commerce Clause, one finds a fundamental source of tension in the notion of state sovereignty and the lurking threat posed to it by Congress' power under the Commerce Clause. In *Maryland*, Appellants argued that the *Fair Labor Standards Act* could not constitutionally be applied to state-operated institutions because federal power "must yield to state sovereignty in the performance of governmental functions."[68] Harlan rejected the argument as untenable since it implied something that was not, as a general doctrine, in the Constitution. Namely, that "the two governments, national and state, are each to exercise its powers so as not to interfere with the free and full exercise of the powers of the other."[69] Referring to *Sanitary District of Chicago v. United States*,[70] he noted that the Court had settled the argument that state matters might constitutionally take precedence over otherwise legitimate federal regulation of commerce. In that case, involving congressional statutory limits on the diversion of water from Lake Michigan, the Court unanimously found that the sanitary district's alleged need for more water than federal law permitted was irrelevant because federal power over commerce "is superior to that of the States to provide for the welfare or necessities of their inhabitants."[71] Submitting again that the commerce power had its limits, Harlan insisted that "valid general regulations of commerce do not cease to be regulations of commerce because a State is involved."[72] As long as the activities engaged in by States are legitimately subject to federal regulation when undertaken by private persons, states too may be required to comply with federal regulation.[73]

In *Maryland*, the concept of enterprise is central to the decision. The Court defined it as "a set or operations whose activities in commerce would be expected to be affected by labor relations, such as wages and hours of any group of employees which is what Congress obviously intended." Defined this way, the Court understood the term to convey limitations on the commerce power. "Neither here nor in *Wickard* has the Court declared that Congress may use a relatively trivial impact on commerce as an excuse for broad regulation of state or private activities."[74]

If labor relations, in particular those which by virtue of wages and hours were unequal, also were said to affect inter-state commerce, might not gender relations likewise have done that? Since they were present in every area of contemporary commerce, and since their institutionalized inequality occasioned a pervasive gender-based violence, did they not also affect inter-state commerce as substantially as labor relations? Obviously, this was what Congress understood to be the case in passing the *VAWA* in 1994, and in providing almost exhaustive evidence demonstrating a negative causal relation between gender-based violence and commerce. Everything suggested that the *Maryland* Court would have accepted the proposition. Why did the *Morrison* Court disagree?

The answer can be found in three related considerations. The first was how to assess the merits of the relevant evidence presented to demonstrate that gender-based violence affects commerce. The second was how Rehnquist understood the language, "whether particular operations affect interstate commerce sufficiently to come under the constitutional power of Congress to regulate them is ultimately a judicial rather than a legislative question, and can be settled finally only by this Court."[75] The third was assessing how the word *sufficient* was being used.

GENDER-BASED VIOLENCE AND COMMERCE

In *Lopez*, Rehnquist observed that Congress was not under an obligation to submit formal findings showing that an activity had substantial effects on commerce. Nevertheless, having such evidence might "enable us to evaluate the legislative judgment that the activity in question substantially affect[s] interstate commerce even though no such substantial effect [is] visible to the naked eye."[76] Unlike in *Lopez*, in *Morrison*, Congress had submitted what Rehnquist referred to as "numerous findings regarding the serious impact that gender-motivated violence has on victims and their families."[77] That such evidence existed, however, was, for him, insufficient on its own to justify the constitutionality of legislation under the Commerce Clause.[78]

While Rehnquist merely referenced the evidence provided by Congress, Souter, in his dissent, laid it out in detail. For example, approximately 50% of victims of rape lost their job or found it necessary to quit work because of the trauma caused by rape.[79] In summarizing another report, Souter noted that gender-based violence inhibited interstate travel by those fearful of gender-based violence. There was also considerable evidence of hesitation to pursue employment in interstate business. Nationally, gender-based violence had substantial consequences for lessening the productivity of its victims, while increasing their medical and other expenses. No less consequential was the reduction in the supply of and the demand for products in commercial traffic between states.[80] This evidence, Souter concluded, provided the grounds for the exercise of congressional power under the Commerce Clause. "The sufficiency of the evidence before the Court to provide a rational basis for the finding cannot seriously be denied." In *Morrison*, he argued, the evidence was far greater than that which the Court accepted in two earlier decisions, involving racial discrimination and commerce.[81] Indeed, "The Act would have passed muster at any time between Wickard in 1942 and Lopez in 1995." Why was the evidence acceptable then, but not now?

METHOD OF REASONING

In a word, because the evidence was substantially weakened, not on its own terms as data generated by means of statistical norms, but because of its reliance on what Rehnquist referred to as a "method of reasoning that we have already rejected as unworkable if we are to maintain the Constitution's enumeration of powers."[82] The method of reasoning was the so-called *but-for* test used in tort law to establish that an injury could not have occurred without a specified action, where injury and the specified action are relatable as consequent and antecedent. In our case, the antecedent was gender-based violence and the consequent was an effect on interstate commerce. The argument Congress was making was that if gender-based violence occurred then there was an effect on interstate commerce. Since the two statements "are related as the antecedent and the consequent of a conditional, then the truth of the antecedent is sufficient for the truth of the consequent and the truth of the consequent is a necessary condition for the truth of the antecedent."[83] Where we have, as in this case, contingently necessary and sufficient conditions, we have causation of the most powerful kind.[84]

It is important to remind ourselves that our perception of *causation* does not come from a sensory experience of *causing* qualities evident in objects or events. What we observe is that events can be constructed as successive and re-occurring. Succession and re-occurrence then afford the logical step of induction and conclusion that specific antecedent events are sufficient for the occurrence of certain consequent events.[85] The practical implication from this logic for our case is that in order to deny gender-based violence as cause, you would have to be able to deny effects on commerce as the consequence since, in a conditional relation, the denial of the truth of the consequent is a sufficient reason to deny the truth of the antecedent. Given the consistency of the evidence and the statistical methods used to generate it, that would be hard to do, especially since the methodology is also able to subtract the rate at which services are used in the absence of violence so as not to overstate the true costs of services used directly because of gender-based violence.[86] In the constitutional order of things, it was for Congress to solicit data through the process of committee hearings of expert testimony and to assess their justification as a rational basis for proposed legislation. Again, in the constitutional order of things as Harlan represented it, Congressional action did not preclude subsequent examination of the evidence by the Court. But, as Souter, in dissenting, observed, "The fact of such a substantial effect is not an issue for the courts in the first instance but for Congress, whose institutional capacity for gathering evidence and taking testimony far exceeds ours."[87] That Congress saw fit to pass the *Act* is a clear statement that the evidence justified its use of the commerce power.[88] For both Harlan and Souter, it would appear, there was a presumption favoring Congress that would require the Court to prove, on factual grounds, that Congress was mistaken. Having already implied that the Court lacked credible ability to generate the factual evidence, let alone disprove it, Souter argued that the Court's constitutional responsibility was to "review the congressional assessment, not for its soundness, but simply for the rationality of concluding that a jurisdictional basis exists in fact."[89]

In contrast, far from seeing a jurisdictional basis, Rehnquist saw a threat to the enumeration of powers as intended in the Constitution. But if the evidence was applied in a way that demonstrated a strong causal relation between gender-based violence and interstate commerce, would that not have justified section 13981, confirming the constitutionality of Congress' claim to regulate gender-based violence under its enumerated powers? If so, then it followed that Congress' interest in regulating gender-based violence under the Commerce Clause, in posing no threat to the enumeration of powers, posed no threat to the balance of power between federal and state government. Clearly questionable here, Rehnquist's argument was questionable elsewhere.

Rehnquist was also concerned that if the Court were to accept Congress' reasoning, it would allow the use of the evidence so that Congress could regulate any crime as long as on aggregate the crime had a substantial impact on employment, production, transit, or consumption. That included murder, or literally any type of violence, Rehnquist argued, since gender-based violence is a subset of all violent crime.[90] It is unfortunate that even as he criticized the reasoning of Congress, he failed to see that his own reasoning was fallacious. To be clear, it was predicated on the logical fallacy of composition which consists in inferring that something is true of the whole from the fact that it is true of some part of the whole. Gender-based violence, while it is undoubtedly violence, is more than that, as we saw from the analysis above. Rehnquist chose to see it only as violence rather than a socioeconomic activity expressing relations of economic inequality between men and women which, in turn, resulted from an institutionalized definition of womanhood as subordinate to manhood.

In this context, gender-based violence has been one of the chosen methods to maintain the subordination of women, as a body of sociological evidence, including the appalling rates of gender-based violence, demonstrated. There can be little doubt that "gender-motivated violence is more than patriarchal prejudices and violent behavior, but rather a fundamental method of ensuring the ongoing subordination of women, including economic subordination."[91] As a result, the presumption of women as subordinate was so ingrained in society that it even found expression in places one might reasonably have expected to be free of such a bias. For example, when the Court ruled that Congress was behaving unconstitutionally when it took steps to protect women against gender-based violence, one has to ask how can protecting a woman's human right to be free from violence be deemed unconstitutional unless at some level of social consciousness one has conceded that violence against women was constitutional? How is it possible to understand the Constitution so as to use it to nullify measures intended to protect women from violence unless it reflected patriarchal notions that were just as institutionalized in our legal system as elsewhere in society? Why see the Constitution in terms that relegated women and the family to a socio-domestic setting that is intentionally subjugating and quite distinct from anything remotely likely to secure economic independence?[92] What would be the point of harboring such notions unless they provided the basis for a social system informed by "a clear power distinction between men and women and the preservation of that division of power"?[93] In other words, a division that renders socially acceptable acting on notions such as "women as a reserve labor force, lower wages for women that provide a labor surplus, unpaid housework done by women, and women as administrators of family consumption."[94] Women have consistently objected to such notions, only to be met with equal resistance in the form of "domestic violence," together with additional abuse inflicted because of being a woman.[95] This would not be the first time in the history of the Court that a majority presented itself as a mirror image of ingrained and unjust social attitudes.

Choosing to see gender-based violence only as a crime of violence, and not a matter of institutionalized injustice, misconstrued the issue central to this case by mistaking a symptom of the problem for the problem itself. Conveniently for Rehnquist's constitutional predilections, this directed the analysis of the case to the constitutional setting of separation of federal and state powers. Here, as a crime of violence, gender-based violence fell under state jurisdiction where it became a judicial not a legislative question that can be settled finally only by the Court.[96] Settled? But how was the matter settled by the Court returning it to the states whose consistent disposition in their courts had been one of complete indifference to securing justice for victims of gender-based violence? According to one report, in 2008, approximately 500 women were raped every day in the United States. The report also found that domestic violence was severely under-reported, and when it was reported, it was rarely prosecuted. But even where it was actually investigated, it had a low conviction rate.[97] The report concluded that "the lack of substantive protective legislation at the federal and state levels and the inadequate implementation of current laws, policies and programs resulted in the continued prevalence of violence against women and the discriminatory treatment of victims."[98] Since the Court's decision, unquestionably, has exacerbated the inadequacy of federal legislation, what constitutional reasoning was so persuasive in making the decision?

FEDERALISM

A leading candidate would have to be Federalism. At one point in his dissent, Souter drew attention to this. Were one to ask why the formalistic distinction between economic and non-economic activity mattered now, after its rejection in *Wickard*, the answer was not because the Court neglected to see causal connections in an integrated economic world. Rather, it was that "in the minds of the majority there is a new animating theory that makes categorical formalism useful again . . . in serving a conception of federalism."[99] What was at stake, Souter argued, was the constitutional justification for the Court's understanding of relations between state and federal governments that it might enforce by imposing limits on an otherwise plenary commerce power. Ultimately, it constituted for Souter a "categorical discount applied today to the facts bearing on the substantial effects test."[100] In more consequential terms, it amounted to regarding the Constitution as an end in itself, when it should be regarded as a means to achieving the people's rights.

Consistent with securing its interest in Federalism, the Court rejected Congress' appeal to section 5 of the Fourteenth Amendment to justify its civil remedy against gender-based violence under the commerce power. According to section 5, Congress was authorized to enforce, through appropriate legislation, the constitutional guarantee that no state shall deprive any person of life, liberty, or property without due process of law, nor deny any person equal protection of the laws. In *Morrison*, Petitioners had claimed that various state justice systems evidenced a widespread bias against victims of gender-based violence. As Rehnquist noted, Congress had presented overwhelming evidence that many participants in state justice systems had consistently turned to erroneous stereotypes in judicial proceedings which resulted in inadequate investigation and prosecution of gender-based violence. Equally in evidence was an attitude of skepticism for the credibility of victims of this violence, together with a pattern of handing down lenient punishment for those convicted of gender-based violence. Since, Petitioners argued, this denied victims equal protection of the laws, Congress was justified in providing a private, civil remedy against perpetrators of this violence, thereby remedying states' bias and deterring any further discrimination in state courts.[101]

In response, Rehnquist observed that the language and purpose of the Fourteenth Amendment is to impose limitations on how Congress may address discrimination. Limitations, that is, that are necessary to avoid dismantling the balance of power between the states and the National Government.[102] To that end, section 5 applied only to state action, not to that of private actors. For confirmation of this distinction, Rehnquist cited two cases, *United States v. Harris* and *Civil Rights Cases*,[103] both from 1883. At issue in *Harris* was a challenge to section 2 of the *Civil Rights Act of 1871*, which was designed to punish private individuals intent on depriving others of equal protection of states' laws. "We concluded," Rehnquist declared, "that this law exceeded Congress' section 5 power because the law was 'directed exclusively against the action of private persons, without reference to the laws of the State, or their administration by her officers.'"[104] In *Civil Rights Cases* (1883), the Court concluded "that the public accommodation provisions of *the Civil Rights Act of 1875* which applied to purely private conduct, were beyond the scope of the Section 5 power."[105] It is worth noting that Rehnquist included, in his rehearsal of cases, that of *Lugar v. Edmondson Oil Co.* (1982), in which the Court declared that "Careful adherence to the "state action' requirement preserves an area of individual freedom by limiting the reach of federal law and federal judicial power.'[106] Applied to *Morrison*, the phrase 'preserves an area of individual freedom' is ambiguous to say the least. *Individual* can refer to men and women; *freedom* can refer to *freedom to* as well as *freedom from*. In the context of the sorry history of states" indifference to violence against women, *freedom to* might reasonably refer to men and their institutionalized ability to inflict violence on women as women, whereas *freedom from* would refer to women and their right as women to be free from the violence of men. As a result, careful adherence to the state action requirement as Rehnquist would have it, could have meant one thing for men and something quite different for women. Congress' appeal to section 5 of the Fourteenth Amendment to justify its civil remedy for gender-based violence could, as a result, be seen as a constitutional measure to counter the indifference of state actors which fosters gender-based violence while it left its victims defenseless. Obviously, gender-based violence occurs on an individual basis which, considered superficially, lends itself to the idea that it is confined to private actors. However, it also occurred so frequently and for the most part with impunity that its prevalence in society had become institutionalized with, as the research showed, states complicit because of their indifference to and discrimination against victims. As Souter observed, thirty-eight Attorneys General supported the enactment of the *Civil Rights Remedy* because of a record of failure on the part of the state-court system to stop gender-based violence. And that record, according to a 1993 U.S. Senate Report, was attributable to "the underlying attitude that this violence is somehow less serious than other crime and to the resulting failure of our criminal justice system to address such violence."[107] It is not unreasonable to think that this underlying attitude of state actors served actively as tacit permission to engage in gender-based violence and gave an unspoken promise of impunity afterward.

Nevertheless, Rehnquist's response consisted in drawing an all but absolute distinction between state and private actors, so as to discount the appeal to the principle of equal protection under the laws. Unlike in *Harris* and *Civil Rights Cases*, however, in *Morrison* "there is not always a bright line dividing those two spheres that permits us to draw a distinction in which the Fourteenth Amendment is not compromised."[108] In *United States v. Guest* (1966), Justice William J. Brennan Jr. dissenting and joined by Chief Justice Earl Warren and Justice Wiliam O. Douglas, questioned this absolute distinction altogether.[109] At the center of the case was the question whether 18 U.S.C. Section 241 of the Criminal Code could be applied in cases of deprivation of rights on public facilities, such as roads or interstate commerce channels, by private actors in connivance with state actors. While the Court held that it could, as long as there was a minimum level of connivance by state actors, Justice Brennan had strong reservations about the necessity of this condition for a correct interpretation of Fourteenth Amendment. Instead, Brennan argued that "Section 241 reaches such a private conspiracy, not because the 14th. Amendment, of its own force, prohibits such a conspiracy, but because Section 241, as an exercise of congressional power under Section 5 of that Amendment prohibits all conspiracies to interfere with the exercise of a 'right . . . secured . . . by the Constitution'" and because the right to equal utilization of state facilities is a "right . . . secured . . . by the Constitution" within the meaning of that phrase as used in section 241.[110] Brennan's disagreement with the Court came from its use of the term "secured," which resulted in a tacit restriction to the effect that private interference with the right in question must be prohibited by the Constitution itself or another federal law. On that condition only can section 241 be applied to private conspiracies to interfere with the right. And since it was the Court's premise that neither the Constitution nor any other federal law prohibited interference from private actors, no application was possible. On the contrary, a right, Brennan countered, can be considered "secured" within the meaning of section 241, " even though only governmental interferences with the exercise of the right are prohibited by the Constitution itself."[111] That is because, with reference to the Constitution, the term "secured" means "is created by," "arising under," or "dependent upon," rather than "fully protected."[112] For example, Brennan noted that the prohibitions and remedies of section 241 were considered to apply to violations of the right to vote in a federal election without reference to whether the violation came from private or public actors.[113] Similarly, the right to use state facilities without discrimination was within the meaning of section 241, "a right created by, arising under and dependent upon the Fourteenth Amendment and consequently a right secured by that Amendment."[114] Citing *Strauder v. West Virginia* (1880), Brennan concluded that

> The Fourteenth Amendment makes no attempt to enumerate the rights it is designed to protect. It speaks in general terms, and those are as comprehensive as possible. Its language is prohibitory; but every prohibition implies the existence of rights.[115]

Unlike Rehnquist's interpretation of the Equal Protection Clause in *Morrison*, Brennan here had decided that nothing in federalism or the Constitution rendered Congress powerless under section 5 of the Fourteenth Amendment to protect the right to equal access to state facilities by punishing "other individuals—not state officers themselves and not acting in concert with state officers—who engage in the same brutal conduct for the same misguided purpose."[116] Moreover, having noted that the language of section 5 of the Fourteenth Amendment was virtually the same as that of section 2 of the Fifteenth Amendment, he noted that the Court had recently held in *South Carolina v. Katzenbach* (1966) that "the basic test to be applied in a case involving Section 2 of the Fifteenth Amendment is the same as in all cases concerning the express powers of Congress with relation to the reserved powers of the States." The definitive definition of which, Brennan insisted, came from John Marshall in *McCulloch v. Maryland* (1819):

> Let the end be legitimate, let it be within the scope of the constitution, and all means which are appropriate, which are plainly to that end, which are not prohibited, but consist with the letter and the spirit of the constitution, are constitutional.[117]

The evidence Congress provided was clear. States, as a matter of course, denied women, in cases of gender-based violence, treatment comparable to that provided to male victims of other crimes. As a state action, it originated with an underlying bias found in state actors. More to the point, it was a bias, "linked intrinsically to the actions and identities of the private actors who were the aggressors."[118] Just as in *DeShaney DeShaney v. Winnebago Cty.*, Rehnquist refused to see that the attitude of state actors was intrinsically linked to the abusive behavior of Joshua's father, so in *Morrison* he made the same mistake through his consistent preference for absolute dichotomies which in their over-simplification of the conditions of human behavior, rendered this decision questionable relative to the facts of the case and, as a consequence, to the application of the law. "The first call of a theory of law is that it should fit the facts. It must explain the observed course of legislation."[119]

Rehnquist, however, was prepared to discount the facts. Here, Justice Stephen Breyer, in his dissent, made a telling observation. The Court was happy to accept Congress' finding that the inadequacy of state remedies against gender-based violence was not a problem in all states. But as Justice Breyer noted, Congress declared it had evidence of constitutional violations from 21 States and added that there was no reason to say that the problem did not exist in any of the other states.[120] What then justified the Court discounting positive evidence of judicial indifference to gender-based violence, preferring instead to rely for its decision on the absence of evidence indicating that the indifference was not alive and well in other states? How could substantial evidence from twenty-one States be ignored? Presumably, that was because the claims of federalism could not be ignored.

There is not a little irony here, given what was at stake in *Morrison*. Rehnquist insisted that "the Framers crafted the federal system of government so that the peoples' rights would be secured by the division of power."[121] Relative to individual rights, federalism was simply a means to secure them. In which case, our understanding of federalism as a means cannot be such as legitimately to prevent the securing of individual rights. In other words, it was rights that were normative, dictating what ought to be done, not federalism, the justification for which rested with its role of securing individual rights. Now if federalism was justified as a means to secure rights, whatever furthered the effectiveness of federalism in this capacity was similarly justified. In assisting federalism, the Commerce Clause contributed, at least indirectly to assuring rights. As a consequence, rights were normative in the case of the Commerce Clause, just as they were in the case of the Fourteenth Amendment. As a consequence, federalism, and along with it the Commerce Clause and the Fourteenth Amendment, may not be construed so as to become instrumental in denying persons the exercise of their constitutional rights, much less their human rights.

HUMAN RIGHTS

What has been lost sight of throughout the Court's review was that violence against women was a gross violation of the human right of women, including Christy Brzonkala, to lead a life free of violence. This right has been confirmed by such international agreements as the Universal Declaration of Human Rights and the United Nations' Declaration on the Elimination of Violence against Women.[122] Not once, however, was this fact acknowledged, let alone considered, whether by the Court's majority or those dissenting. Instead, they confined their review to whether gender-based violence can be considered a commercial or non-commercial activity, the behavior of private or public actors. They failed to see that any constitutional conclusion arrived at on the basis of these two considerations was merely a matter of deciding what might or might not have been done under Congress' enumerated powers, and not what ought to have been done for victims of gender-based violence as a matter of natural justice. The former is a matter of constitutional possibilities, as evidenced in the differences between the Court majority and those dissenting; the latter is a matter of ethical prescription. There is no doubting the importance of the Constitution and the respect owed it in both our legal and governmental systems. For all that however, since one of its critical roles has been to confirm human rights, not originate them, it must cede to the demands of human rights as prior when constitutional priorities, regarded incorrectly as ends in themselves, threaten the exercise of human rights. For example, what is entailed in the Fourteenth Amendment of the Constitution does not ultimately emanate from the Constitution but derives from the fact, acknowledged by the Constitution itself, that all human beings are born equal.

This equality was there from the beginning, long before the Constitution. But when it came time, at the birth of this nation, the Framers of the Constitution had the wisdom to adapt their vision of the nation to the requirements of the human right to equal treatment of humans as humans in its most comprehensive form. As a result, while the justices of the Supreme Court swear a civic oath to uphold the Constitution, they are under a prior ethical obligation, derived from natural law, as the ground of constitutional law, to exercise their judicial review from the perspective of law as just, not merely law as so ordered. Justices of the Court, in fulfilling their obligations to the Constitution, do not exhaust their prior moral obligation as human beings to respect the human rights of their fellow human beings, despite the Constitution, should that become necessary. The judicial review in *Morrison* should have started with the human rights violation and then worked back from there to determine how to interpret the Constitution to provide the redress that was called for because of the violation which of course was an ethics issue before it was a constitutional issue. The Court, under the sway of its legal positivism, neglected, as a result, to give any consideration to the priority of human rights over constitutionally based rights. Instead, it was content mistakenly to confine its review to a rehearsal o its case history regarding Congress' enumerated powers regarding the Commerce Clause and the Fourteenth Amendment as though they were the only issues to be considered. As was clear from that rehearsal, there was, evident over time, a consistently diverse range of interpretation regarding both, all of it constitutionally reasonable. It should not be surprising because it was not unusual the outcome was a degree of reasonable uncertainty that is usually resolved arbitrarily by a majority of justices deciding the position of the Court. Given the certainty of the human right of women to be free from violence, the

Court had a logically and ethically prior obligation to turn to the overriding authority of the Constitution's natural law groundings for the correct judgment. Instead, Rehnquist's strained effort to distinguish "commercial" from "non-commercial activity," and his even more strained attempt to distinguish "private from public actors," while he replaced "rational basis analysis" with his novel standard for interpreting the Commerce Clause, led the Court to a conclusion questionable constitutionally and devoid of any moral content. If anything, they only confirmed "how the judicial system can suffer from the same implicit bias against women that Congress was trying to deter with the enactment of VAWA."[123]

The Court's failure to meet its ethical obligation can be traced to Rehnquist's basic, and impoverished theory of law:

> If a society adopts a constitution and incorporates in that constitution safeguards of individual liberty, these safeguards do indeed take on a general moral rightness or goodness. They assume a general social acceptance, neither because of any intrinsic worth, nor because of any unique origins in someone's idea of natural justice but instead simply because they have been incorporated in a constitution by a people.[124]

If one adopts such a positivist view of the Constitution in particular, or law in general, it follows that one would find no difficulty in saying, as Rehnquist did, "it is, I believe, impossible to justify the sacrifice of even a portion of our historic individual freedom for a purpose such as giving blacks, Latinos and Jews the right to be served in local motels, hotels and restaurants."[125] But why anyone would think that, must have to do with the mistaken belief that freedom is divisible, when in fact it is indivisible. As a human right, freedom is "had by every human being simply insofar as he or she is human."[126] Further, it has to be exercised reciprocally in the sense that, since human rights are enjoyed in common, they require to be exercised with appropriate consideration of others, especially where one's exercise is likely to affect others.[127] To speak of freedom as individual freedom is to speak of freedom as something of the essence of an individual or person. Since freedom of access to the services of hotels and restaurants is an expression of individual freedom, it cannot be denied without compromising the integrity of the freedom of which it is an expression, and along with it the integrity of the individual who enjoys this freedom as integral to individuality or personhood. If whites, Christians and atheists enjoy freedom of access to hotels and restaurants as an extension of their human right to freedom, then so equally should blacks, Latinos, and Jews "unless there is a general and relevant principle of differentiation."[128] Anyone who appreciates the need for reasoned argument is unlikely to insist that a difference in the color of one's skin or national origin, for example, is sufficient to constitute a general and relevant reason for differentiation. Anyone who does, however, incurs errors of both logic and ethics.[129]

This two-fold error, in Rehnquist's case, was his claim that a general social acceptance, rather than the intrinsic merit of justice, is sufficient for law to take on a general moral rightness. Were one to apply this to slavery which had general social acceptance in the United States but no longer does, one would logically have to accept that at one point in time ownership by white persons of black persons, because they were black, was morally right. But now, in the absence of such acceptance, it no longer enjoys that moral rightness. But what if general social acceptance regarding slavery were to return to its earlier position? In that case, logic would dictate that slavery would regain its moral rightness. From the perspective of ethics, Rehnquist's error lay in his failure to see that "the principle that no person should be treated differently from any or all other persons unless there is some general and relevant reason that justifies this difference in treatment is a fundamental principle of morality, if not rationality itself."[130]

This line of thinking was evident in *Morrison* when Rehnquist, again minimizing the question, argued that state-sponsored gender discrimination violated equal protection unless undertaken in pursuit of important governmental goals and the discrimination was substantially related to reaching these goals.[131] The discrimination referred to was the bias consistently shown by state courts against women who were victims of gender-based violence. This was nothing less than to consider gender-based violence as secondary to the pursuit of important government goals. As long as such goals existed, they presumably provided a general and relevant reason that justified treating women who were victims of gender-based violence differently from men in similar legal contexts. It is hard to believe that a justice of the United States Supreme Court, writing for the majority, would argue that there were important government goals that justified overlooking a human right confirmed as it is, for example, by the Universal Declaration of Human Rights, and who was prepared to restrict the language and purpose of the Fourteenth Amendment in order to prevent it from being constitutionally instrumental in providing any remedy for the violation of the right. Hard, that is, unless we recall that the Justice was one who espoused a philosophy of law that logically led to the belief that a woman's right to lead her life free of gender-based violence lacked any intrinsic worth. If, however, the Constitution lacks intrinsic value, is there any reason to believe it is as normative as Rehnquist appeared to believe in his review in *Morrison*?

Moreover, this is also the same Justice who closed the Court's opinion in *Morrison*, writing, with reference to Brzonkala's allegations, that if they "are true, no civilized system of justice could fail to provide her a remedy."[132] But does not the U.S. Constitution embody a civilized system of justice? And if civilized in Aristotlean terms, would it not be at its foundation ethical? If so, how can it be allowed to entertain an understanding of federalism that would, in its name, tolerate something as uncivilized as state courts' indifference to the plight of women who are the victims of gender-based violence? Some twenty-one state attorneys general had recognized the state courts' indifference and, in an exercise of cooperative federalism, turned to Congress for a remedy which Rehnquist declared unconstitutional. In its place, the best Rehnquist could offer was to declare that, "under our federal system that remedy must be provided by the Commonwealth of Virginia."[133] Obviously, his words did not constitute an order from the Court to the Commonwealth of Virginia. Rehnquist was merely saying that if there was to be a remedy, it can only come from Virginia. In Kantian terms, it was nothing more than a hypothetical imperative. The provision of a remedy was contingent on Virginia's wanting to provide it. In this case, this is to say that the exercise of the human right of women to be free from gender-based violence is at the discretion of government. On the contrary, government, whether state or federal, is under a prior moral obligation, based on the notion of law as just, to respect and foster their right.

What won the day was the legal formalism Justice Harry Blackmun complained of in *DeShaney*. In *Morrison*, the Constitution was regarded as an end in itself, not a means to justice, and its decision rested on questionable distinctions drawn between commercial and non-commercial activity, between private and public actors. Federalism prevailed over the common good. The result was to perpetrate a gross injustice that no ethical system of law could tolerate.

NOTES

1. U.S. Supreme Court, *United States v. Morrison*, 529 U.S. 598 (2000), at 627, https://supreme.justia.com/cases/federal/us/529/598/ (accessed October 23, 2020).

2. *United States v. Morrison*, 529 U.S. 598 (2000), at 603.

3. U.S. Congress, *Violence Against Women Act (VAWA)*, 42 U.S.C. 13701–14040 (1994), sec. 13981, https://www.govinfo.gov/app/details/USCODE-1996-title42/USCODE-1996-title42-chap136-subchapI-partA-sec13701 (accessed October 23, 2020).

4. U. S. District Court, Eastern District of Pennsylvania, *United States v. Morrison*, 99–5 (2000), https://www.oyez/cases/1999/99-5 (accessed March 30, 2019); see also *United States v. Morrison*, 529 U.S. 598 (2000), at Syllabus.

5. U.S. Congress, *Violence Against Women*, sec. 13981 (b).

6. U.S. Congress, *Violence Against Women*, sec. 13981 (b).

7. *United States v. Morrison*, 529 U.S. 598 at 624–25.

8. *United States v. Morrison*, 529 U.S. 598 at 627.

9. U.S. Supreme Court, *United States v. Lopez*, 514 U.S. 549 (1995), at 608, https://supreme.justia.com/cases/federal/us/514/549/ (accessed October 23, 2020).
10. *United States v. Morrison*, 529 U.S. 598 at 608.
11. *United States v. Morrison*, 529 U.S at 634.
12. *United States v. Morrison*, 529 U.S 598 at 628.
13. U.S. Congress, *Gun-Free School Zones Act*, 18 U.S.C. (101st Cong., 2nd sess.) (1990), sec. 922 (q)(1)(A), https://www.congress.gov/bill/101st-congress/senate-bill/2070/ (accessed October 23, 2020).
14. *United States v. Morrison*, 529 U.S. 598 at 610.
15. *United States v. Morrison*, 529 U.S. 598 at 610, citing *United States v. Lopez*, 514 U.S. 549 at 560.
16. *United States v. Morrison*, 529 U.S. 598 at 610.
17. *United States v. Morrison*, 529 U.S. 598 at 611.
18. *United States v. Morrison*, 529 U.S. 598 at 612.
19. *United States v. Morrison*, 529 U.S. 598 at 612.
20. *United States v. Morrison*, 529 U.S. 598 at 636.
21. *United States v. Morrison*, 529 U.S. 598 at 613.
22. *United States v. Morrison*, 529 U.S. 598 at 613.
23. Surbhi S, "Differences Between Economic and Non-Economic Activities," *Key Differences* (June 20, 2016), https://keydifferences.com/difference-between-economic-and-non-economic-activities.html (accessed October 23, 2002).
24. S, "Differences."
25. Tanis Day, Katherine McKenna, and Audra Bowlus, "The Economic Costs of Violence Against Women: An Evaluation of the Literature," brief prepared for Secretary-General of Canada, United Nations, London, Ontario (2005), https://www.un.org/womenwatch/daw/vaw/expert%20brief%20costs.pdf (accessed October 23, 2020).
26. Day et al., "Economic Costs," 27.
27. Day et al., "Economic Costs," 27.
28. Day et al., "Economic Costs," 27.
29. Day et al., "Economic Costs," 28.
30. Day et al., "Economic Costs," 25.
31. Mara Bolis and Christine Hughes, "Women's Economic Empowerment and Domestic Violence: Links and Lessons for Practitioners Working with Intersectional Approaches," *OXFAM* (2015), https://s3.amazonaws.com/oxfam-us/www/static/media/files/Womens_Empowerment_and_Domestic_Violence_-_Boris__Hughes_hX7LscW.pdf (accessed October 23, 2020).
32. Bolis and Hughes, "Women's Economic Empowerment," 4n1.
33. Center for Disease Control and Prevention (CDC), "Costs of Intimate Partner Violence Against Women in the United States," (2003), https://www.cdc.gov/violenceprevention/pdf/IPVbook-a.pdf (accessed October 23, 2020).
34. *United States v. Morrison*, 529 U.S. 598 at 602.
35. Bolis and Hughes, "Women's Economic Empowerment," supra 3.
36. Bolis and Hughes, "Women's Economic Empowerment," 4.
37. Bolis and Hughes, "Women's Economic Empowerment," 4.

38. Bolis and Hughes, "Women's Economic Empowerment," 4.
39. Bolis and Hughes, "Women's Economic Empowerment," 5.
40. Bolis and Hughes, "Women's Economic Empowerment," 6.
41. Gita Ramjee and Brodie Daniels, "Women and HIV in Sub-Sharan Africa," *AIDS Research and Therapy* 10, no. 30 (2013), https://doi.org/10.1186/1742-6405-10-30 (accessed October 23, 2020). See also Geeta Rao Gupta, Justine O. Parkhurst, Jessica A. Ogden, Peter Aggleton, and Ajay Mahal, "Structural Approaches to HIV Prevention," *Lancet* 372, no. 9640 (2008): 764–75, https://doi.org/10.1016/s0140-6736(08)60887-9 (accessed October 23, 2020).
42. *United States v. Morrison*, 529 U.S. 598 at 610.
43. *United States v. Morrison*, 529 U.S. 598 at 610.
44. *United States v. Morrison*, 529 U.S. 598 at 611.
45. *United States v. Lopez*, 514 U.S. 549 at 551.
46. *United States v. Lopez*, 514 U.S. 549 at 553.
47. *United States v. Morrison*, 529 U.S. 598 at 616, see U.S. Supreme Court, *Gibbons v. Ogden*, 22 U.S. 1 (1824), at 9 Wheat. 1, 189–90, https://supreme.justia.com/cases/federal/us/22/1/ (accessed October 23, 2020).
48. *Gibbons v. Ogden* at 196.
49. *Gibbons v. Ogden* at 194–95.
50. Rehnquist citing Chief Justice Marshall in *McCulloch v. Maryland*, 4 Wheat 316 (1819), at 405.
51. U.S. Supreme Court, *Wickard v. Filburn*, 317 U.S. 111 (1942), at 121, https://supreme.justia.com/cases/federal/us/317/111/ (accessed October 23, 2020).
52. *United States v. Lopez*, 514 U.S. 549 at 556.
53. *Wickard v. Filburn* at 125.
54. *United States v. Lopez*, 514 U.S. 549 at 556–57.
55. *United States v. Lopez*, 514 U.S. 549 at 557.
56. *United States v. Lopez*, 514 U.S. 549 at 557.
57. U.S. Supreme Court, *Maryland v. Wirtz*, 392 U.S. 183 (1968), at 190, https://supreme.justia.com/cases/federal/us/392/183/ (accessed October 23, 2020); see U.S. Supreme Court, *Katzenbach v. McClung*, 379 U.S. 294 (1964), at 303–4, https://supreme.justia.com/cases/federal/us/379/294/ (accessed October 23, 2020).
58. See *United States v. Lopez*, 514 U.S. 549 at 557n2.
59. See U.S. Supreme Court, *Hodel v. Virginia Surface Mining and Reclamation Assn., Inc.*, 452 U.S. 264 (1981), at 311, https://supreme.justia.com/cases/federal/us/452/264/ (accessed October 23, 2020).
60. See U.S. Supreme Court, *Heart of Atlanta Motel, Inc. v. United States*, 379 U.S. 241 (1964), at 273, https://supreme.justia.com/cases/federal/us/379/241/ (accessed October 23, 2020).
61. *Maryland v. Wirtz* at 190.
62. *Maryland v. Wirtz* at 190.
63. U.S. Congress, *Fair Labor Standards Act* (*FLSA*), 29 U.S.C. 201, et seq. (1938), https://www.law.cornell.edu/uscode/text/29/chapter-8 (accessed October 24, 2020).
64. *Maryland v. Wirtz* at 190n13.
65. *Maryland v. Wirtz* at 191.

66. *Maryland v. Wirtz* at Syllabus.
67. *Maryland v. Wirtz* at 194.
68. *Maryland v. Wirtz* at 195.
69. *Maryland v. Wirtz* at 195; See U.S. Supreme Court, *Case v. Bowles*, 327 U.S. 92 (1946), at 101, https://supreme.justia.com/cases/federal/us/327/92/ (accessed October 23, 2020).
70. U.S. Supreme Court, *Sanitary District of Chicago v. United States*, 266 U.S. 405 (1925), https://supreme.justia.com/cases/federal/us/266/405/ (accessed October 23, 2020).
71. *Sanitary District v. United States* at 426.
72. *Maryland v. Wirtz* at 196–97.
73. *Maryland v. Wirtz* at 197.
74. *Maryland v. Wirtz* at 197n27.
75. *United States v. Morrison*, 529 U.S. 598 at 614.
76. *United States v. Lopez*, 514 U.S. 549 at 563.
77. *United States v. Morrison*, 529 U.S. 598 at 599.
78. *United States v. Morrison*, 529 U.S. 598 at 604.
79. Justice Souter, dissenting *United States v. Morrison*, 529 U.S. 598 at 634; see S. Rep. No. 102–197, at 53 (citing Ellis, Atkeson, & Calhoun, "An Assessment of Long-Ter Reaction to Rape," *Journal of Abnormal Psychology* 90, no 3 (1981): 264).
80. *United States v. Morrison*, 529 U.S. 598 at 614, citing H.R. Conf. Rep. No. 103–711, (1994) at 385.
81. See *Heart of Atlanta Motel, Inc. v. United States*, and *Katzenbach v. McClung*.
82. *United States v. Morrison*, 529 U.S. 598 at 615.
83. Thomas F. Green, *The Activities of Teaching* (1782) (New York: McGraw-Hill, 1971), 110.
84. Green, *Activities of Teaching*, 118.
85. See fuller discussion of the "but-for" test above in *DeShaney v. Winnebago Cty. Dept. of Soc. Serv*, 812 F.2d 298 (7th Cir. 1987), https://casetext.com/case/deshaney-v-winnebago-cty-dept-of-soc-serv/ (accessed October 19, 2020); aff'd, 109 S. Ct. 998 (1989).
86. See United Nations expert brief by Day, McKenna, and Bowlus, "The Economic Costs of Violence Against Women."
87. Justice Souter, dissenting *United States v. Morrison*, 529 U.S. 598 at 628.
88. Justice Souter, dissenting *United States v. Morrison*, 529 U.S. 598 at 628.
89. Justice Souter, dissenting *United States v. Morrison*, 529 U.S. 598 at 628.
90. Justice Souter, dissenting *United States v. Morrison*, 529 U.S. 598 at 624.
91. Shaakirrah R. Sanders, and Anbal Rosario Lebrón, "*Morrison v. United States*, 529 U.S. 598 (2000)," in *Feminist Judgment: Rewritten Opinions of the United States Supreme Court*, ed. Kathryn M. Stanch, Linda L. Berger, and Bridget J. Crawford (New York: Cambridge University Press, 2016), 461.
92. ShaSanders and Lebrón, "*Morrison v. United States*, 529 U.S. 598 (2000)," 447–67.
93. Gayle Rubin, "The Traffic in Women: Notes on the 'Political Economy' of Sex," in *Toward an Anthropology of Women*, ed. Rayna R. Reiter (New York: Monthly

Review Press, 1975), 169–83; as cited by Sanders and Lebrón, "*Morrison v. United States*, 529 U.S. 598 (2000)," 461

94. See Rubin, "The Traffic in Women," 160; as cited by Sanders and Lebrón, "*Morrison v. United States*, 529 U.S. 598 (2000)," 461

95. Sanders and Lebrón, "*Morrison v. United States*, 529 U.S. 598 (2000)," at 461

96. *United States v. Morrison*, 529 U.S. 598 at 615.

97. Rashida Manjoo, "Report of the Special Rapporteur on Violence Against Women, its Causes and Consequences," *United Nations Human Rights*, addendum 5, nos. 11, 13, 16 (June, 2011), https://www.ohchr.org/en/issues/women/srwomen/pages/srwomenindex.aspx (accessed October 23, 2020).

98. Manjoo, "Report of the Special Rapporteur," see Conclusions and Recommendations no. 113.

99. Justice Souter, dissenting *United States v. Morrison*, 529 U.S. 598 at 644.

100. Justice Souter, dissenting *United States v. Morrison*, 529 U.S. 598 at 644.

101. *United States v. Morrison*, 529 U.S. 598 at 600.

102. *United States v. Morrison*, 529 U.S. 598 at 620.

103. U.S. Supreme Court, *United States v. Harris*, 106 U.S. 629 (1883), https://supreme.justia.com/cases/federal/us/106/629/ (accessed October 24, 2020); U.S. Supreme Court, *Civil Rights Cases*, 109 U.S. 3 (1883), https://supreme.justia.com/cases/federal/us/109/3/ (accessed October 24, 2020).

104. *United States v. Morrison*, 529 U.S. 598 at 621; See *United States v. Harris* at 639.

105. *United States v. Morrison*, 529 U.S. 598 at 621.

106. U.S. Supreme Court, *Lugar v. Edmondson Oil Co., Inc.*, 457 U.S. 922 (1982) at 936, https://supreme.justia.com/cases/federal/us/457/922/ (accessed October 24, 2020).

107. Justice Souter, citing S. Rep. No. 103–138 at 38, in *United States v. Morrison*, 529 U.S. 598 at 631.

108. Sanders and Lebrón, "*Morrison v. United States*, 529 U.S. 598 (2000)," 462–63.

109. U.S. Supreme Court, *United States v. Guest*, 383 U.S. 745 (1966), https://supreme.justia.com/cases/federal/us/383/745/ (accessed October 24, 2020).

110. *United States v. Guest*, Justice Brennan dissenting at 777.

111. *United States v. Guest* at 778.

112. *United States v. Guest* at 779.

113. *United States v. Guest* at 780.

114. *United States v. Guest* at 780.

115. U.S. Supreme Court, *Strauder v. West Virginia*, 100 U.S. 303 (1880), at 310, https://supreme.justia.com/cases/federal/us/100/303/ (accessed October 24, 2020).

116. *United States v. Guest*, Justice Brennan dissenting at 784.

117. *McCulloch v. Maryland*, 4 Wheat 316, at 421.

118. *McCulloch v. Maryland* at 463.

119. Oliver W. Holmes, Jr., *The Common Law* (Boston: Little, Brown, 1881; repr. Chicago: American Bar Association, 2009), 142, https://books.google.com/books?id=VeFg0o5T9O0C (accessed October 24, 2020).

120. *United States v. Morrison*, 529 U.S. 598, Justice Breyer dissenting at 666.

121. *United States v. Morrison*, 529 U.S. 598, at 616n7.
122. *United States v. Morrison*, 529 U.S. 598, at 616n7.
123. Sanders and Lebrón, "*Morrison v. United States*, 529 U.S. 598 (2000)," 467.
124. William H. Rehnquist, "The Notion of a Living Constitution," *Texas Law Review* 54, no. 693 (1976): 1–9, http://lc.org/071218TheNotionofaLivingConstitution.doc.pdf (accessed October 24, 2020).
125. David G. Savage, "The Rehnquist Court," *Los Angeles Times*, September 29, 1991, https://www.latimes.com/archives/la-xpm-1991-09-29-tm-4832-story.html (accessed October 24, 2020).
126. Alan Gewirth, *The Community of Rights* (Chicago: University of Chicago Press, 1996), 6.
127. Gewirth, *Community of Rights*, 6.
128. Richard Wasserstrom, "Rights, Human Rights, and Racial Discrimination," in *Human Rights*, ed. A. I. Melden (Belmont, CA: Wadsworth Publishing, 1970), 107.
129. Wasserstrom, "Rights, Human Rights," 107.
130. Wasserstrom, "Rights, Human Rights," 103.
131. *United States v. Morrison*, 529 U.S. 598, at 620.
132. *United States v. Morrison*, 529 U.S. 598, at 627.
133. *United States v. Morrison*, 529 U.S. 598, at 627.

Bibliography

Acton, Harry Burrows. "Herbert Spencer." *Encyclopaedia Britannica.* April 23, 2020. https://www.britannica.com/biography/Herbert-Spencer (accessed October 5, 2018).
Adler, Mortimer J., "Does the End Ever Justify the Means?" *SCI Library.* Reprint. February 2001. https://www.cooperative-individualism.org/adler-mortimer_does-the-end-justify-the-means-2001.htm (accessed September 8, 2018).
Aquinas, St. Thomas. "First Part of the Second Part." In *Summa Theologica.* 2nd and revised ed. Translated by Father of the English Dominican Province. New Advent, Online Edition, 1920. https://www.newadvent.org/summa/2.htm (accessed October 15, 2020).
Aristotle. *The Nicomachean Ethics.* Translated by J. A. K. Thomson. New York; Harmondsworth, UK: Penguin Books, 1965.
Authorized King James Version. Oxford: Oxford University Press.
Baker, Sir Ernest. *Tradition of Civility.* Cambridge: Cambridge University Press, 1948.
Bernstein, David E. "Freedom of Contract." *Liberty of Contract, in Encyclopedia of the Supreme Court of the United States,* edited by David S. Tanenhaus (2008): 1–10. George Mason University Law and Economics Research Paper Series No. 08-51. http://ssrn.com/abstract id=1239749 (accessed August 31, 2018; December 13, 2018).
———. "*Lochner* Era Revisionism, Revised: *Lochner* and the Origins of Fundamental Rights Constitutionalism." *Georgetown Law Journal* 82, no. 1 (2003): 1–61. George Mason University Law & Economics Research Paper No. 03-18. https://papers.ssrn.com/sol3/papers.cfm?abstract_id=395620 (accessed October 17, 2020).
Bezilla, Robert, and George H. Gallup International Institute. "Teenage Attitudes and Behavior Concerning Tobacco-Report of the Findings." ICPSR 6252 (1992). https://doi.org/10.3886/ICPSR06252.v1 (accessed October 22, 2020).
Bolis, Mara, and Christine Hughes. "Women's Economic Empowerment and Domestic Violence: Links and Lessons for Practitioners Working with Intersectional

Approaches." *OXFAM* (2015). https://s3.amazonaws.com/oxfam-us/www/static/media/files/Womens_Empowerment_and_Domestic_Violence_-_Boris__Hughes_hX7LscW.pdf (accessed October 23, 2020).

CaseBriefs. "DeShaney v. Winnebago County." *Bloomberg Law*. 1989. https://www.casebriefs.com/blog/law/evidence/evidence-keyed-to-waltz/nonfeasance/deshaney-v-winnebago-county/ (accessed October 19, 2020).

Centers for Disease Control and Prevention (CDC). "Cigarette Smoking-Attributable Mortality and Years of Potential Life Lost-United States, 1990." *Morbidity and Mortality Weekly Report* 42, no. 33 (August 27, 1993): 645–49. https://www.jstor.org/stable/41965095 (accessed October 22, 2020).

———. "Costs of Intimate Partner Violence Against Women in the United States." (2003). https://www.cdc.gov/violenceprevention/pdf/IPVbook-a.pdf (accessed October 23, 2020).

———. "Reasons for Tobacco Use and Symptoms of Nicotine Withdrawal Among Adolescent and Young Adult Tobacco Users-United States, 1993." *Morbidity and Mortality Weekly* 43, no. 41 (1994): 745–50.

Centers for Disease Control and Prevention (CDC), M. C. Farrelly, J. W. Bray, and Research Triangle Institute. "Response to Increases in Cigarette Prices by Race/Ethnicity, Income, and Age Groups—United States, 1976-1993." *Morbidity and Mortality Weekly Report* 47, no. 29 (July 31, 1998): 605–28. https://www.cdc.gov/mmwr/PDF/wk/mm4729.pdf (accessed October 22, 2020).

Chemerinsky, Erwin. "Substantive Due Process." *Touro Law Review* 15, no. 4 (1999): 1500–1534 (Article 15). https://digitalcommons.tourolaw.edu/lawreview/vol15/iss4/15 (accessed October 18, 2020).

Chuang, Jane. "Who Should Win the Garbage Wars? Lessons from the Low-Level Radioactive Waste Policy Act." *Fordham Law Review* 72, no. 6 (2004): 2403–69. https://ir.lawnet.fordham.edu/flr/vol72/iss6/5 (accessed October 21, 2020).

Cicero, Marcus Tullius. *On the Laws*. Translated by David Fott. Ithaca, NY: Cornell University Press, 2014. https://www.ninrac.org/classical/cicero/documents/de-legibus (accessed September 5, 2020).

———. *De Legibus (On the Laws)*. In The Political Works of Marcus Tullius Cicero: Comprising his Treatise on the Commonwealth; and his Treatise on the Laws. vol. 2, trans. Francis Barham, Esq. London: Edmund Spettigue, 1841-1842. https://oll.libertyfund.org/titles/cicero-treatise-on-the-laws (accessed October 15, 2020).

———. *On the Republic*. In The Political Works of Marcus Tullius Cicero: Comprising his Treatise on the Commonwealth; and his Treatise on the Laws. 2 vols., translated by Francis Barham, Esq. London: Edmund Spettigue, 1841-1842. https://oll.libertyfund.org/titles/546 (accessed October 15, 2020).

———. *On the Republic*. Translated by Clinton W. Keyes. Cambridge, MA: Harvard University Press, 1928. http://www.attalus.org/translate/republic3.html (accessed September 5, 2020).

Colish, Marcia L. *The Stoic Tradition from Antiquity to the Early Middle Ages*. Vol. 1. *Stoicism in Classical Latin Literature*. New York: E. J. Brill, 1990.

Cornell Law School. "Lochner Era." *Legal Information Institute*. https://www.law.cornell.edu/wex/lochner_era (accessed October 16, 2020).

Dahl, Robert A. *Democracy and its Critics*. New Haven, CT: Yale University Press, 1989.
Day, Tanis, Katherine McKenna, and Audra Bowlus. "The Economic Costs of Violence Against Women: An Evaluation of the Literature." Brief prepared for Secretary-General of Canada. United Nations. London, Ontario (2005). https://www.un.org/womenwatch/daw/vaw/expert%20brief%20costs.pdf (accessed October 23, 2020).
d'Entrèves, Alessandro Passerin. *Natural Law: An Introduction to Legal Philosophy*. London: Hutchinson University Library, 1964.
Dewey, John. *The Ethics of Democracy*. University of Michigan Philosophical Papers, 2nd series, 1. Ann Arbor: Andrews & Co., 1888.
Dreilinger, Samantha. "Fall-Out: *New York v. United States* and the Low-Level Radioactive Waste Problem." *Northwestern Journal of Law and Social Policy* 5, no. 1 (2010): 183–205. https://paperity.org/p/83996251/fall-out-new-york-v-united-states-and-the-low-level-radioactive-waste-problem (accessed November 19, 2016).
Dworkin, Ronald. *Freedom's Law: The Moral Reading of the American Constitution*. Oxford: Oxford University Press, 1996; 2005.
Encyclopaedia Britannica. "Lochner v. New York." *Encyclopaedia Britannica*. https://www.britannica.com/print/article/345714 (accessed August 29, 2018).
Endicott, Timothy. "Law and Language." *Stanford Encyclopedia of Philosophy*, edited by Edward N. Zalta (Summer 2016 ed.). https://plato.stanford.edu/archives/sum2016/entries/law-language/ (accessed October 19, 2020).
Feinberg, Joel. *Harmless Wrongdoing*. Oxford: Oxford University Press, 1988.
Gale, Fred. "Economic Structure of Tobacco-Growing Regions." *Tobacco Situation and Outlook*. U.S. Department of Agriculture. Economic Research Service, TBS-241 (April 1998): 40–47.
Gerken, Heather K. "Our Federalism(s)." *William & Mary Law Review* 53, no. 5 (2012): 1549–73. https://scholarship.law.wm.edu/wmlr/vol53/iss5/3 (accessed August 4, 2016).
Gewirth, Alan. *The Community of Rights*. Chicago: Chicago University Press, 1996.
Glendon, Mary Ann. *Rights Talk: The Impoverishment of Political Discourse*. New York: Free Press, 1991.
Gostin, Lawrence O., ed., *Public Health Law and Ethics: A Reader*. 2nd and Revised ed. Berkeley: University of California Press, 2010.
Green, Leslie, and Thomas Adams. "Legal Positivism." *Stanford Encyclopedia of Philosophy*. edited by Edward N. Zalta (Winter 2019). http://plato.stanford.edu/entries/legal-positivism/ (accessed April 29, 2020).
Green, Thomas F. *The Activities of Teaching*. New York: McGraw-Hill, 1971.
Greenhouse, Linda. "The Supreme Court and a Life Barely Lived." *New York Times*, January 7, 2016. https://www.nytimes.com/2016/01/07/opinion/the-supreme-court-and-a-life-barely-lived.html (accessed October 19, 2020).
Grotius, Hugo. The Rights of War and Peace. Edited by Jean Barbeyrac and Richard Tuck. Introduction by Richard Tuck. 3 vols. Indianapolis: Liberty Fund, 2005. https://oll.libertyfund.org/titles/1425 (accessed April 20, 2020).

———. The Rights of War and Peace, including the Law of Nature and of Nations. Translated from the Original Latin of Grotius, with Notes and Illustrations from Political and Legal Writers, by A. C. Campbell, A.M. Introduction by David J. Hill. New York: M. Walter Dunne, 1901. https://oll.libertyfund.org/titles/553 (accessed April 24, 2020).

Gupta, Geeta Rao, Justine O. Parkhurst, Jessica A. Ogden, Peter Aggleton, and Ajay Mahal. "Structural Approaches to HIV Prevention." *Lancet* 372, no. 9640 (2008): 764–75. https://doi.org/10.1016/s0140-6736(08)60887-9 (accessed October 23, 2020).

Hamilton, Alexander. "The Federalist No. 28." *Yale Law School.* https://avalon.law.yale.edu/18th_century/fed28.asp (accessed August 1, 2016).

———. "The Federalist No. 82." In *The Debate on the Constitution Federalist and Antifederalist Speeches Articles and Letters During the Struggle over Ratification Part One September 1787 February 1788* edited by Bernard Bailyn part 2 493–97 New York Library of America 1993

Hare, R. M. [Richard Mervyn]. *The Language of Morals* (1952). Oxford: Clarendon Press, 1960; 2003.

Hart, H. L. A. [Herbert Lionel Adolphus]. *The Concept of Law* (1961). Oxford: Oxford University Press, 2012.

———. "Positivism and the Separation of Law and Morals." *Harvard Law Review* 71, no. 4 (1958): 593–629. https://doi.org/10.1093/acprof:oso/9780198253884.003.0003. Quoted in "Legal Positivism." *Wikipedia,* https://en.wikipedia.org/wiki/Legal_positivism#cite_note-1 (accessed August 31, 2018).

Hodges, Andrew. *Alan Turing: The Enigma.* Princeton, NJ: Princeton University Press, 2014.

Holmes, Oliver W., Jr. *The Common Law.* Boston: Little, Brown, 1881. Reprint. Chicago: American Bar Association, 2009. https://books.google.com/books?id=VeFg0o5T9O0C (accessed October 24, 2020).

———. "The Path of the Law." *Harvard Law Review* 10, no. 8 (1897): 457–78. http://moglen.law.columbia.edu/LCS/palaw.pdf (accessed October 18, 2020).

Institute of Medicine (IOM). *Ending the Tobacco Problem: A Blueprint for the Nation.* Edited by Richard J. Bonnie, Kathleen Stratton, and Robert B. Wallace. Washington, DC: National Academies Press, 2007.

———. *Growing Up Tobacco Free: Preventing Nicotine Addiction in Children and Youths.* Edited by Barbara S. Lynch and Richard J. Bonnie. Washington, DC: National Academies Press, 1994.

Jha, Prabhat, Chinthanie Ramasundarahettige, Victoria Landsman, Brian Rostron, et al., "21st-Century Hazards of Smoking and Benefits of Cessation in the United States." *New England Journal of Medicine* 368 (2013): 341–50. https://www.nejm.org/doi/10.1056/NEJMsa1211128 (accessed October 22, 2020).

Kahn-Freund, Otto. *Labour and the Law.* Hamlyn Lectures 24th ser. London: Stevens, 1972. https://doi.org/10.1093/iclqaj/22.1.199 (accessed October 18, 2020).

Kant, Immanuel. *Critique of Practical Reason.* Translated by Lewis White Beck. Upper Saddle River, NJ: Prentice Hall, 1993.

———. *Groundwork of the Metaphysic of Morals*. Translated and analyzed by H. J. Paton. New York: Harper Torch Books/The Academy Library, 1964.

———. *The Metaphysics of Ethics*. Translated by J. W. Semple. Edited and Introduction by Rev. Henry Calderwood, 3rd ed. Edinburgh: T & T Clark, 1886. https://oll.libertyfund.org/titles/1445 (accessed October 10, 2020).

———. *Rechtslehre*. In *Die Metaphysik der Sitten* (1797), *47. Translated by J. W. Semple. Edited with introduction by Rev. Henry Calderwood. 3rd ed. Edinburgh: T. & T. Clark, 1886. https://oll.libertyfund.org/titles/1443 (accessed December 10, 2020).

Kearney, Richard C. Low-Level Radioactive Waste Management: Environmental Policy, Federalism, and New York." *Publius* 23, no. 3 (1993): 57–73. https://www.jstor.org/stable/3330842 (accessed October 21, 2020).

"Labour Law." *Wikipedia*. Last edited October 7, 2020. https://en.wikipedia.org/wiki/Labour_law (accessed September 7, 2018).

A Law Dictionary, Adapted to the Constitution and Laws of the United States. By John Bouvier, S.v. "Impairing the Obligation of Contracts." N.d., https://legal-dictionary.thefreedictionary.com/Impairing+the+obligation+of+contracts (accessed December 13, 2018).

"Lochner v. New York." *Wikipedia*. Last edited October 2, 2020. https://en.wikipedia.org/wiki/Lochner_v._New_York (accessed October 17, 2020).

Locke, John. *An Essay Concerning The True Original, Extent and End of Civil Government* (1690). In *The English Philosophers From Bacon To Mill*, edited by Edwin A. Burtt, 404-9. New York: Modern Library, 1939.

———. *The Two Treatises of Civil Government* (1689; 1764), in *Classics of Liberty: The Enhanced Editions*, https://oll.libertyfund.org/page/john-locke-two-treatises-1689 (accessed December 10, 2020).

Longeway, John. "Medieval Theories of Demonstration." *Stanford Encyclopedia of Philosophy* (Spring 2009), edited by Edward N. Zalta. https://plato.stanford.edu/entries/demonstration-medieval (accessed October 15, 2020).

Madison, James. "The Federalist No. 46." In *The Debate on the Constitution Federalist and Antifederalist Speeches Articles and Letters During the Struggle over Ratification Part One September 1787-February 1788* edited by Bernard Bailyn part 2 109–15. New York Library of America 1993.

Maine, Henry James Sumner. *Ancient Law, Its Connection with the Early History of Society, and Its Relation to Modern Ideas*. London: John Murray, 1861.

Manjoo, Rashida. "Report of the Special Rapporteur on Violence Against Women, its Causes and Consequences." *United Nations Human Rights*. Addendum 5, nos. 11, 13, 16 (June, 2011). https://www.ohchr.org/en/issues/women/srwomen/pages/srwomenindex.aspx (accessed October 23, 2020).

McCartney, Steve, and Rick Parent. "2.9 Social Contract Theory." In *Ethics in Law Enforcement*, 30-32. Victoria, BC: BC Campus, 2015. https://opentextbc.ca/ethicsinlawenforcement/open/download?type=pdf (accessed October 18, 2020).

McBride, Alex. *Lochner v. New York* (1905). https://www.thirteen.org/wnet/supremecourt/capitalism/landmark_lochner.html (accessed November 14, 2020).

McCulloch v. Maryland, 4 Wheat 316 (1819).

Merriam Webster Online Dictionary. s.v. "Legal Right." 2020. https://www.merriam-webster.com/dictionary/legal%20right (accessed November 14, 2020).

Mill, John Stuart. "On Liberty" (1859). In *On Liberty. In The English Philosophers From Bacon to Mill*, edited by Edwin A. Burtt, 949-60. New York: Random House, 1939.

Morris, Herbert. "Persons and Punishment." In *Human Rights*, edited by A. I. Melden. Belmont. CA: Wadsworth Publishing, 1970.

Murphy, Mark. "The Natural Law Tradition in Ethics." Stanford Encyclopedia of Philosophy (Summer 2019). Edited by Edward N. Zalta. https://plato.stanford.edu/archives/sum2019/entries/natural-law-ethics (accessed October 15, 2020).

National Research Council, Commission on Geosciences, and Committee to Review New York State's Siting and Methodology Selection for Low-Level Radioactive Waste Disposal. *Review of New York State Low-Level Radioactive Waste Siting Process.* Washington, DC: National Academy Press, 1996. https://www.nap.edu/catalog/5325/review-of-new-york-state-low-level-radioactive-waste-siting-process (accessed November 19, 2016).

Nelson, Russell M. "Addiction or Freedom." *Church of Jesus Christ of Latter-Day Saints.* From a conference address delivered October 1988. https://www.churchofjesuschrist.org/study/new-era/1989/09/addiction-or-freedom?lang=eng (accessed October 22, 2020).

Newberry, William F. "The Rise and Fall and Rise and Fall of American Public Policy on Disposal of Low-Level Radioactive Waste." *South Carolina Environmental Law Journal* 3, no. 1 (1993): 43–73.

New York Baking Companies. "Unions: The Baking Industry in the State of New York." *Ward Baking Company* (2005): 1–3. http://www.wardbakingcompany.com/library/docs/New YorkBakingCompanies.pdf (accessed October 18, 2020).

New York State. Court of Appeals. *People v. Lochner.* 177 N.Y. 145 (1904). https://cite.case.law/ny/177/145/ (accessed August 29, 2018).

New York State. Supreme Court. Appellate Division, Fourth Department. *People v. Lochner.* 73 N.Y. App. Div. (1902). https://casetext.com/case/people-v-lochner-3 (accessed August 29, 2018).

New York Times Editorial Board. "Justice Kennedy's Plea to Congress." *New York Times.* April 4, 2015, SR 10. https://www.nytimes.com/2015/04/05/opinion/sunday/justice-kennedys-plea-to-congress.html (accessed October 20, 2020).

Nicholls, Donald. "My Kingdom for a Horse: The Meaning of Words." (2005) 121 LQR 577. In fulfillment of Doctor of Philosophy in Law, Victoria University of Wellington, 2012.

Nock, Albert Jay. "Spencer." N.d. https://oll.libertyfund.org/pages/spencer-by-albert-jay-nock (accessed December 10, 2020).

"Notes on Labor, 1875-1900." *Georgetown Preparatory School.* http://claver.gprep.org/sjochs/labor.htm (accessed September 1, 2018).

Nowell-Smith, P. H. *Ethics.* Baltimore, MD: Penguin Books, 1961.

Nuclear Information and Resource Services (NIRS). "'Low-Level' Radioactive Waste Is Not Low Risk." *NIRS.* April 2009. https://www.nirs.org/wp-content/uploads/factsheets/llwnolowrisk.pdf (accessed October 20, 2020).

O'Connor, Anahad. "Putting a Number on Smoking's Toll." *New York Times* (New York), January 29, 2013, D4. Online January 23, 2013, https://well.blogs.nytimes.com/2013/01/23/putting-a-number-to-smokings-toll/ (accessed October 22, 2020).

Penguin Dictionary of Philosophy. Edited by Thomas Mautner. London: Penguin Books, 1997.

Plato (ΠΛΑΤΩΝ). *Crito (ΚΡΙΤΩΝ)* (c. 399 BCE). Translated by Cathal Woods and Ryan Pack. San Francisco: Creative Commons, 2007-2012. https://www.pitt.edu/~mthompso/readings/crito.pdf (accessed October 15, 2020).

Pope Leo XIII. *Rerum Novarum, Encyclical of Pope Leo XIII on Capital and Labor* (1891). http://www.vatican.va/content/leo-X111/encyclicals/documents/hf_1-X111_enc_15051891_rerum-novarum (accessed December 10, 2020).

Price, J. "Teen Smoking, Marijuana Use Increase Sharply, Study Shows." *Washington Times*, December 16, 1995.

Ramjee, Gita, and Brodie Daniels. "Women and HIV in Sub-Sharan Africa." *AIDS Research and Therapy* 10, no. 30 (2013). https://doi.org/10.1186/1742-6405-10-30 (accessed October 23, 2020).

Rehnquist, William H. "The Notion of a Living Constitution." *Texas Law Review* 54, no. 693 (1976): 1–9. http://lc.org/071218TheNotionofaLivingConstitution.doc.pdf (accessed October 24, 2020).

Rorty, Richard. "Human Rights, Rationality, and Sentimentality." In *On Human Rights: The Oxford Amnesty Lectures, 1993*, edited by Stephen Shute and Susan Hurley, 111-34. New York: Basic Books, 1993.

Rubin, Gayle. "The Traffic in Women: Notes on the 'Political Economy' of Sex." In *Toward an Anthropology of Women*, edited by Rayna R. Reiter, 157-210. New York: Monthly Review Press, 1975.

Russell, Bertrand. *My Philosophical Development*. London: Routledge, 1995.

S, Surbhi. "Differences Between Economic and Non-Economic Activities." *Key Differences* (June 20, 2016). https://keydifferences.com/difference-between-economic-and-non-economic-activities.html (accessed October 23, 2002).

Sanders, Shaakirrah R., and Anbal Rosario Lebrón. "*Morrison v. United States*, 529 U.S. 598 (2000)." In *Feminist Judgment: Rewritten Opinions of the United States Supreme Court*, edited by Kathryn M. Stanch, Linda L. Berger, and Bridget J. Crawford, 447-67. New York: Cambridge University Press, 2016.

Savage, David G. "The Rehnquist Court." *Los Angeles Times*, September 29, 1991. https://www.latimes.com/archives/la-xpm-1991-09-29-tm-4832-story.html (accessed October 24, 2020).

Schwanke, Crystal. "Early 20th Century Unemployment." *Lovetoknow.* https://jobs.lovetoknow.com/Early_20th_Century_Unemployment (accessed August 31, 2018).

Singer, Peter. "R. M. Hare's Achievements in Moral Philosophy." Talk for Memorial Service at St. Mary's Church, Oxford, May 25, 2002. *Utilitas* 14, no. 3 (2002): 1–10. https://www.utilitarian.net/singer/by/20020525.pdf (accessed October 15, 2020).

Smith, Garrett M. "*DeShaney v. Winnebago County*: The Narrowing Scope of Constitutional Torts." *Maryland Law Review* 49, no. 2 (1990): 484–508. https://digitalcommons.law.umaryland.edu/mlr/vol49/iss2/9 (accessed October 19, 2020).

Soifer, Aviam. "Moral Ambition, Formalism, and the 'Free World' of DeShaney." *George Washington Law Review* 57, no. 6 (1989): 1513–32. https://ssrn.com/abstract=1539685 (accessed October 19, 2020).

Stole, Lars A. "Lectures on the Theory of Contracts" (1993; rev. 1999). *Yale CampusPress*. http://campuspress.yale.edu/dirkbergemann/files/2011/01/lectures.pdf (accessed December 19,2018).

Sunstein, Cass R. "Lochner's Legacy." *Columbia Law Review* 87, no. 5 (1987): 873–919. https://www.jstor.org/stable/1122721 (accessed October 16, 2020).

Tuckness, Alex, "Locke's Political Philosophy." *Stanford Encyclopedia of Philosophy*, edited by Edward N. Zalta (2005; Winter 2020 ed.). https://plato.stanford.edu/entries/locke-political/ (accessed August 2, 2018).

U.S. Bureau of Labor Statistics. "American Labor in the 20th Century." By Donald M. Fisk (2001; repr. 2003): 1–8. https://www.bls.gov/opub/mlr/cwc/american-labor-in-the-20th-century.pdf (accessed October 17, 2020).

U.S. Congress. *Annex Nicotine in Cigarettes and Smokeless Tobacco Is a Drug and These Products Are Nicotine Delivery Devices Under the Federal Food, Drug, and Cosmetic Act*: Jurisdictional Determination. 61 FR 44619 (August 28, 1996). https://www.govinfo.gov/content/pkg/FR-1996-08-28/pdf/X96-20828.pdf (accessed October 22, 2020).

———. *Comprehensive Smokeless Tobacco Health Education Act.* 15 U.SC. 4401–4408 (1986). https://www.ftc.gov/enforcement/statutes/comprehensive-smokeless-tobacco-health-education-act-1986 (accessed October 22, 2020).

———. Congressional Record-House (99th Cong., 1st sess.). Vol. 131, Part 27, December 19, 1985. https://www.congress.gov/bound-congressional-record/1985/12/19, or https://www.congress.gov/99/crecb/1985/12/19/GPO-CRECB-1985-pt27-2.pdf (accessed October 21, 2020).

———. *Consumer Products Safety Act (CPSA).* 15 U.S.C 2051-2089, PL 92-573, 86 Stat. 1207 (1972). https://www.cpsc.gov/PageFiles/105435/cpsa.pdf?epslanguage=en (accessed October 22, 2020).

———. *Fair Labor Standards Act (FLSA).* 29 U.S.C. 201, et seq. (1938). https://www.law.cornell.edu/uscode/text/29/chapter-8 (accessed October 24, 2020).

———. *Family Smoking Prevention and Tobacco Control Act.* PL 111-13 (111th Cong., 1st sess.) (2009). https://www.congress.gov/bill/111th-congress/house-bill/1256 (accessed October 23, 2020).

———. *Federal Cigarette Labeling and Advertising Act.* 15 U.S.C. 1331-1340, 21 U.S.C. 387c (1966). https://www.ftc.gov/enforcement/statutes/federal-cigarette-labeling-advertising-act (accessed October 22, 2020).

———. *Food, Drug, and Cosmetics Act (FDCA).* 21 U.S.C. 301 (1938). https://www.loc.gov/item/uscode1934-006021009/ (accessed October 22, 2020).

———. *Food, Drug, and Cosmetics Act (FDCA).* 21 U.S.C. 301 (1938). https://www.loc.gov/item/uscode1934-006021009/ (accessed October 22, 2020).

———. *The Low-Level Radioactive Waste Policy Act.* Pub. L. 96-573 (1980). 94 Stat. 3347, 94 Stat. 3348, 94 Stat. 3349 (96th Cong. 2nd sess.) December 22, 1980. https://www.govinfo.gov/link/statute/94/3347 (accessed October 20, 2020).

———. *The Low-Level Radioactive Waste Policy Amendments Act*, Pub. L. 99-240 (1985) H.R. 1083 (99th Cong. 1st sess.) (January 15, 1996), https://www.congress.gov/bill/99th-congress/house-bill/1083 (accessed October 21, 2020).

———. *Regulations Restricting the Sale and Distribution of Cigarettes and Smokeless Tobacco Products To Protect Children and Adolescents*. 60 FR 155, 41321–41338 (August 11, 1995). https://www.govinfo.gov/content/pkg/FR-1995-08-11/pdf/95-20051.pdf (accessed October 22, 2020).

———. *Regulations Restricting the Sale and Distribution of Cigarettes and Smokeless Tobacco Products To Protect Children and Adolescents*. 61 FR 168, 44396–44618 (August 28, 1996). https://www.govinfo.gov/content/pkg/FR-1996-08-28/pdf/X96-10828.pdf (accessed October 22, 2020).

———. *Violence Against Women Act (VAWA)*, 42 U.S.C. 13701–14040 (1994), sec. 13981, https://www.govinfo.gov/app/details/USCODE-1996-title42/USCODE-1996-title42-chap136-subchapI-partA-sec13701 (accessed October 23, 2020).

U.S. Court of Appeals. *Action on Smoking and Health ASH v. Harris*. 655 F.2d 236 (D.C. Cir. 1980). https://law.justia.com/cases/federal/appellate-courts/F2/655/236/65200/ (accessed October 20, 2020).

———. *DeShaney v. Winnebago Cty. Dept. of Soc. Serv*. 812 F.2d 298 (7th Cir. 1987). https://casetext.com/case/deshaney-v-winnebago-cty-dept-of-soc-serv/ (accessed October 19, 2020). aff'd, 109 S. Ct. 998 (1989).

———. *Doe v. New York City Department of Social Services*. 649 F. 2d 134 (2nd Cir. 1981). https://casetext.com/case/doe-v-new-york-city-dept-of-social-services-2 (accessed October 19, 2020).

———. *Estate of Bailey by Oare v. County of York*. 768 F. 503, 510-511 (3rd Cir. 1985). https://casetext.com/case/estate-of-bailey-by-oare-v-county-of-york (accessed October 19, 2020).

———. *FERC v. Mississippi*. 456 U.S. 742 (1982). https://supreme.justia.com/cases/federal/us/456/742/ (accessed October 20, 2020).

———. *Hodel v. Virginia Surface Mining and Reclamation Assn., Inc*. 452 U.S. 264 (1981). https://supreme.justia.com/cases/federal/us/452/264/ (accessed October 20, 2020).

———. *In the Matter of Baby "K" (Three Cases)*. 16 F.3d 590 (4th Cir. 1994). https://h2o.law.harvard.edu/cases/4272 (accessed October 15, 2020).

———. *National Nutritional Foods Ass'n v. FDA*. 504 F.2d 761 (2d Cir. 1974). https://openjurist.org/504/f2d/761/national-nutritional-foods-association-v-food-and-drug-administration (accessed October 22, 2020).

U.S. Department of Health and Human Services (HHS). *Healthy People 2000: National health Promotion and Disease Prevention Objectives, A Strategy for Improving the Health of Americans by the End of the Century*. Atlanta: CDC, 1990. https://www.cdc.gov/nchs/healthy_people/hp2000.htm (accessed October 22, 2020).

U.S. Department of Health and Human Services (HHS). Office on Smoking and Health. *Preventing Tobacco Use Among Young People: A Report of the Surgeon General*. Vol. 43, No. RR-4. Atlanta: CDC, 1994. https://www.cdc.gov/mmwr/PDF/rr/rr4304.pdf (accessed October 22, 2020).

U.S. Department of Labor. "Government Regulation of Workers' Safety and Health, 1877-1917," by Judson MacLaury. N.d. https://www.dol.gov/general/aboutdol/history/mono-regsafeintrotoc (accessed October 18, 2020).

U. S. District Court. Eastern District of Pennsylvania. *United States v. Morrison*. 99–5 (2000). https://www.oyez/cases/1999/99-5 (accessed March 30, 2019).

U.S. National Archives. The Constitution of the United States. https://www.archives.gov/founding-docs/constitution-transcript (accessed October 18, 2020).

U.S. Nuclear Regulatory Commission (U.S. NRC). "Low-Level Radioactive Waste (LLW)." April 10, 2017. Last updated June 29, 2020. https://www.nrc.gov/reading-rm/basic-ref/glossary/low-level-radioactive-waste-llw.html (accessed October 20, 2020).

U.S. Supreme Court. *Allgeyer v. Louisiana*. 165 U.S. 578 (1897). https://supreme.justia.com/cases/federal/us/165/578/ (accessed October 18, 2020).

———. *Brown v. Board of Education*. 347 U.S. 483 (1954). https://www.law.cornell.edu/supremecourt/text/347/483 (accessed October 15, 2020).

———. *Case v. Bowles*. 327 U.S. 92 (1946). https://supreme.justia.com/cases/federal/us/327/92/ (accessed October 23, 2020).

———. *Chevron U.S.A Inc. v. Natural Resources Defense Council, Inc.* 467 U.S. 837 (1984). https://supreme.justia.com/cases/federal/us/467/837/ (accessed October 22, 2020).

———. *Civil Rights Cases*. 109 U.S. 3 (1883). https://supreme.justia.com/cases/federal/us/109/3/ (accessed October 24, 2020).

———. *DeShaney v. Winnebago County Department of Social Services*. 489 U.S. 189 (1989). https://www.law.cornell.edu/supremecourt/text/489/189 (accessed October 19, 2020); https://supreme.justia.com/cases/federal/us/489/189/ (accessed October 19, 2020).

———. *Dred Scott v. Sandford*. 60 U.S. 393 (1856). https://caselaw.findlaw.com/us-supreme-court/60/393.html (accessed October 15, 2020).

———. *Estelle v. Gamble*. 429 U.S. 97 (1976). https://supreme.justia.com/cases/federal/us/429/97/ (accessed October 19, 2020).

———. *ETSI Pipeline Project v. Missouri*. 484 U.S. 495 (1988). https://supreme.justia.com/cases/federal/us/484/495/ (accessed October 22, 2020).

———. *Ewing v California*. 538 U.S. 11 (2003). https://supreme.justia.com/cases/federal/us/538/11/ (accessed October 20, 2020).

———. *FDA v. Brown & Williamson Tobacco Corporation*. 529 U.S. 120 (2000). https://supreme.justia.com/cases/federal/us/529/120/case.html (accessed October 22, 2020).

———. *Furman v. Georgia*. 408 U.S. 238 (1972). https://supreme.justia.com/cases/federal/us/408/238/ (accessed October 20, 2020).

———. *Gibbons v. Ogden*. 22 U.S. 1 (1824). https://supreme.justia.com/cases/federal/us/22/1/ (accessed October 23, 2020).

———. *Harmelin v. Michigan*. 501 U.S. 957 (1991). https://supreme.justia.com/cases/federal/us/501/957/ (accessed October 20, 2020).

———. *Heart of Atlanta Motel, Inc. v. United States*. 379 U.S. 241 (1964). https://supreme.justia.com/cases/federal/us/379/241/ (accessed October 23, 2020).

———. *Hodel v. Virginia Surface Mining and Reclamation Assn., Inc.* 452 U.S. 264 (1981). https://supreme.justia.com/cases/federal/us/452/264/ (accessed October 23, 2020).

———. *Holden v. Hardy.* 169 U.S. 366 (1898). https://supreme.justia.com/cases/federal/us/169/366/ (accessed October 17, 2020).

———. *Jacobson v. Massachusetts.* 197 U.S. 11 (1905). https://supreme.justia.com/cases/federal/us/197/11/ (accessed October 17, 2020).

———. *Katzenbach v. McClung.* 379 U.S. 294 (1964). https://supreme.justia.com/cases/federal/us/379/294/ (accessed October 23, 2020).

———. *Lochner v. New York.* 198 U.S. 45 (1905). https://supreme.justia.com/cases/federal/us/198/45/ (accessed October 17, 2020).

———. *Lockyer v Andrade.* 538 U.S. 63 (2003). https://supreme.justia.com/cases/federal/us/538/63/ (accessed October 20, 2020).

———. *Lugar v. Edmondson Oil Co., Inc.* 457 U.S. 922 (1982). https://supreme.justia.com/cases/federal/us/457/922/ (accessed October 24, 2020).

———. *Maryland v. Wirtz.* 392 U.S. 183 (1968). https://supreme.justia.com/cases/federal/us/392/183/ (accessed October 23, 2020).

———. *New York v. United States.* 505 U.S. 144 (1992). https://supreme.justia.com/cases/federal/us/505/144/ (accessed October 15, 2020).

———. *Northern Securities Co. v. United States.* 193 U.S. 197 (1904). https://supreme.justia.com/cases/federal/us/193/197/ (accessed October 18, 2020).

———. *Ogden v. Saunders.* 25 U.S. 213 (1827). https://supreme.justia.com/cases/federal/us/25/213/ (accessed October 18, 2020).

———. *Otis v. Parker.* 187 U.S. 606 (1903). https://supreme.justia.com/cases/federal/us/187/606/ (accessed October 18, 2020).

———. *Parke v. Raley.* 506 U.S. 20 (1992). https://supreme.justia.com/cases/federal/us/506/20/ (accessed October 20, 2020).

———. *Plessy v. Ferguson.* 163 U.S. 537 (1896). https://www.law.cornell.edu/supremecourt/text/163/537 (accessed October 15, 2020).

———. *Sanitary District of Chicago v. United States.* 266 U.S. 405 (1925). https://supreme.justia.com/cases/federal/us/266/405/ (accessed October 23, 2020).

———. *Solem v. Helm.* 463 U.S. 277 (1983). https://supreme.justia.com/cases/federal/us/463/277/ (accessed October 20, 2020).

———. *Strauder v. West Virginia.* 100 U.S. 303 (1880). https://supreme.justia.com/cases/federal/us/100/303/ (accessed October 24, 2020).

———. *Trop v. Dulles.* 356 U.S. 86 (1958). https://supreme.justia.com/cases/federal/us/356/86/ (accessed October 20, 2020).

———. *United States v. Guest.* 383 U.S. 745 (1966). https://supreme.justia.com/cases/federal/us/383/745/ (accessed October 24, 2020).

———. *United States v. Harris.* 106 U.S. 629 (1883). https://supreme.justia.com/cases/federal/us/106/629/ (accessed October 24, 2020).

———. *United States v. Lopez.* 514 U.S. 549 (1995). https://supreme.justia.com/cases/federal/us/514/549/ (accessed October 23, 2020).

———. *United States v. Morrison.* 529 U.S. 598 (2000). https://supreme.justia.com/cases/federal/us/529/598/ (accessed October 23, 2020).

———. *United States v. Rutherford.* 442 U.S. 544, 556 (1979). https://supreme.justia.com/cases/federal/us/442/544/ (accessed October 22, 2020).

———. *Wickard v. Filburn.* 317 U.S. 111 (1942). https://supreme.justia.com/cases/federal/us/317/111/ (accessed October 23, 2020).

———. *Williamson v. Lee Optical, Inc.* 348 U.S. 483 (1955). https://supreme.justia.com/cases/federal/us/348/483/ (accessed October 18, 2020).

Warner, Kenneth E. "The Economics of Tobacco: Myths and Realities." *Tobacco Control Journal* 9, no. 1 (2000): 78–89. http://dx.doi.org/10.1136/tc.9.1.78 (accessed October 22, 2020).

Wasserstrom, Richard. "Rights, Human Rights, and Racial Discrimination." In *Human Rights*, edited by A. I. Melden. Belmont, CA: Wadsworth, 1970.

West Virginia State. *Board of Education v. Barnette.* 319 U.S. 624, 638 (1943). https://supreme.justia.com/cases/federal/us/319/624/ (accessed October 20, 2020).

Williamson v. Lee Optical, Inc. 348 U.S. 483 (1955). https://supreme.justia.com/cases/federal/us/348/483/ (accessed December 5, 2020).

Wilson, John. *Language and the Pursuit of Truth.* Cambridge: Cambridge University Press, 1969.

Index

abuse, 77–88, 92–98, 121, 181, 185, 209; Abusive Conduct Policy, 165–66. *See also* U.S. Supreme Court, *DeShaney*
action, xv, 31, 179; and the Due Process clause, 89, 93; duty to, 79–86, 96; and ethics, 26, 159; and freedom, 69, 183; and God, 13; human, 3, 8, 10–12, 15, 30, 34, 66, 81; in-, 77–80, 83–87, 90–97; and justification, 10, 12, 153; and the law, 3, 7, 10, 16, 66, 118–20, 125, 179–80, 185; and morals, 13, 67; and objectivity, 10; and reason, 3; and rights, 34, 44, 63, 81; and smoking, 137, 148
Action on Smoking and Health (ASH), xv, 137
Adler, Mortimer J., 53
adolescents, 133, 140–42, 148, 154, 157 *See also* children; juveniles
altruism, 22
Amendments (U.S.), 18, 176; Eighth, 110–13; Eleventh, 105; Fifth, 105; *A fortiori*, 97, 152; Fourteenth, 18–21, 44–47, 50–51, 60–61, 67, 69, 70n17, 77–78, 85, 166, 182–89; Tenth, 105–6, 109, 126. *See also* constitution; Declaration of Independence; *Low-Level Radioactive Waste Policy Amendment Act* (1980); U.S. Supreme Court *Amendment Act* (1985), 105, 107–9, 119
anarchy, 67
apartheid, 23. *See also* slavery
Aquinas, St. Thomas, 2, 4, 8–13, 24, 37n35, 65–66, 135
Aristotle, 6, 9–11, 16, 23–24, 146, 190
assault, 165, 171; hearing process in higher education, 165–66; sexual, 165. *See also* abuse; violence
Athens, 5, 30; and Athenians, 29–30
autonomy, 7, 12, 46, 56, 63, 90, 117

Baker, Sir Ernest, 4
behavior, 22, 26, 28, 31, 66, 82, 84–86, 137, 152; action v. inaction, 77, 94; direction of, 30; and ethics, 3, 28, 31, 34, 36, 57, 64, 68, 153; good v. bad, 25, 64; and humans, 5–7, 9, 16, 32, 68, 77, 81, 90–91, 93, 97, 110, 112, 185; and justice or the law, 8, 64–65, 68, 82, 98, 107, 112; moral properties, 12, 25, 34, 61, 65, 153, 159; normative, 10, 21, 32, 153, 157; public and private, 186–87; and rights, 33, 61; rules of conduct, 32; self-or other-regarding, 12, 25, 32, 57–58, 61, 123, 135; and violence as

control, 172–73, 180, 185; voluntary v. non-voluntary, 57, 66. *See also* morals; violence
beings, 68; human, vi, 3–8, 14, 22–26, 29, 35 81, 83, 89, 97, 135, 187
Bernstein, David E., 47, 61, 66
black(s), 17, 20; and inclusion in the U.S. Constitution, 17; ownership of by whites, 189; and separation from whites in laws, 18–19, 188–89. *See also* race; slavery
Black, Hugo, 175
Blackman, Harry A., 77, 85, 93, 96, 98n1, 190
Brennan, William J., Jr., 81, 85, 90–96, 113–14, 184–85
Breyer, Stephen, 134, 144–45, 147, 149–52, 159, 186
Britain. *See* United Kingdom
Brown v. Board of Education. *See* U.S. Supreme Court

Carneades, 5–6, 23–24
causation, 77, 80, 96, 179
Centers for Disease Control and Prevention (CDC), xv, 142, 170
certiorari, 79, 134, 143, 166
children, 31, 81, 91, 112, 133, 140, 141–42, 154, 170; *See also* adolescents; juveniles
choice, 7, 18, 26, 33, 44, 63, 85, 107, 110, 121, 137, 144–45, 153, 157. *See also* Hobson
Christians, 11, 188. *See also* God/gods;
Cicero, Marcus Tullius, 2, 5–8, 11, 23, 65, 114, 126
cigarettes. *See* smoking
civil rights. *See* rights
commerce, 43, 106, 169, 174–75; Clause, 166–67, 173–78, 180, 186–88; foreign/international, 147, 167; gender-based violence and, 177–79; internal/intrastate, 174; interstate, 19, 167–68, 173–80, 184; and power, 106, 167, 174, 176–77, 180, 182; protection of, 176; racial discrimination and, 179; sources of, 174. *See also* legislation
community, 3, 10, 15, 30, 54, 68, 123–25; of justice, 6; political, 114; rights/interests of vs. that of the individual, 3, 14, 32, 35, 55; scientific, 58. *See also* Gewirth
compensation, 47–48, 52, 58, 96. *See also* remedy
competence, 90
competition, 47, 176
compliance, 22, 25, 29, 45, 64–65, 107, 147; non-, 22
consequences, 1, 4, 15, 20, 27, 50, 94, 127, 177–79; accountability, 80, 94; affect on others or the public, 25, 104, 120, 122, 125; avoidance of, 145; disagreeable, 65; good or bad, 66, 82, 86, 89, 125, 146–48; and the law, 53, 65, 84, 95–96, 108, 119; material, 64; other-regarding, 25, 66, 123, 154; regressive, 155–56; and rights, 62, 86–87, 186
constitution, iii, vi, ix, 1–2, 15; framework of, 15, 56, 114; original intent of, 15–16, 18–20; principles of, 15–16, 18, 56, 106, 158; protections of, 89, 91, 93; and public policy, 21, 35, 108; and slavery, 2, 17–18, 23, 25. *See also* Amendments (U.S.); contracts; federalism; Food and Drug Administration; freedom; Gerwirth; law; legislation; order; U.S. Constitution
Consumer Products Safety Act. *See* legislation
contract, ix, 15, 24, 27, 56–59, 64–65, 68, 97; in the Constitution, 60–61, 83; and employee/employers, 43–49, 51–70, 155; encroachment on, 47, 53; enforcement of, 55, 61; and ethics, 63; freedom of/to, 47, 51, 56–61; legitimacy of, 57; notion of, 56; obligations of, 61; and the

Index

Peckham argument, 47–49; right of, 47, 54–60, 62–63; terms of, 60–61; social, 11–12, 68, 83–84, 97, 103–27; theories, 11, 63. *See also* Gewirth; Hart; Holmes; U.S. Constitution; U.S. Supreme Court, *FDA* and *Lochner*
control, 4–5, 10, 20, 22, 32, 54–55, 57, 92, 115, 134, 138, 150, 155–56, 159, 170, 172–75
courts, ii–iii, v–vi; appeals, 1, 143 and cases examined, 1, 3–4, 36, 77 circuit, 1, 78–79, 134, 142 decisions of, xiii, 58, 79, 90, 93, 106, 116–17, 124, 126, 152, 174, 182 function of, 1 indifference of, 58–62, 77, 181, 186, 190 jurisprudence, 1, 3, 15, 20, 35, 113, 135, 152 understanding, 19, 44, 144, 167, 182 *See also* Justices by name; legislation; precedent; U.S. Court of Appeals; U.S. Supreme Court, cases by name
crime, 89, 112–13, 166–68, 180–81, 183, 185
Criminal Code, 184 *See also* law; legislation; U.S. Supreme Court
crisis, 104, 109, 117–20
Crito. *See* Plato

damage(s), 48, 64, 78, 96, 105–6, 120, 166
Declaration of Independence (U.S.), 16–18, 158
democracy (-itc), 21, 35–36, 51, 67, 121, 123
d'Entreves, A. P. [Alessandro Passerin], 4, 13, 36, 36n5, 69 Natural Law, 23
deontology, 1
Department of Social Services (DSS), ix, xv, 2, 77–84, 86–87, 90–98
DeShaney v. Winnebago County. See U.S. Supreme Court
Dewey, John, 35–36
dignity, 69, 113

discrimination, 94, 179, 182–84, 189. *See also* gender; racism
disobedience, 66
Doe v. New York City Department of Social Services (1987), 82
Douglas, William O., 61, 184
Dred Scott v. Sandford. See U.S. Supreme Court
due process. *See* Amendment, Fourteenth
duty (-ies), 5–6, 22, 31, 64, 69, 79, 83, 86–89, 91, 97–98, 139

economy (-ics), 33, 44, 149, 154; advantages, 56; and behavior, 57; conditions, 55; and equality/inequality, 180; and legislation, 51; non-, 167, 169, 173, 182; and policy/regulation, 43, 61, 143, 167, 173, 175; power, 170–73; and rights, 35, 43; socio-, 122, 180; subordination, 181; theory of, 51; and the tobacco industry, 147–50, 152, 154–59, 168; and victimization, 55, 168–73. *See also* commerce, Clause; Gewirth
empowerment, 170, 172–73
employment/jobs, 19, 47, 49, 51, 60, 62, 92, 123, 155, 170, 178; compensation, 48, 154; and contracts, 46, 51–52, 155; and health, 46; and laws, 44, 180; and power, 52; un-, 47; work day/week, 43–52, 55, 58–59, 69, 70n17, 169, 171, 176–77; and working conditions, 176–77. *See also* labor; law, labor
enactment. *See* legislation
envy, 9
equality, 12, 24, 97, 187; absolute, 18; economic, 180; human, 6–7, 14–15, 19, 25, 69–70, 135; in-, 19, 52, 171–73, 177; and the law, 19, 22; political, 18; and respect, 171. *See also* Cicero; rights; slavery
Estelle v. Gamble. See U.S. Supreme Court

ethics, 1–36; discourse of, 26, 153; and grounding of law, 36, 188; history of, 1; as internal, 2, 64, 66; and norms, 10, 34, 153; notion of, 25, 111; "ought" vs. "can," 1, 25–27, 30–31, 34, 36, 112; relationship to the law, 2. *See also* Aristotle; behavior; contracts; freedom; Gewirth; good; Hare; individualism; Kant; language; law, logic; morals; natural theory; obligation; perspective; positivism; risk; theory; U.S. Supreme Court

Euclid, 8

Europe, 13, 61–62. *See also* cities and countries by name;

evidence, 27, 173, 180; and contacts, 52, 60; and contradiction, 33; credibility of, 96, 179–80, 182; empirical, 28, 168, 176; non-consideration of, 50; objective/subjective, 137; referred to in legal judgments, 45, 47, 50, 52, 54, 86–87, 151, 158–59, 178–80, 185–87; relevancy of, 178; self-, 13; statistical/scientific, 133–36, 139–40, 179; sufficient v. insufficient, 58, 78, 80, 82, 84–85, 92, 95–96, 109, 136–37, 165, 168, 176, 178, 186; undeniable, 86

evil. *See* good

federalism, 105–7, 110; description of, 115–17, 182–86; doctrine of, 114; and individual rights, 186; and power, 123, 125; referred to in legal judgments, 120–26, 182–85, 190; and the states, 118–19, 121, 190

feminism, 171

FDA v. Brown and Williamson Tobacco. *See* U.S. Supreme Court

Food and Drug Administration (FDA), xv, ix, xv, 134; jurisdiction of, 133–40, 142–43, 146, 149–51; and intervention, 138, 140–41, 144–45, 148, 150, 153; policies of, 136, 138; and public health, 141, 143, 146–47, 152; and violation of the Constitution, 153–54, 158. *See also* U.S. Supreme Court, *FDA*; U.S. Court of Appeals, *Nutritional Foods v. FDA*

forbearance, 23–25

formalism, ix, 77, 85, 93, 104, 111, 116, 123, 190; v. human rights, 165, 182. *See also* Federalism

freedom, 34, 55, 69, 89, 91, 97, 157, 188; of action, 13, 89; and the Constitution, 79; and contracts, 47, 51, 56–57, 59–61, 70; constraint of, 69; and ethics, 34; *from* and *to*, 183; and the liberty of others, 54; and power, 12, 183; rights and well-being, 34–35, 54–55, 62–63, 87. *See also* Amendments, Fourteenth; Gewirth

gender, ii, ix; bias, 167, 174, 181–82, 185, 188–89; and the Commerce Clause, 178–80; and crime, 166, 168; discrimination, 189–90; and economics, 168–73; equality v. inequality, 170–73, 177–78, 189; and identity, 171–72; and wages, 177, 181. *See also* assault; violence, gender-motivated

Germany, 31, 62. *See also* Nazism

Gewirth, Alan, 3, 32–36, 63, 87–88; *The Community of Rights*, 32, 68; "economic constitution," 35; and ethical individualism, 54–55; and Holmes, 63–64; *Principle of Generic Consistency*, 35

Glendon, Mary Ann, 61–62

good, xiii, 116, 136, 146; v. bad, 6, 25, 64–66, 79; and behavior, 25, 65; common, 2, 10, 12, 14, 50, 106, 109, 114–17, 121, 123, 125–26, 190; concept of, 9, 24, 32, 79; and ethics, 26, 28; and evil, 3, 8–9; and humans, 24, 55, 63–64, 68, 122; and the law, 3, 10–11, 15, 33, 47, 65–66, 82–83,

114, 188; of man, 64–65; and morals, 32; and order, 18, 121–22. *See also* Aquinas; Aristotle; Cicero
governance, 15, 21, 44, 67, 88, 105, 115, 117, 120–21, 123
government, 7, 117, 189; American system, 53; British, 14; democratic form, 21, 35–36, 51, 67, 121, 123; despotic, 14; failure of, 14, 66, 165; federal, 104–10, 115, 117–18, 125, 182; inaction by, 79–80, 85–87, 91–97; interference, 45, 55, 58–60, 85–89, 184; legislative branches, 50, 137, 167; overreach, 79, 106, 107; and paternalism, 41, 57; power of, 7, 13–14, 21, 47, 50, 55, 57, 70n17, 105–10, 113, 115–17, 125, 128n22, 144, 156, 166–67, 174–87; regulation, 107–9, 122, 125, 139, 149, 174, 177; sovereignty, 105–7, 109–10, 114, 116–17, 121, 123, 126–27, 177; systems of, 15, 53, 114, 115, 123, 167, 175, 186–87; and tyranny, 79, 114, 121. *See also* Federalism; states
greed, 9
Grotius, Hugo, 2, 11–14 *See also* law, natural theory
God/gods, 6, 13, 24 *See also* Christians; law; Stoics
gun(s), xv, 167–68, 173 *See also* legislation, *Gun-Free School Zones Act of 1990*

happiness, 10, 14, 115
Harding, Warren, 61
Hare, R. M., 3, 26–32, 35, 67, 153; *The Language of Morals*, 3. *See also* ethics; Kant
Harlan I, John Marshall (as Justice 1877–1911), 20–21, 45, 50, 52–53
Harlan II, John Marshall (as Justice 1955–1971), 43, 121–22, 175–77, 179–80

Hart, H. L. A. [Herbert Lionel Adolphus], 2–3, 21–25, 33, 47; "master group," 23
health, ix, xv, 141–42; care, 145, 148, 171; costs, 154–55, 169–70; and employees, 45–46, 50–52, 58–59; and the law, 44–46, 50, 58–59, 103, 114, 138–39, 147–48, 153; mental, 60, 171; public, ix, 43–44, 46, 50, 59, 103, 111, 126, 140–41, 146, 152; and risk/hazards, 45–46, 49–50, 60, 124, 140, 147–49, 151–52, 157. *See also* Action on Smoking and Health (ASH); Centers for Disease Control and Prevention; Food and Drug Administration; legislation; smoking
Health and Human Services (HHS), xv, 135
Hill, David J., 13–14
Hitler, Adolf, 62, 94. *See also* Nazism; socialism
HIV, 172
Hobbes, Thomas, 11, 15
Hobson, Thomas, 107, 145; free choice, 63
Holden v. Hardy. See U.S. Supreme Court
Holmes, Oliver Wendell, Jr., 50–54, 63–67, 69; good man v. bad man, 64–65
human beings. *See* beings
human law. *See* law
Hume, David, 23–24

ideology, ii, 44–45
Illinois, 103
IMAGE (project), 172–73
immigration, 47
imperatives, 26–28; and indicative, 12, 27–30, 79, 122, 152; moral, 26
independence, 14, 16, 18, 54–55, 126, 158, 181
individual (-ism), 6, 32, 91, 94; and behavior, 66–68; and conflict, 12; and control, 32, 87, 89; and ethics,

25, 32, 54; and freedom, happiness, and liberty, 10, 12, 55, 79, 83, 87, 89, 97, 116, 125, 183; and justice, 7, 79, 88, 183; and identity, 171; life/mind, 6; and morality, 54–55, 154; and natural law, 15, 23; rights of, 11–12, 15, 32–33, 35, 44–48, 54–55, 59, 122, 186, 188; and (self-)interest, 33–34, 44, 56, 57; and society, 6, 10, 12, 14–15, 25, 33, 54–55, 97, 154; and the states, 2, 32–34, 88, 121, 185; v. Statism, 55. *See also* Grotius; Hart

injustice. *See* justice

Institute of Medicine (IOM), xv, 142

intersectionality, ii, 171. *See also* feminism

interest, 7, 107, 116, 173, 182; community/common good, 12, 15, 32, 34, 43, 46, 50, 60, 109, 114, 116, 123; competing, 14, 34, 116, 125; economic, 55; groups, 156; and liberty, 44, 78–79, 83–84, 86–89, 91, 93, 96–98, 125; of others, 22, 33–34; personal, 12, 33, 67, 121; protected, 59, 87, 91, 105; property, 44, 87–88; public, 51, 59, 103, 112, 114, 117, 120, 148–49, 156; self-/individual, 11–12, 15, 32, 33–34, 36, 44, 54, 65, 68, 125; states, 2, 48, 90, 108–9, 112–15, 124, 174

interference. *See* government; legislation

intervention, 15; government, 54–55, 57–59, 86, 133, 136, 138, 153, 156; paternalistic, 57; regulatory, 140–41, 144–45, 148; state, 63–64, 91, 96

intuitions, 33

Jacobson v. Massachusetts. *See* U.S. Supreme Court

Jefferson, Thomas, 2, 14–21

Jew (-ish), 31, 188. *See also* Nazism

jobs. *See* employment

Journeymen Bakers Union of New York, 48

jurisprudence. *See* court

justice, ii–iii, 52, 55, 85, 117, 153, 165, 168, 189; centrality of, 7, 24; and community or society, 6–7, 10, 24, 114, 158; criminal, 110, 112, 173, 184; and effectiveness or punishment, 28, 112; and equality, 23, 25; and gender, 181–82; in-, 2, 11, 21, 30, 43, 56, 90, 96, 98, 111, 120, 168, 173, 181, 190; and law, 5, 7, 21, 23, 96, 135, 189; natural and nature of, 5–6, 8, 13, 187–88; as a right, 5, 12, 15, 89; social, 66, 173; universal, 10, 19–20, 88, 135

juveniles, 95. *See also* adolescents; children

Kahn-Freund, Otto, 51–52

Kant, Immanuel, xi, 4, 10, 190; and ethics, 67–70; and the law, 4, 36, 69; *The Metaphysics of Ethics*, xi; morals and conduct, 10, 67–68. notion of "kingdom," 68–69; *See also* law

Kemmeter, Ann, 81–84, 86, 92

Kennedy, Anthony M., 110–13, 134

Kentucky, 103

labor, 44, 50, 155, 176–78; and bargaining, 52; conditions in the workplace, 49–52, 57–58, 176–77; contracts, 45, 48, 58–59; and employers, 47, 52; exploitation of, 47–48, 54; involuntary, 47, 62–63; and laws, 44, 46–47, 49, 51–52; reform, 58; voluntary, 54; and women, 181. *See also* employment; health; law, legislation, *Fair Labor Standards Act of 1938*, *National Labor Relations Act*; slavery

language, 1, 5, 28–29, 90, 94, 97, 157, 171, 174–78; of the day, 17; and dishonesty, 17; of ethics, 26–27, 153; interpretation of, 87–88, 90, 183, 185, 189; meaning of, 17, 47, 49, 85–87, 90, 137–39, 148–49, 153;

and mood, 27; and morality, 3, 27, 153; and natural law, 20, 24, 27; ordinary, 17

Latino/a, 188

law, ii–iii, vi, ix, xi, 1–4; common, 44, 64, 68, 81–82; conditions of, 60; constitutional, vi, 81–82, 89, 110–11, 114, 128n34, 187; ethics and law, 2, 10, 66; and failure to protect, 82, 86; formulation of, 4, 8–14, 21–22, 97; and God as author of, 6, 13; human, 4, 9–10, 13–14; of the land, 4, 128n19, 154; *lex ut jussum*, 107, 135; *lex ut justum*, 107, 135; and mental status, 91; natural, 2–15, 18, 20–21, 23–24, 33, 35–36, 65–66, 88–89, 135, 154, 158–59, 187–88; and objectivity, 3, 27, 29, 66; prohibitions in, 10, 43–47, 60, 65, 105, 110, 112, 148, 184–85; purpose of, 4, 20, 23, 107; rule of, 21; true, 5–7, 14, 66, 114; universality, 5, 9–10, 12, 15, 68; validity of, 21–22, 113; violations of, 30, 44, 78–80, 98, 105, 184, 186–87, 189; of war, 14. See also actions; behavior; blacks; consequences; d'Entreves; employment; equality; ethics; good; health; justice; Kant; labor; legislation; liberty; logic; morals; New York; obligation; philosophy; police; positivism; property; reason; sense; U.S. Constitution; U.S. Supreme Court

legislation, 55, 59, 104–8, 126, 133, 138, 176; *Civil Rights Act* (1871), 183; *Civil Rights Act* (1875), 183; *Civil Rights Cases* (1883), 183–84; *Civil Rights Remedy*, 183; *Comprehensive Smokeless Tobacco Health Education Act* (1966), 138; and the Constitution, 15, 20–21, 44–46, 51, 53, 110, 119, 138, 147, 154, 166, 178, 182; *Consumer Products Safety Act* (*CPSA*), xv, 138; enactment, 50, 53, 139, 183, 188; and equality/justice, 18, 21, 51; *Fair Labor Standards Act of 1938* (*FSLA*), xv, 176–77; *Family Smoking Prevention and Tobacco Control Act* (2009), 159; *Federal Cigarette Labeling and Advertising Act of 1966* (*FCLAA*), xv, 138, 148–49; *Federal Food, Drug, and Cosmetics Act of 1938* (*FDCA*), xv, 133–40, 142–51, 153–54, 158; *Gun-Free School Zones Act of 1990* (*GFSZA*), xv, 167, 173; interpretation of, 149–50, 185; and interference with freedom/rights, 45, 54–55, 58–60, 85–89, 184; *Interstate Commerce Act* (1887), 174; invalidation of, 166; *National Labor Relations Act* (*Wagner Act*) (1937), 51, 174, 176; *New York State Low-Level Radioactive Waste Disposal Act of 1986* (*LLRW*), xv, 122; *Public Utility Regulatory Policies Act of 1978* (*PURPA*), xv, 109; and "pure reason," 69; *Sherman Anti-Trust Act* (1889), 174; and the states, 43, 46, 92, 104–5, 112, 117, 125, 167, 174, 181; *Violence Against Women Act of 1994* (*VAWA*), 166, 178, 188. See also courts; economics; Federalism; law; U.S. Supreme Court;

liberty (-ies), ix, 54, 67, 108, 110, 114; as absolute, 67; depravation or encroachment of, 44, 46–47, 53, 57–58, 69, 80, 85–86, 89, 93, 95, 116, 182; enjoyment of, 57, 97; failure to act, 82, 84, 89; and imprisonment/incarceration, 88–89; interests, 83–84, 86–89, 91, 93, 96–98, 107; in the law, 50, 59, 66, 69, 77, 79, 89, 91, 94, 97, 121, 125, 139, 150, 158, 188; of others, 54, 112; protection of, 59, 78, 86, 91; and race, 18–19; and rights, 3, 14, 16–17, 51, 57–58, 60, 67, 78. See also Amendments; U.S. Constitution

life, 6, 25, 33, 49–50, 80, 152; of a child, 94; and a civil society, 11, 14; expectancy, 158; free of violence, 186, 189; human, 6, 9–11; and liberty / pursuit of happiness, 14–15, 44, 46, 69, 85–89, 94, 97–98, 182; loss of, 134–35; and morality, 64, 66; as prison sentence, 110–12; public, 114, 126
Lochner v. New York. See U.S. Supreme Court
Locke, John, 15, 97, 157
logic, 3, 6, 28, 45, 179; and ethics, 26, 32, 189; and language, 26–27, 31, 49, 90; laws of, 22, 27, 29
logos, 6–7. *See also* reason
Low-Level Radioactive Waste Policy Amendment Act (1980), 104, 114, 119, 122

Maine, Henry James Sumner, 56
market, 44, 134, 136, 140, 142, 146–48, 150, 154–55, 172; black, 148; pre-approval, 143–44
Marshall, John, 174, 185
Marshall, Thurgood, 85
Massachusetts, 43
Matter of Baby "K." See U.S. Court of Appeals
metaphysics, xi, 24, 90. *See also* Kant
methods (-ology), 25, 28, 64, 169; of reasoning, 179–82
Mill, John Stuart, 54, 122; Harm Principle, 54–55
morals (-ity), 1, 16, 189; as commodities, 62; and the common good, 14; correctness, 8; and ethics, 25; indifference, 53; judgment, 27–28, 32, 110–11, 153–54; justification, 33, 120; and the law, 5, 12, 21–24, 65, 111–14; and minimalism, 15; nature of man, 13–14, 15; non-, 27, 29; norms/ standards, 21–22, 33, 54, 154; social, 23, 25; union, 13; values, 9, 27.

See also action; Aquinas; behavior; good; Hare; imperatives; individual; Kant; language; life; obligation; punishment
mores, 9, 19, 23, 25, 33
Murphy, Mark, 8, 10–11
mutuality, 33, 35, 63, 67

National Academy of Sciences, 157
National Governors' Association, 104, 107–8, 118–19
National Labor Relations Act (1935), 51, 174, 176
natural law. *See* law, natural
Nazism, 31, 62. *See also* Germany; Hitler
Nevada, 103–4, 118, 120
New Deal. *See* Roosevelt
New York (State of), ii, ix, xv, 15, 43, 58, 103; actions of, 50; and breach of faith, 125–26; Court of Appeals, 46, 105; legislation/laws of, 43–44, 46, 50–52, 63, 69, 109, 123–25; New York Bureau of Statistics of Labor, 50; New York City, 45, 82; and *not-in-my-backyard*, 123; relationship to other states, 126–27; Supreme Court of, 46; rights of, 66; waste disposal in, 103, 105, 108–9, 115–16, 121–22, 125. *See also* intervention; Journeymen Bakers Union of New York; legislation; U.S. Supreme Court
New York v. United States. See U.S. Supreme Court
Nock, Albert Jay, 55
norms, 8–10, 21–22, 32–36, 93, 153–54, 179. *See also* ethics
not-in-my-backyard (NIMBY), xv, 123
Nuclear Information and Resource Services (NIRS), xv, 104. *See also* waste

oath, 187
obedience, 5, 66

objective, 3, 10–12, 14, 32, 63–64, 67–69, 111, 113, 137, 159 *See also* Gewirth

obligation, 12, 81–83, 85; affirmative, 87, 90; concept of, 64; and contracts, 55, 60–61; and contradiction, 34; and ethics, 187–88; and humans, 14, 33, 56, 92; and the law, 2, 73n80, 90, 120, 125–27, 139, 159, 178, 187–88; moral, 125–27, 153–54, 187, 190. *See also* Grotius; states

O'Brien, Denis, 46–47

O'Connor, Sandra Day, 15, 103–14, 116–17, 119–123, 125–16, 134, 136, 143–44, 150–54, 157–59

Office of the Surgeon General (OSG), xv, 142

ownership, 8, 22, 105, 120, 122, 126; of humans, 189. *See also* slavery

order, 9, 18; and the Constitution, 56, 179–80; legal, 25, 78, 83, 94, 190; and natural law, 9; "second," 15, 56; societal, 55

OXFAM America, 170–72

paternalism, 51, 57, 59

Peckham, Rufus, 46–53, 57–60, 63. *See also* U.S. Supreme Court, *Lochner*

perspective, 13, 20, 25, 27, 43, 45, 63, 91, 107, 119, 170, 187; and ethics, 79, 87, 111, 189; and federalism, 117, 120; and legal positivism, 87, 158; universal, 4, 9, 135

philosophy: of the law, 175, 189

Plato: *Crito*, 29–30

Plessy v. Ferguson. See U.S. Supreme Court

police, 66, 78, 92–93, 169; law enforcement, 78; powers of, 46–49, 52–53, 57, 59–60, 64, 70n17

policy (-ies), xv, 21; and the courts, 53, 112, 136, 138; and economics, 43; federal, 104, 107–9, 117, 151–52, 156; and justice/equality, 21, 112–13, 155, 182; public, 21, 35; purposes of, 54–55; and race, 20; and sexual assault, 165–66; and the states, 118–19

Pope Leo XIII, 43

positivism (-ist), vi, 1, 90, 98; constitutional, 125; and ethics, 81; and the law, 3, 36, 63, 87–90, 152, 188; legal, 2, 4, 11, 21–26, 47, 53, 61–62, 64, 81–82, 85, 87, 96, 107, 111, 117, 135, 152, 158, 187. *See also* Hart

Posner, Richard A., 78–86

power, 117, 123, 125, 171; abuse of, 92; balance of, 57, 106, 110, 116, 123, 180, 183; division of, 110, 121, 181, 186; enumeration of, 179–80; and equality/inequality, 52; executive, 97;-less, 52, 57, 185; separation of, 50, 110; and society, 171; sources of, 15; use of, 153. *See also* commerce; economy; employment; empower; federalism; freedom; government; police; state; system; U.S. Congress

precedent (-ce), 60, 82, 85, 87, 97, 106, 177; *stare decisis*, 2, 16; super, 2

prima facie, 57, 62

privacy (-te), 12, 56, 79, 86–87, 92, 95, 98, 121, 177, 182–88, 190

progressivism, 6, 36, 58, 155

property, 8, 22, 46, 49, 69, 70n17, 85, 94, 97–98, 152, 166, 182; humans as, 17; and natural law, 12; notion of, 22; personal/private, 12–13, 44, 97, 122; right to own, 33, 85–89; "work," 35. *See also* slavery

punishment, 28, 153, 165, 182; capital, 28; cruel and unusual, 110–11, 113; fear of, 5, 64; inhumane, 89; morality of, 111–13

race, 171; and Africans in the U.S., 17–18; human, 6–7, 17, 33; and inferiority, 18–20; and rights, 19. *See also* black(s); slavery

racism, 2, 19–20, 179. *See also* the *Separate Car Act* (1890)
radioactivity. *See* waste
rape. *See* assault; violence
rationalism, 11
reason, 3, 5; *but-for* test, 179, 193n85; defy, 26; human, 5, 7–10, 25; laws of, 9; no, 51, 57, 78–79, 139, 186; and nature, 5, 8–9; practical, 3–4, 8–9, 11, 16, 69, 135; principles of, 8–10, 12, 30, 36, 37n35, 135; pure, 3–4, 9–10, 69; speculative, 8, 135. *See also* action; Cicero; Kant; legislation; logos; methods; U.S. Supreme Court
reciprocity, 33, 67
regressive (-ion), 2, 56, 155–56
regulation, 44, 124, 144; challenge to, 142; and commerce, 173–74, 176–77; of employers/labor, 43, 58, 176; of the federal government, 108–9, 122, 139, 142, 154, 156–57, 177; of products, 109, 139, 142, 145–46, 148–49, 152, 154, 156, 158; v. prohibition, 45; and public health, 146–48; of the state, 107–8, 125, 177
Rehnquist, William, 79, 85–88, 92, 94–96, 134, 166–69, 173–86, 188–90; and the Due Process clause, 79, 86–88, 90, 97–98; and positivism, 88–90, 96; and Posner, 79–80, 85
relativism (-ist), 2, 9, 11, 26, 68
remedy (-ies), ix, 6, 48, 96, 112, 144, 146, 152, 165, 182–84, 186, 189–90
right(s), 3, 11–13; absolute, 49, 67, 121; antecedent, 66–67; assertion of, 12, 14, 51; civil, 5, 13, 62, 183–84; community of, 3, 13–14, 32, 35, 55, 68; concept of, 11–12; human, iii, ix, 13, 16, 32, 34–35, 54–56, 62, 83, 87–89, 110, 165, 170, 181, 186–90; limits of, 48, 60; notion of legal, 60; of the state, 15; unalienable, 14. *See also* action; behavior; community; consequences; constitutions; contract; economy; equality; federalism; formalism; Gewirth; Grotius; justice; individualism; legislation, *Civil Rights Act*s; liberty; property; race; United Nations; U.S. Constitution
risk, 81, 86, 170; of abuse/violence, 79, 82–83, 95, 121, 170–72; to employees, 57, 62–63; and ethics, 153; and exploitation, 54, 57; to health, 46, 49, 104, 116, 134, 137, 142, 144–45, 148, 151–52, 157; and police, 64; and radioactive waste, 104, 124
Robert Wood Johnson Foundation, 154
Rome, 5
Roosevelt, Franklin D., 61
    New Deal, 61
Rorty, Richard, 33

Scalia, Antonin G., 113, 134
segregation, 2, 19–20, 112. *See also* Amendments (U.S.); slavery
self-interest, 11, 15, 32–34, 68, 125
self-preservation, 9, 13, 24
Seneca, 13
sense, 6, 23, 27, 30, 35, 51, 64, 93, 97, 146, 153, 156–57, 168, 188; common, 24, 143, 145, 148; of equality, 69; of justice, 8; of the law, 4, 12, 64; non-, 67; of obligation, 92; of purpose, 3
Separate Car Act (1890), 18
shibboleth, 54
Singer, Peter, 35
slavery, 2, 18, 33, 48, 53–55, 189; and the African race, 17; anti-, 25; comparison to apartheid, 23; owners of, 17. *See also* constitution; Declaration of Independence
smoking, 133–59; and addiction, 133, 135–37, 139–42, 145–51, 157–58; and advertising, xv, 133–34, 138–39, 141–42, 148–49; and banning, 141–42, 144–48; cigarettes, xv, 133,

135–41, 144–52, 155–57; commodity or drug (tobacco), 133, 135–36, 138–39, 142–44, 146–49, 151–52; deaths, 133–35, 140–42, 144, 152; decline of, 139, 141, 145–47, 155; and life expectancy, 158; manufacturers, 133–34, 136–37, 139, 141–42, 145, 150–51, 154, 157; and minors, 133; policies, 156; regulations, ix, 133–40, 142–52, 154–59; and smokeless tobacco, 135–36, 138, 139–41. *See also* Food and Drug Administration; health; legislation, *FDCA* and *FCLAA*; U.S. Supreme Court, *FDA v. Brown and Williamson Tobacco*

socialism, 62. *See also* Hitler

society, 3, 6, 9, 12, 52, 67, 158, 168; civil, 11–12; coercion by, 54–55; contingency-based, 33, 35; as democratic, 67; and equality, 25, 52, 172–73, 181; human to industrial, 52, 54–55; and individual liberty, 188; law and justice, 7–8, 11, 21–24, 35–36, 53, 64, 66, 88; members of, 10, 14, 23–25, 32–33, 53–55, 67, 84, 97, 114; mores of, 19, 23; norms of, 21, 34; pluralistic, 14; protection of, 12; stability of, 12; standards, 35; systems or structures of, 21, 23–24, 54–55, 97, 114, 169, 181; universal, 68; viability of, 23–25. *See also* democracy; Mill

Socrates, 29–30

Souter, David, 134, 167, 173, 178, 180, 182–83

South Carolina, 103–4, 118, 120, 185

South Carolina v. Katzenbach (1996). *See* U.S. Supreme Court

sovereignty. *See* states

Spencer, Herbert, 51, 54–55

stare decisis. See precedent

states, 2, 6–7, 10; obligation of, 79, 85, 87, 90–91, 125–26; power of, 13, 48, 50, 53, 70n17, 181; processes/system, 108, 167; prohibition of interference, 55, 60, 85, 184; responsibilities of, 89, 104, 125; sovereignty of, 105–10, 114, 116–17, 126–27, 177; wards of, 51, 169. *See also* states by name; commerce, Clause; federalism; individualism; interest; intervention; legislation; policy; regulation; rights; unions; United States; U.S. Congress; U.S. Constitution; U.S. Supreme Court; waste

Statism, 55

Stoics (-ism), 6, 11. *See also* philosophy

Strauder v. West Virginia (1880). *See* U.S. Supreme Court

sui juris, 48

Sunstein, Cass R., 44

system, 58, 62, 68, 92, 120, 124, 128n34, 156, 181, 190; coercive, 22; federal, 15, 113, 186, 190; of government, 53, 114–17, 123, 167, 174–75, 187; health-care, 145, 148; justice, 110, 112, 165, 182–84, 188–89; legal, 21, 47, 181; logical, 47; of power, 171, 174

taxes, 52, 154–56. *See also* smoking

teleology, 1

Territory v. Ah Lim (1890), 67

theory (-ies), ii, 185, 188; contact/game, 63; and the economy, 51, 62; empirical, 36; ethics and law, 2, 10, 66; and Euclid, 8; feminist, 171; formalism, 182; of language, 27; natural law, 2–6, 8–15, 21, 23–24, 33, 35–36, 66, 135; positivist, 36; social contract, ix, 11–12, 68, 84, 97, 103. *See also* law, theories

Thirty Years' War, 13

tobacco. *See* smoking

tolerance, 12, 22–25

tyranny, 79, 114, 121

unions: as organization, 13, 48, 51; as the United States, 15, 68, 109, 115–16
United Kingdom (Britain), 14, 46 law of as model, 46
United Nations, 169; Declaration on the Elimination of Violence against Women, 186, 189; Universal Declaration of Human Rights, 186
United States, Code of, 147, 184 independence of Thirteen Colonies, 14–15 *See also* Jefferson; U.S. agencies by name;
U.S. Congress, 19, 50, 104; authority of, 137–38, 149, 166–67, 175, 182; authorization of the FDA, 134, 138, 142–48; hearings of, 2, 179–80; and labor, 176–78; as mediator between states, 119; powers of, 105–9, 127n9, 174–75, 179–80, 183, 185, 187; and public health, 126, 140, 150; Record of, 108; vs. state regulation, 107–8, 114, 125, 134, 143, 168, 174–75; Supremacy Clause, 108–9. *See also* commerce, Clause; legislation; smoking
U.S. Constitution, 2, 47, 79, 105, 128n19, 128nn21–22, 157, 166, 189; and African persons, 17–18; duty to provide protections, 79, 86, 91, 98; founders/framers/framework, 15, 17–19, 56–57, 60, 79–80, 114, 157, 186–87; personal rights, 17 and states' rights, 15, 115, 117; and tort, 81–82, 98, 179; view of role, 15–16; violations of, 44, 78–79, 98, 105, 184, 186–87, 189. *See also* Amendments; contracts; constitution
U.S. Court of Appeals, 78, 137, 166; Fourth Circuit, 1, 134, 142; *In the Matter of Baby "K" (Three Cases)* (1994), 1; *Nutritional Foods Association v. Food and Drug Administration* (1974), 137; Seventh Circuit, 78; Third Circuit, 79

U.S. Supreme Court, vi, 1–4, 16, 36, 189; *Brown v. Board of Education of Topeka* (1954), ix, 19–20; *DeShaney v. Winnebago County Department of Social Services*) (1989), ix, 2, 16, 77–98, 185, 190; *Dred Scott v. Sandford* (1856), 16; *Estelle v. Gamble* (1976), 89, 91–92; *FDA v. Brown and Williamson Tobacco Corporation* (2000), 2, 133–59; *Gibbons v. Ogden* (1824), 174; *Holden v. Hardy* (1898), 47, 49; *In the Matter of Baby "K" (Three Cases)* (1994), 1; *Jacobson v. Massachusetts* (1905), 43; *Lochner v. New York* (1905), ix, 2, 43–70; *New York v. United States* (1992), ix, 2, 15, 103–27; *Northern Securities Co. v. United States* (1904), 51; *Plessy v. Ferguson* (1896), 18, 20–21; *Otis v. Parker* (1903), 51; *South Carolina v. Katzenbach* (1996), 185; *Strauder v. West Virginia* (1880), 185; *United States v. Guest* (1966), 184; *United States v. Lopez* (1995), 167; *United States v. Morrison* (2000), ix, 2, 165–90; use of ethics reasoning, 1–3; *Williamson v. Lee Optical of Oklahoma* (1955), 61; *Youngberg v. Romeo* (1982), 91. *See also* legislation
utilitarianism, 1, 10

Virginia Polytechnic Institute, 165–66
virtue, 5, 7, 9, 11–12, 16, 56, 61, 65, 116, 177
violence, 6, 180; by abuse/harm/injury, 31, 77, 80–84, 89, 96; avoidance or tolerance of, 22; behavior, 180; and crime, 168, 180–84; decrease in, 172–73; domestic (DV), 170, 172, 181; economic cost of, 169–73, 178–80; freedom from, 83, 166, 171, 181, 183, 186; gender-motivated, ix, 165–90; and government, 79,

86–87, 166; indifference to, 181, 183, 186, 190; by intimate partner (IPV), xv, 171; National Violence Against Women Survey, 170–71; and punishment, 28, 89, 182; random acts, 166; and rape/sexual, 165–66, 171–72, 178, 181. *See also* abuse; assault; legislation, *VAWA*;

Wagner Act. *See National Labor Relations Act*
Warren, Earl, 184
Washington (State of), 103–4, 118–20 Supreme Court, 67
waste, xv; disposal of, 103–6, 108–10, 115, 118–19, 121–27; generators of, 106, 109, 118–19, 122, 124; nuclear/radioactive, 15, 103–4, 109, 116, 118, 122–24; regulation of, 109; and the states, 120–22, 125–26. *See also Low-Level Radioactive Waste Policy Amendment Act*; U.S. Supreme Court, *New York*
well-being, 12, 34–35, 54, 62–63, 87, 89, 104, 170
West Virginia, 185
White, Byron R., 117–20, 125–26
will (of humans), 10, 21–22, 28, 48, 54, 65, 67–69
Williamson v. Lee Optical of Oklahoma. *See* U.S. Supreme Court
Wilson, John, 28
Wisconsin, 78–81, 85–86, 89, 91–94, 96, 98
work. *See* employment
World Health Organization (WHO), xv, 142

Youngberg v. Romeo. *See* U.S. Supreme Court

About the Author

T. Patrick Hill is Associate Professor at the Edward J. Bloustein School of Planning and Public Policy, Rutgers University, where he teaches courses in ethics, law, and thinking. He is a member of the Newborn Screening Review Committee for the New Jersey Department of Health and Senior Services, and has served as ethics consultant to the Cancer Institute of New Jersey. He is the coauthor of "Ethical Issues in Geriatric Gastroenterology," in *Geriatric Gastroenterology* (Springer, 2021), and the author of "Conscience: Its Use and Abuse, in Sightings," *The Divinity School* (University of Chicago, 2019).

www.ingramcontent.com/pod-product-compliance
Lightning Source LLC
Chambersburg PA
CBHW061712300426
44115CB00014B/2651